# The Cost of Free Speech

# The Cost of Free Speech

## Pornography, Hate Speech, and their Challenge to Liberalism

Abigail Levin
*Niagara University, New York*

First published 2010 by
PALGRAVE MACMILLAN

Palgrave Macmillan in the UK is an imprint of Macmillan Publishers Limited, registered in England, company number 785998, of Houndmills, Basingstoke, Hampshire RG21 6XS.

Palgrave Macmillan in the US is a division of St Martin's Press LLC, 175 Fifth Avenue, New York, NY 10010.

Palgrave Macmillan is the global academic imprint of the above companies and has companies and representatives throughout the world.

Palgrave® and Macmillan® are registered trademarks in the United States, the United Kingdom, Europe and other countries

ISBN 978-0-230-23768-1          hardback

This book is printed on paper suitable for recycling and made from fully managed and sustained forest sources. Logging, pulping and manufacturing processes are expected to conform to the environmental regulations of the country of origin.

A catalogue record for this book is available from the British Library.

A catalogue record for this book is available from the Library of Congress.

10   9   8   7   6   5   4   3   2   1
19   18   17   16   15   14   13   12   11   10

Printed and bound in Great Britain by
CPI Antony Rowe, Chippenham and Eastbourne

*To T.L.S. and E.L.S., whose freedom of expression
is delightfully unregulated.*

# Contents

# Acknowledgements

So many people have played vital roles in helping me better formulate the ideas in this book. I owe a profound debt of gratitude to Wayne Sumner and David Dyzenhaus, who were both wonderful advisors when this project started out as a dissertation at the University of Toronto. Their insight, good humor, and faith in me as a student were invaluable. Rae Langton also made very helpful comments on an earlier draft. Thanks also to *Public Affairs Quarterly* for their permission to reprint an earlier version of what is now Chapter 3 in this work.

During the revision process I have had the support of my wonderful colleagues at Niagara University, and the eagle eye of Rebecca Mendelson, whose patience and attention to detail were indispensable at the late stages of revision. My ever-supportive husband Rob made me endless cups of tea, and kept the cats entertained while I was working. What more could I ask for?

# Introduction

On the classical liberal view, constitutional rights protect the individual from certain kinds of interference with basic liberties by the state. The theoretical concern informing such rights is of course the familiar anxiety about abuse of government power. In order to check this concern, centered particularly around state interference in private morality, liberalism has developed the notion of the state's role as a neutral facilitator of a 'marketplace of ideas,'[1] within which citizens may freely debate competing notions of the good life, with the state favoring no one view over another. Closely tied to this view is the idea that equality among citizens is to be thought of as almost interchangeable with state neutrality – what it means for the state to treat its citizens equally is for the state to treat its citizens neutrally.

However, this traditional view of the relationship between the marketplace of ideas, equality, and neutrality seems to be in crisis today, as it has become clear that contemporary society is by no means operating as classical liberal theorists had envisioned – as a free marketplace of ideas, where diverse views are considered openly and in a spirit of genuine inquiry. On the contrary, our systemically racist, sexist, and homophobic society has had the effect that certain dominant racist, sexist, and homophobic views have become so deeply held as not to be amenable to rational discussion, with the effect that minorities' and women's voices are not heard fairly in the marketplace.

If this is indeed the case, then our culturally oppressive society, by which I mean a society that permits the unchecked cultural formation of attitudes and beliefs about inequality,[2] calls into question the typical liberal remedy of equality as neutrality, and seems to demand a new approach in the interest of ensuring a more robustly equal society.

Put another way, through the lens of a cultural oppression framework, beliefs about inequality have the potentially devastating effect of so undermining their recipient's self-respect and understanding of her equal moral worth as to preclude that recipient from having access to the liberal ideal of forming her own conception of the good life. As Andrew Kernohan (1998: 88) presents the problem in his book *Liberalism, Equality, and Cultural Oppression*:

> To come to know the good, people require a cultural environment free of practices that would enculturate false and undermining beliefs about value.... In an inegalitarian culture, many of the beliefs that people take up from their cultural environment are based on beliefs about the moral inequality of persons.... If people base their ends in life on these false evaluations, their highest-order interest in coming to know the good will have been harmed.

If Kernohan's scenario describes our contemporary condition, then the liberal ideal of state neutrality as facilitating each citizen's conception of the good would be ineffective, as it would in fact facilitate conceptions of the good that deny the equal worth of persons. In a culturally oppressive society, if the liberal state is indeed committed to facilitating each citizen's ability to realize her good, then the state must take steps to remedy the conceptions of the good that deny the equal moral worth of persons, rather than maintain neutrality about such conceptions.

This book will examine two paradigmatic cases of harms caused by culturally oppressive speech – the harm to women in general in the case of pornography, and the harms to racial, religious, and sexual minorities (both to the particular targets of the speech and to the affected group as a whole) in the case of hate speech. These harms, I will argue, accrue because the proliferation of pornography and hate speech in the marketplace of ideas has three deleterious consequences: First, the dominant culture comes to believe what I will argue is the message of pornography and hate speech – that women and minorities have inferior moral worth. Second, women and minorities themselves come to believe this message. Finally, if women and minorities believe this message, they will be less likely to attempt to rebut it in the marketplace, or their attempted rebuttals will be disregarded by the dominant culture.

Speaking very broadly, the targets of pornography and hate speech – women and minorities – claim that their right to equality or their right to freedom of expression is being violated by the speech in question, because pornography and hate speech are limiting their opportunity to enter into the marketplace of ideas. Conversely, the speakers claim that to limit their speech is a violation of their own rights to equality and to freedom of expression.

Several questions arise from the issue of how to resolve the conflict between these two claims. How are competing rights claims best adjudicated and how are they in fact adjudicated? How can one conceptualize the nature of the harm caused by cultural oppression? Can such a conception be accommodated by liberalism, or is remedying the harms of cultural oppression too much of a departure from the liberal principle of state neutrality? These issues form the major lines of inquiry of this study.

I will argue that the harms of cultural oppression ought to be remedied by the state, and that such a remedy in fact follows from the core principles of egalitarian liberalism. This argument is intended as a twofold critique of the value of state neutrality. The first line of critique comes from the first three chapters, which offer a critique of neutrality from within the egalitarian liberal tradition, albeit not within the dominant line of thinking within that tradition. The thrust of this critique is that state neutrality is undesirable for the reason that it allows a culturally oppressive culture to flourish, unchecked by the state, and that such a culture is anathema to the fundamental goals of liberalism itself.

Chapters 4, 5, and 6 offer a critique of state neutrality from outside of the liberal tradition, from contemporary continental political philosophy. The core of the arguments here will be to the effect that state neutrality is not merely undesirable but impossible in principle. It is my hope that these two arguments – from within liberalism and from outside of it – can be taken together to form a critique of liberal state neutrality to which liberals will be receptive, either from the angle of the undesirability of neutrality, or from the angle of its impossibility. In either case, my aim is always sympathetic to the egalitarian liberal project, and I hope that my arguments concerning the weaknesses of state neutrality will ultimately lead to a more robust, and activist, liberalism, better able to meet its commitments to its own core value of treating its citizens with equal concern and respect.[3]

In Chapter 1, I will set out three strands of egalitarian liberal theory, which, taken together, provide a background set of views amenable to discussing cultural oppression. These views are: J.S. Mill's harm principle, Joseph Raz's view of rights as in part justified by the common interest, and Ronald Dworkin's notion of rights as correctives for the failures of utilitarianism in treating citizens with equal concern and respect.

In Chapters 2 and 3, I will argue that while the framework articulated in Chapter 1 provides a starting point for the justification of state intervention in cases of cultural oppression, neither Mill nor Dworkin goes so far as to contemplate active state intervention for the promotion of equality at the direct expense of freedom of expression. Both Mill's and Dworkin's views on this question will be discussed in these chapters, as well as criticisms of their views, especially as offered by feminists and critical race theorists who find fault with the effects of state neutrality.

I will conclude this discussion by arguing, first, that both Mill and Dworkin have important but overlooked lines of thinking that would actually facilitate an activist liberalism, and secondly, that the criticisms offered by feminists and critical race theorists reveal that the liberal state's delimiting of the scope of the right to freedom of expression does not in all cases preserve the state's core commitment to equality; and that in some cases, particularly in cases of cultural oppression, the state's deployment of rights operates to promote oppression.

Given this, the central question for the egalitarian liberal becomes how to ensure that the state's granting of a particular right in a particular circumstance will in fact promote equality, as opposed to promoting oppression. In Chapters 4, 5, and 6, I will argue that this question is illuminated by three strands of thought not normally considered by Anglo-American political philosophy but which I believe offer very fruitful critiques of the very possibility, let alone desirability, of state neutrality. Instead of seeing the state as neutral, all three of these lines of thought see the state as a powerful actor in the marketplace of ideas. In Chapter 4, I will undertake an analysis of the nature and operation of speech acts, as articulated by J. L. Austin and contemporary interpreters of his work. Through this analysis, the state's speech, particularly in its judicial decisions, will come to be seen as illocutionary speech acts, which carries the implication that state speech contains a great deal of power normally overlooked in mainstream liberal discourse.

In Chapter 5, the idea of state speech as bound up with state power becomes more explicit, and the consequences of this view are given more nuance by an analysis of the nature of power and discourse as articulated by the leading continental theorist of power, Michel Foucault. I argue in Chapters 4 and 5 that these two theories – speech act theory and power as discourse – taken together, reveal that rights themselves are to be seen as instruments of state power. This insight is crucial to the central argument of the book: that the state as a neutral facilitator of private ideas is untenable and must be dropped if the liberal state is to fulfill its goal of equal concern and respect for all of its citizens. I argue that Foucault and Austin demonstrate that judicial decisions of the state are a paradigmatic instance of authoritative state speech and state power, which is entirely unavoidable and anything but neutral. Given that, the best option for the egalitarian liberal state is to acknowledge its role as speaker, and aim to use its speech in the service of equality.

This argument is further developed in Chapter 6, which addresses the traditional reasoning given by liberals for resisting state activism in the service of equality: fear of censorship. In recent years, theorists from the continental tradition, led by Judith Butler, have argued that censorship is in fact a much more pervasive and thoroughgoing phenomenon than the liberal account has admitted. If Butler's 'new' censorship is in fact the correct way of understanding the phenomenon, then the state is implicated in censorship at a much deeper, and indeed unavoidable, level than had previously been theorized. Again, the thrust of this argument is to demonstrate that the liberal ideal of neutrality is, of necessity, untenable, and ought to be abandoned in the service of the central liberal goal of the promotion of equality.

The final two chapters of the book examine how a liberal state no longer tied to neutrality might act in the service of equality. Chapter 7 conceives of how what I will call an 'activist' liberal state might operate to remedy the harms of cultural oppression. My argument here will be twofold. First, the state may engage in legally non-binding activist speech in the marketplace, in the form of state resources being expended to model and encourage discourse about diversity, such as through public service announcements on television and other media. The aim of such measures would be to remedy the oppressive speech of private actors in the marketplace with liberatory state speech. Second, and more controversially, the judiciary may render decisions about freedom of expression in ways that are guided by the value of equal concern and respect, rather than being guided by the perceived imperative to retain neutrality.

Chapter 8 will demonstrate that the idea of an activist liberal state in the service of equality may already be working in practice, and not just in theory. I will analyze the leading United States, Canadian, and European cases on pornography and hate speech to demonstrate that a more egalitarian result has in fact been reached in these cases in Canada and Europe than has currently been reached in the US jurisprudence. Equality, here, implies protection for individuals and groups both against a hostile background of societal cultural oppression and against the background of the power wielded by the state itself. Unconsciousness of the workings of both cultural oppression and state power, I believe, has led to inegalitarian results in these cases in the US. However, Canada and Europe – on both the state and international levels – provide compelling examples of egalitarian jurisprudence guided by the very principles for which I am arguing.

The arguments in this book attempt to demonstrate – both from within the liberal tradition and from outside of it – that neutrality is not a salve for inequality, but is rather in many instances an enactor of it; the arguments serve to highlight the role of state power in the hopes that a liberal state more aware of its own power will curb its unwitting inegalitarianism when given the tools and responsibility to engage in activism on behalf of equality. It is my hope that this book will clarify liberalism's core commitments and make clear that the liberal commitment to neutrality, if there even is one, is merely instrumental in nature, and ought to be jettisoned in our current culturally oppressive climate in the hopes of making our culture one amenable to the laudable and classical liberal goals of a vigorous, robust, and diverse discussion of the good life.

# 1
# Harm, Equality, and the Common Interest: Towards a Framework for an Activist Liberalism

## 1.1 An uneasy triad: Liberty, equality, and neutrality

On most egalitarian liberal accounts,[1] constitutional rights are seen as protecting the individual from certain kinds of interference with basic liberties by the state. The theoretical concern informing such rights is of course the familiar anxiety about abuse of government power. In order to check this concern, centered particularly around state interference in private morality, liberal theorists – both classical and contemporary – have developed the familiar, even clichéd, notion of the state's role as a neutral facilitator of a 'marketplace of ideas,' within which competing notions of the good life may be articulated freely, with the state favoring no one view over another. If the state's role is confined to neutral facilitation of private citizens' ideas, then the state's confinement in that role is apt to render it benign.

Further, such a marketplace is thought to preserve our constitutional right to freedom of expression – what could better facilitate freedom of expression than an unregulated forum? – and many egalitarian liberal theorists believe that it preserves our constitutional right to equality as well. The state's guarantee of equality among citizens – in the US, the guarantee of 'equal protection of the laws' enshrined in the Fourteenth Amendment (see Appendix B for the text of the First and Fourteenth Amendments) – can be understood as being facilitated by state neutrality in the marketplace of ideas. In other words, what it means to be treated equally by the state is to be treated neutrally by the state.

This traditional concern about abuse of state power and its remedy in the marketplace, however, seems to be in crisis today, as it has become clear to many theorists that contemporary society is by no means operating as classical liberal theorists had envisioned – as a free market-place of ideas, where diverse views are considered openly and in a spirit of genuine inquiry. On the contrary, our systemically racist and sexist society has the effect that certain racist or sexist views have become so prolific as to flood the marketplace, and so deeply held as not to be amenable to rational discussion. Thus, the views of racial minorities and women are not heard in the marketplace, posing a threat to their rights of both liberty, especially the liberty of freedom of expression, and equality. It is the project of this book to try to resolve this crisis of the marketplace in terms friendly to the egalitarian liberal. In other words, I believe the challenges posed to the marketplace from systemic racism, sexism and homophobia are not insurmountable for egalitarian liberal-ism, but they will require a reframing of egalitarian liberal priorities, which I shall outline.

Another way to cast this is to say that our current situation as a society which practices cultural oppression – by which I mean a society which permits the unchecked cultural formation of attitudes and beliefs about inequality – calls into question the liberal insistence that equality is being facilitated if neutrality is maintained by the state, and seems to demand that the egalitarian liberal state take a new approach in the interest of ensuring a more robustly equal society.

A particularly problematic consequence of cultural oppression for the egalitarian liberal is that the proliferation of racist and sexist opinions – which are, at bottom, opinions about inequality – have the effect of so undermining their targets' self-respect and sense of equal moral worth as to preclude the targeted group from having access to their highest-order interests in knowing the good.

If this is indeed the consequence of cultural oppression, and I argue in what follows and in Chapter 2 that it is, then the egalitarian liberal ideal of state neutrality as facilitating each citizen's ability to formulate their own conception of the good – through equal access to the market-place of ideas – would be ineffective. I argue that the egalitarian liberal state is fundamentally committed – through the values underlying its core constitutional obligations – to treating its citizens with equal con-cern and respect, and only committed to neutrality instrumentally, insofar as it serves the goal of facilitating equal concern and respect. Since the egalitarian liberal state is committed to facilitating each citizen's ability to realize their good, which presupposes treatment with equal concern and respect, then in an inegalitarian culture, the state must take steps to remedy that inequality, rather than remaining neutral concerning it.

There are two traditional, highly influential, liberal arguments against state intervention in the liberty of citizens in order to protect equality, and both make use of the notion of state neutrality. These two arguments, far from settling the issue in favor of neutrality in preference to intervention, instead show that the roots of the conflict between liberty and equality run as deep as the idea of neutrality itself. Very generally, since this is well-worn territory,[2] one argument for state neutrality holds that all citizens ought to receive 'neutral concern' from the government, which means that they shall receive concern equal to that given to others, regardless of their conception of the good life, as long as their conception does not violate the rights of others. They will receive this equal – that is, neutral – concern from the state regardless of whether their conception of the good life is shared by others or not – in other words, whether or not their lifestyle is a minority position.

According to this view, neutral concern is the best way of promoting equality among citizens; it is the purpose of neutrality to ensure that citizens are not discriminated against by the government by virtue of their holding minority lifestyles. Thus, this view of neutrality sees it as the very mechanism for enhancing the equality of citizens in the first instance; consequently, a departure from neutrality in the name of equality is seen as nonsensical. Articulated in this way, state neutrality appears to be of a piece with the aims of egalitarian liberalism in securing equal treatment of citizens.

However, the traditional justification of neutrality, from Mill onwards, also makes use of another argument, to the effect that the reason to afford different, competing, visions of the good life equal, or neutral, concern, is that at present we as a culture are ignorant about what constitutes the good life or lives. Thus, any or all of these visions of the good life, articulated freely in the marketplace, may be true or valuable to the community as a whole, and the undecided individual is best served by a state which allows her to sample all of these diverse visions in making up her own mind about her own lifestyle. The state's function, then, is to ensure that its citizens are afforded an environment wherein they may have maximal opportunity to freely choose their own lifestyles, or ideas of the good life, from all of the available options. In other words, the state's role is to maximize the liberty of its citizens to choose how to live their lives. On this view, then, neutrality, rather than equality, is justified as a necessary condition for liberty. Equality is instrumental for liberty, on this view, rather than an end in itself.

This second argument, then, may be at odds with my argument about the desirability of state intervention in the elimination of harms caused by cultural oppression. If the state's role is to facilitate neutrality in the service of liberty, then intervention to prohibit cultural oppression may have the effect of violating the liberty of the oppressors, not to mention the liberty of their potential listeners, who may be deprived of hearing their version of the good, and are thus less at liberty to adopt it for themselves. This raises the traditional problem of the tension between liberty and equality in liberal theory, and I aim to offer a potential resolution of it in the later chapters of this study through an analysis of social power. For now, however, it must suffice to say that the idea of the neutrality of the liberal state already betrays a tension in its justification – between liberty and equality – and thus it is not altogether to depart from the notion of state neutrality to argue, as I will, on the side of equality rather than on the side of liberty in particular cases.

I will argue for such a departure from state neutrality in particular cases, for particular groups of people – cases where cultural oppression is operative and where current egalitarian liberal thinking has been thus far unable to take such discrimination on board. In so doing, I will rely on three influential and current egalitarian liberal theories which, taken together, set up a viable framework within which a liberal interventionist state is intelligible and defensible. These three theories are John Stuart Mill's harm principle, and his corollary right to liberty of self-determination; Joseph Raz's view – joined by Owen Fiss's and Cass Sunstein's readings of the United States' freedom of expression jurisprudence – of rights as properly seen as protective of the common interest as well as protective of the individual; and the egalitarian liberalism of Ronald Dworkin. In this chapter, I will present and defend these three theories, and in subsequent chapters I will attempt to work out criteria to determine when the liberal state, thus conceived, ought to intervene to prevent harm to its citizens.

## 1.2   J. S. Mill: Rights, interests, and the activist state

Mill's *On Liberty* (1978; first published 1858) provides the most influential framework for the contemporary egalitarian liberal understanding of the relation between the state and the citizen. I will treat the book more thoroughly, especially with regard to its arguments about freedom of expression, in Chapter 2, but at this point it is worth discussing Mill's liberalism and his characterization of rights in quite general and brief terms.

The central subject at issue in *On Liberty* is of course the issue of civil liberty – the nature and limits of the power that can be legitimately exercised by society over the individual, where the primary concern is abuse of state power over individuals. Historically, the issue of the relationship between the state and the individual was preoccupied with a concern that the monarch, established to protect the weakest people, may abuse that power; and so rights, guaranteeing certain key civil liberties, were needed as a sphere of immunity that the monarch could not legitimately infringe upon.

Although we have of course replaced the monarchy with democracy, the same concern of abuse of power remains, according to Mill – only now it is put in terms of the 'tyranny of the majority' of citizens over the minority, and so we need the same rights to guard against such tyranny.[3] In other words, the majority, in principle, has the same ability to infringe upon the civil liberties of the minority as monarchical power does, and so the issue of the necessity of rights remains untouched in these two systems of government. This characterization of the need for rights as arising out of concern about the tyranny of the majority is echoed in Dworkin's contemporary formulation of the necessity of rights in a liberal democracy, which I will turn to later in this chapter.

It is important to note, however, that in this formulation of concern about the tyranny of the majority, Mill is not only concerned with the power of the state over individuals, but with the power of some individuals over others as well. The discussion in *On Liberty* raises the general question of what to do when liberty in a matter of individual freedom interferes with someone else's pursuits, and the notion of the tyranny of the majority refers not only to a democratically elected majority government, but also to the harms that a majority of private citizens can inflict upon other citizens. The scope of Mill's concern in this regard is of interest to the argument of this study because it implicitly premises an activist liberal state insofar as Mill sees it as the state's task to prevent not only its own interference with private individuals in certain cases, but also its task to prevent private citizens from interfering in certain cases.

For Mill, then, the question is how to justly limit the power of the majority – government or citizen – from tyrannizing the minority. Mill (1978: 9) proposes the answer in his articulation of his famous harm principle:

[T]he sole end for which mankind are warranted, individually or collectively, in interfering with the liberty of action of any of their number, is self-protection. That the only purpose for which power can be rightfully exercised over any member of a civilized community, against his will is to prevent harm to others.

Mill justifies this notion of maximal liberty consistent with the prevention of certain harms on utilitarian grounds, based on the 'permanent interests of man as a progressive being' (p.10) – our collective interest in progress would be compromised, at too great a cost, if we were to forgo the harm principle and instead allow thoroughgoing liberty. I will return to the notion of our collective interest in progress later in this chapter, to argue that Mill's conception of rights, in opposition to that of Dworkin but similarly to Raz, sees our individual and collective interests as dovetailing at a certain point. But for now, it is important only to note that our interest in progress as a society and as a species, then, authorize on utilitarian grounds the subjection of individual 'spontaneity,' as Mill puts it, to external control only in respect to those actions which concern other people. The idea here is that if we are harming others through our actions, society cannot progress optimally, and our progress as individual human beings is necessarily an urgent interest of ours as a collective.

Of course a central question applied to Mill's formulation is what kind of harms are sufficient to warrant interference with individual liberties, and Mill concedes that there is always a certain degree of interference with others in any action at all, and thus 'harm' in the sense which warrants state intervention cannot merely mean any kind of interference. To avoid such an over-broad application of the harm principle, Mill limits it to covering only such harms that constitute an interference with a certain vital interest. Thus, only harms to vital interests, which Mill deems to be synonymous with rights, are sufficient to warrant an interference with liberty:

> Everyone who receives the protection of society owes a return for the benefit, and the fact of living in society renders it indispensable that each should be bound to observe a certain line of conduct toward the rest. This conduct consists, first, in not injuring the interests of one another, or rather certain interests that, either by express legal provision or by tacit understanding, ought to be considered as rights. (1978: 73)

So the harms that the state ought to intervene to prevent are not simply any case where one person's action interferes with another person's interest, but rather only those cases where the action interferes with an interest of such magnitude that that interest is protected legally through the imposition of a right by the state.

This formulation, now commonplace in modern liberal society, thus narrows the question of when the state is justified in interfering in private life, or must tailor its own, otherwise interfering actions, to the question of what interests ought to be considered important enough to be deemed rights, and thus worthy of protective action by the state. I will turn to the question of what these interests are shortly, first by investigating Chapter V of *Utilitarianism*, where Mill discusses the fundamental interest in security, and then by discussing what Mill says about our fundamental right to liberty or autonomy in *On Liberty*. The discussion of his most famous right, to freedom of expression, which is a corollary of the right to liberty, however, will be taken up in Chapter 2.

Thus far in Mill's formulation, though, the harm principle can be understood to mean that the state must intervene to prevent actions, either of its own or of others, which violate rights. Everything turns, then, on the question of what ought to be considered a right, since (1978: 73): '[t]he acts of an individual may be hurtful to others or wanting in due consideration for their welfare, without going to the length of violating any of their constituted rights,' in which case the state should not intervene. There is a fair amount of harm allowable in Mill's liberalism, then, but it is only allowable insofar as it falls short of the threshold of an interest sufficient to be deemed a right; there is only an obligation to prevent harm when there is a positive and identifiable duty owed to that person (1978: 80):

> ...[W]ith regard to the merely contingent or, as it may be called, constructive injury which a person causes to society by conduct which neither violates any specific duty to the public, nor occasions perceptible hurt to any assignable individual except himself, the inconvenience is one which society can afford to bear, for the sake of the greater good of human freedom.

It is interesting to note the utilitarian justification offered for the allowing of harms that fall short of rights violations. It is not that Mill thinks that such harms are too trivial to merit the attention of the state, but rather that the cost of the harm is, on balance, worth the benefit of increased freedom. Thus, for Mill, the state's task is to strike the correct balance between prevention of harm and maximization of freedom or liberty most consistent with the utilitarian aim of maximizing happiness for the greatest number of citizens.

Respect for liberty is important, according to Mill, in that it provides one with the opportunity to define one's own style of life, which Mill considers the basis of his liberalism. He writes, famously (1978: 12):

> No society in which these liberties are not, on the whole, respected is free, whatever may be its form of government.... The only freedom which deserves the name is that of pursuing our own good in our own way, so long as we do not attempt to deprive others of theirs or impede their efforts to obtain it.

Thus, Mill sees the liberty to define one's own good as a presupposition of freedom, and the only societies which offer the true possibility of freedom are those which guarantee maximal liberty consistent with the prevention of certain harms. Societies where this fundamental freedom of defining one's own good is respected are societies that will offer their citizens the greatest possibility of happiness, on the presupposition that happiness is best facilitated by an individual's ability to choose the lifestyle that they believe will make them happiest.

This ability of the individual to choose the lifestyle that they believe will make them happiest is fundamental to understanding not only what Mill understands the right to liberty to be, but what he understands liberalism itself to be. For Mill, the underpinning of both is the value to the individual and to society in diversity of opinion and lifestyle. Mill's notion of our permanent interests as progressive beings, which was his chief concern, flourishes under conditions of diversity of opinion and lifestyle, as it is necessarily an empirical question which opinions are true and which lifestyles are most conducive to happiness; thus, we need a society where conditions are such that we can experiment and find out the best of a diverse range of options. Thus, a liberal society is one where such conditions obtain, and the right to liberty is the mechanism by which such conditions are secured.

The right to liberty, then, is key to understanding Mill's political and ethical theory, and very pertinent to the question of the legitimacy of state intervention in cases of cultural oppression. Many commentators have cashed out Mill's fundamental right to liberty in terms of a right to liberty of self-development (see Donner 1992), as opposed to a right to autonomy (Gray 1996 argued for the autonomy view), and I will follow the former line of interpretation in my discussion of Mill. This understanding of the right to liberty runs as follows: Mill's chief departure from Benthamian utilitarian theory was in his rejection of Bentham's crude felicific calculus for happiness, and his insistence on a hierarchy of goods. Once this hierarchy is premised, Mill needs to establish how it is that agents can come to know and to access this hierarchy and make choices based upon it for their lives. In order that agents may come to be in a position to judge the true value of the various goods presented to them by their culture, they must be broadly educated – intellectually, emotionally, and ethically – such that they may develop the critical capacity to discern the higher goods from the lower. Such educated individuals are Mill's famous 'competent judges,' and it is this process of education that can be said to be realized through the right to liberty of self-development. For Mill, the function of society is to train all of us, to one degree or another, depending on our natural capacities and talents, to become such judges of the good, and it is our right to be given access to this developmental process.

The justification behind this schema of self-development is, of course, utilitarian: what it is to be a competent judge is to be able to weigh the good *to society overall* of a particular choice, rather than merely the good to the particular agent. Thus, overall welfare is increased by the existence of these judges making choices in its interest. For the purposes of this study, the right to the liberty of self-development is of use as an entry into discussing the harms of cultural oppression as a violation of this right. For instance, when members of a minority population are the targets of a discriminatory admissions policy, one way of characterizing the harm done to them is to say, for example, that their ability to access the resources available for self-development is impeded.

Another way of casting the harms of cultural oppression in terms of denial of the right to liberty of self-development is to maintain that when a woman or minority receives views of their unequal moral worth from the majority culture, their internalization of those views causes them to be unable to come to know their true good. Since the content of the culturally oppressive view claims that they are unequal, their internalization of this view would cause them to feel unworthy of their true good, or even unable to formulate many possible goods, because they would see themselves as precluded from them. As Kernohan puts it (1998: 66), views of the unequal moral worth of women, for example, can undermine a particular woman's knowledge of the good:

> ... if she depends on them in her deliberations about the good and they lead her into mistaken beliefs about her good. Domestic work

carries a social meaning that makes it seem obligatory to many women and optional to most men. Suppose a woman accepts this assumption and builds a vision of her life on this basis. If domestic work had carried a more egalitarian social meaning, she would have made another choice about her life. Suppose also that this life is in fact wrong for her; devoting her life to her professional career would have been a better choice for her. An inegalitarian distributional assumption has directly undermined her knowledge of the good.

The discussion in Chapter 2 will reveal that this formulation is strikingly compatible with Mill's own characterization of the plight of women in *The Subjection of Women* (1997; first published 1869), offering another reason to believe that the present project of a state that is activist in fighting the harms of cultural oppression would meet with Mill's assent.

Mill's discussion of what interests are sufficient to be deemed rights continues in *Utilitarianism* (1977; first published 1861), and it is useful to examine briefly that text. In Chapter V, Mill explicitly deals with the question of the reconciliation of rights with utilitarian theory, and he famously writes (1977: 1013):

> To have a right, then, is, I conceive, to have something which society ought to defend me in the possession of. If the objector goes on to ask why it ought, I can give him no other reason than general utility. If that expression does not seem to convey a sufficient feeling of the strength of the obligation, nor to account for the peculiar energy of the feeling, it is because there goes to the composition of the sentiment, not a rational only but also an animal element – the thirst for retaliation; and this thirst derives its intensity, as well as its moral justification, from the extraordinarily important and impressive kind of utility which is concerned.

This grounding the justification of rights in the interests of utility is, as many commentators from Mill's own time and since have noted, somewhat unsatisfying; or, to put it perhaps more generously, it is as satisfying as the notion of utility itself is satisfying. As the discussion in Chapter 3 will reveal, it is perhaps this unsatisfactoriness that leads Dworkin to posit quite the opposite justification of the necessity of rights: as trumps against utility.

Mill is well aware that the utilitarian justification of rights does not quite have a bedrock sort of appeal, and devotes much of his argument in Chapter V to an indirect defense of utility – essentially, that deontological theories do not do any better in justifying rights. He writes (1977: 1013–14):

> If the preceding analysis, or something resembling it, be not the correct account of the notion of justice – if justice be totally independent of utility, and be a standard per se, which the mind can recognize by simple introspection of itself – it is hard to understand why that internal oracle is so ambiguous, and why so many things appear to be either just or unjust, according to the light in which they are regarded. We are continually informed that utility is an uncertain standard, which every different person interprets differently, and that there is no safety but in the immutable, ineffaceable, and unmistakable dictates of justice, which carry their evidence in themselves and are independent of the fluctuations of opinion. One would suppose from this that on questions of justice there could be no controversy.... So far is this from being the fact that there is as much difference of opinion, and as much discussion, about what is just as about what is useful to society.

Of course, this debate is as yet unresolved, and I will turn shortly to Dworkin's opposing view of rights as trumps on utility, rather than indicators of it. However, it is noteworthy that nothing for my purposes turns on the question of whether or not rights are best understood as instruments of utility or checks on it; all that is needed is for rights to be justified by reference to a fundamental interest, which is compatible with either Mill's or Dworkin's characterization.

Mill claims that rights are such because they are of paramount utility, and he of course recognizes that such a characterization entails that they cannot be considered to be absolute – 'particular cases may occur in which some other social duty is so important as to overrule any one of the general maxims of justice.' (1077: 1019). I will return to this caveat shortly, but so far in his account in *Utilitarianism*, Mill has not revealed which interests are of such paramount utility as to merit the standing of right, though *On Liberty* reveals that a chief interest is liberty of self-development. In that work as well, as Chapter 2 will show, Mill famously highlights liberty of expression as worthy of right-status, because of its utility in furthering the interests of a democratic society.

In *Utilitarianism*, however, he enumerates two other interests that he finds sufficiently important to general utility to enshrine as rights. The first is our interest in security, which is

> ...to everyone's feelings the most vital of all interests. All other earthly benefits are needed by one person, not needed by another; and many of them can, if necessary, be cheerfully foregone or replaced by something else; but security no human being can possibly do without; on it we depend for all our immunity from evil and for the whole value of all and every good, beyond the passing moment; since nothing but the gratification of the instant could be of any worth to us, if we could be deprived of anything the next instant by whoever was momentarily stronger than ourselves. (Mill 1977: 1013)

Security here seems to mean the ability of the individual to rely on the continued efficacy of established expectations; the right to security is the right to faith in a certain regularity of societal norms and rules. In part, this is achieved by having a consistently enforced system of laws, but it also seems to refer to less formal social and ethical norms. That such an interest is of sufficient import to the general utility to be given status as a right should be obvious: if we were not assured of the regularity of societal norms, we would be in a constant state of anxiety, and spend all of our time guarding our property and bodies. Such an interest seems logically prior to the interest in liberty of self-development; having a basic level of security in the regularity and predictability of social life seems a precondition to any other endeavor we undertake, including the project of self-development.

Mill then enumerates another interest belonging to the select group worthy of state protection: our interest in equality. He writes that: 'All persons are deemed to have a *right* to equality of treatment, except when some recognized social expediency requires the reverse.' (Mill 1977: 1019, emphasis in the original). This is an interest that Dworkin will adopt and develop as primary, though, notably, without Mill's caveat. I will take up the right to equality in much more detail in my discussion of Dworkin, so I will leave it unelaborated for now.

For Mill, then, our interest in security is paramount; our interest in liberty of self-development guaranteed except when it harms the rights of others; and our interest in being treated as an equal also qualifies as of sufficient value to general utility to be considered a right. All three of these interests are relevant to my discussion of the harms suffered by women and minorities as a result of cultural oppression: the right to security is violated when, for example, hate speech is not consistently protected under the law; the right to liberty of self-development is violated when, for example, higher education admissions policies are discriminatory; the right to equality is violated when, for example, pornography is upheld as free expression in spite of its role in circulating views about women's inequality.

Thus, if state intervention in cases of cultural oppression is going to accord with Mill's formulation, the problem with cultural oppression must be formulated not merely with respect to its harm to our interests in general or to its harm to the welfare of its victims, but rather in terms of its harm to a particular right. Therefore, I will maintain that the harms of cultural oppression are such that they ought to warrant the protection offered by the harm principle, for three reasons. First, there is a primary, positive right to equality that is violated in the case of cultural oppression. Second, independently of any such right to equality, and even allowing that such a right is controversial enough not to be granted, there is still a case consistent with Mill for preventing the harms caused by cultural oppression because those harms prevent those affected by them from enjoying what is certainly a fundamental right – the right to liberty of self-determination. Finally, there is a reason to consistently address and resolve these hard cases through the legal system, because a failure to do so is a violation of the right to security.

For my purposes, then, given this brief look at Mill, I need only note that Mill's articulation of the liberal state is by no means a neutral state – rather, the state can and must depart from its neutrality whenever a right is violated and do what is necessary to restore the right. The state, then, for Mill, is activist in preventing those harms that are seen as pressing enough interests to be considered rights. Both Mill's harm principle – in delineating the sphere of interests sufficient to merit state interference with individual liberty – and the rights to security, liberty of self-development, and equality, in more fully explicating what our primary interests are, are consistent with my argument that the liberal state ought to take the harms of cultural oppression more seriously. Further, these arguments lend the weight of one of liberalism's most formidable thinkers to the argument.

Before turning to Raz, Fiss, and Sunstein, and then to Dworkin, there is one further point about Mill worth addressing, because it highlights both an important contrast to Dworkin and an important affinity with Raz, Fiss, and Sunstein, and more importantly because it speaks to a conception of rights as part of a system of community values, rather than at odds with them, as Dworkin would have it. This understanding of rights may be a welcome consequence of Mill's utilitarianism, in that a conception of rights as against the community interest would be, if not impossible, then at least difficult to justify within a utilitarian framework, for the reason that a mere individual's interest would be insufficient to overwhelm the interest of the rest of the community.

I will argue, along with Mill and later with Raz, Fiss, and Sunstein, who echo this viewpoint – that this conception of rights as of a piece with community interests is compatible with the view of the activist liberal state that I am advocating: if rights exist in order to further the community interest, it is much easier to justify an activist state, so long as that state is acting in the community interest. Further, it is more plausible to envision a genuine community interest in a society free of cultural oppression than it is to envision a society with a genuine community interest in such discrimination.

That said, it is worth briefly investigating Mill's view of rights as supportive of the community's overall welfare. As Mill's discussion of rights has just illuminated, he often invokes a caveat in the same breath that he enumerates a right: 'All persons are deemed to have a right to equality of treatment, except when some recognized social expediency requires the reverse'; 'particular cases may occur in which some other social duty is so important as to overrule any one of the general maxims of justice.' Such exceptions are of course vital to the consistency of Mill's utilitarian account of rights, but more importantly, they seem to indicate an understanding of the relationship between individual and community interests as reciprocal.

Mill's understanding of the nature of this reciprocity is seen at several points throughout *On Liberty*. One such place is found in a passage seen earlier in this chapter:

> Everyone who receives the protection of society owes a return for the benefit, and the fact of living in society renders it indispensable that each should be bound to observe a certain line of conduct toward the rest. This conduct consists, first, in not injuring the interests of one another, or rather certain interests that, either by express legal provision or by tacit understanding, ought to be considered as rights. (Mill 1978: 73)

On this formulation, rights are embedded in the very fabric of our lives as a society as much as they are embedded in the conception of the individual; we exist as individuals in a society, and there is no way of discussing the interests of one without discussing the interests of the other. The reciprocity here is that we receive, as individuals, certain benefits from society (the protection of the law, for example) – and in return for these benefits, we owe society a guarantee that we will behave in such a way that does not violate the interests that have been deemed important enough both to other individuals and to society as a whole, to be considered rights. Our respect for rights here arises out of our duties as citizens of a society, rather than in spite of them. As well, this passage reveals the close relationship between such an understanding of rights and utilitarianism – the mention of the respect for rights as indispensable, presumably to the general welfare, highlights their connection to utility.

Put in this way, the corollary that rights are not ultimate, but rather instrumental, features of our attempt to strike a balance between individual and societal interests seems more palatable. Indeed, it has been taken up as a way of justifying the relatively progressive contemporary Canadian *Charter* jurisprudence, which I will take up at greater length in Chapters 7 and 8. Keeping this Millian formulation firmly in mind throughout this study will help to ground my argument regarding the legitimacy of the state's use of rights as part of a campaign of activism in the interest of equality, rather than viewing rights as an impediment to such a campaign.

Further, it is worth concluding from the preceding discussion of the rights that Mill sees as fundamental – the rights to security, to liberty of self-development, and equality – that the benefits that these rights confer are as much societal as they are individual: the right to security cashes out as a right to a smoothly running society – one with stable laws and expectations; the right to liberty of self-development relies on a societal system of education wherein individuals are raised to learn to make the decisions about beliefs and lifestyles that best benefit society as a whole; and the right to equality can be seen as of a piece with the right to security – we can have no security, in Mill's sense of the term, if we are not assured that the rules of the society apply equally to each of us. So at every turn, in Mill's framework, we have justifications of rights being offered both in terms of benefits to individuals as well as benefits to society.

This understanding of the relationship between individual and society as reciprocal is further evidenced in the following passage from *On Liberty*:

There are also many positive acts for the benefit of others which he may rightfully be compelled to perform; such as, to give evidence in a court of justice; to bear his fair share in the common defense, or in any other joint work necessary to the interest of the society of which he enjoys the protection; and to perform certain acts of individual beneficence, such as saving a fellow-creature's life, or interposing to protect the defenseless against ill-usage, things which whenever it is obviously a man's duty to do, he may rightfully be made responsible to society for not doing. A person may cause evil to others not only by his actions but by his inaction, and in either case he is justly accountable to them for the injury. The latter case, it is true, requires a much more cautious exercise of compulsion than the former. To make any one answerable for doing evil to others, is the rule; to make him answerable for not preventing evil, is, comparatively speaking, the exception. Yet there are many cases clear enough and grave enough to justify that exception. (Mill 1978: 10–11)

This passage emphasizes that the relationship between the individual and the society is quite a strong one, and one that should not be understood as an imposition on the individual's freedom.[4] On the contrary, Mill views our obligations to each other in a much more holistic way – as much as we are individuals, we are members of society, and ideally, neither of these identities is at odds with, or hierarchically related to, the other.

This kind of understanding of the relationship between the individual and the society is more compatible with an activist liberal state than an account that sees the individual and the society as pitted against one another, for the reason that if society and the individual are mutually supportive of one another, state activism is less apt to be thought of as an encroachment into individual liberty, but rather as ultimately supportive of it. To this end, Mill can be read with Raz, Fiss, and Sunstein as supportive of a liberal framework of reciprocity, rather than a liberal framework of adverse interests, which theorists such as Dworkin and Nozick support. Interestingly, though Mill's view of the reciprocity between state and individual in the justification of rights seems deeply tied to his utilitarian outlook, Raz articulates a similar view that could be read independently of any commitment to utilitarianism.[5] I will now turn to discuss Raz's viewpoint of the relationship between the state and the individual, as well as the role of rights in that relationship.

## 1.3   Joseph Raz: Rights and the common interest

In 'Rights and Individual Well-Being' (1992), Raz sets out to dispute the idea that rights are about protecting individual interests against those of the community. According to Raz, it is a mistake to characterize rights as representing the individual's interest as against the interests of others, though this has certainly been the prevailing contemporary view, as exemplified in Dworkin's influential account. Rather, what Raz terms 'the common good' informs the justification of rights, such that the interests of the individual and the interests of the society coincide and both form vital components of the way that we justify the assigning of rights.

Raz argues for the conclusion that the justification of rights must be found in part in the interests of the common good, by examining a puzzle that arises when we look only to the interest of the individual right-holder to ground our justification of a right. He finds that the interest of the individual in what she has a right to is not a sufficient justification for the existence of the right, thus giving rise to the question of what else may ground the justification of the right:

> On the one hand, typically rights are to what is or is thought to be of value to the right-holder. On the other hand, quite commonly the value of a right, the weight it is to be given or the stringency with which it is to be observed do not correspond to its value to the right-holder. Since rights are, generally speaking, to benefits, to what is in the interest of or is valuable for the right-holder, it is plausible to suppose that that interest is the basis of the right, i.e., that the reason for the right, its justification, is the fact that it serves the right-holder's interest. But in that case we would also expect the weight or importance of the right to correspond to the weight or importance of the interest it serves. Since this is clearly not the case, since the weight of rights diverges from the weight of the interests they serve one would expect that the reasons for or justification of rights relate to considerations other than those interests. But if so why do rights dovetail with interests? Why do we generally have rights only to what is in our interest? Can this be a mere coincidence? (Raz 1992: 128–9)

Raz thinks that this puzzle of the imperfect overlap between the weight of rights (very strong) and the interests that they serve in the individual (less strong) is resolved by reference to the notion that rights also serve the interests of the common good; when we take this into consideration, the overlap becomes more commensurate – we accord rights such grave weight because not only do they serve the individual, they serve society as a whole, the common interest, at the same time.

So, the characterization of rights as interests of the right-holder seems to be an insufficient basis for the justification of the existence and gravity of rights. Instead, Raz contends, we need to acknowledge that the right is justified by the fact that by serving the interest of the right-holder, it serves the interest of some others, and the interest of these others contributes to determining the weight due to the right. The interests of these others matter, however, only when they are served by serving the right-holder's interests – only when helping the right-holder is the proper way to help others.

Raz gives a persuasive example to illustrate this relationship between the right-holder and others:

> I, as a parent, have, in English law, a right to a periodic payment known as a child benefit, which I receive because I am a parent and because benefiting me is a good way of benefiting my child. People who support invalid parents or spouses have similar rights to reductions in their tax liability, and there are many other examples. In all of them the weight of the right does not match the right-holder's interest which it serves, because in all of them the right is justified by the fact that by serving the interest of the right-holder it serves the interest of some others, and their interest contributes to determining the weight due to the right. (Raz 1992: 133)

This example illustrates that the rights-to-interests ratio becomes much more explicable once we factor the interests of third parties into the justificatory account of the right. Raz feels that these examples support a twofold understanding of what I will call the 'reciprocal interests' justificatory framework of rights:

> On the one hand, rights are sometimes justified by the service they secure for people other than the right-holder. On the other, other people's interests count for the justification of the right only when they are harmoniously interwoven with those of the right-holder, i.e., only when benefiting him is a way of benefiting them, and where by benefiting them the right-holder's interest is served. (Raz 1992: 134)

At this point, the parallels between Mill's and Raz's accounts become clear. For both theorists, rights support both the right-holder and others, and when we take those others into account, the weight of the right becomes more intelligible. As the previous excerpts from *On Liberty* and *Utilitarianism* reveal, Mill sees rights as supportive not only of the individual's interest, but as necessarily, *qua* utilitarian, supportive of the community interest.

Raz's examples up until this point have exclusively concerned the interests of third-party dependents, and one is justified in wondering if perhaps these parties are special cases, rather than general instances. Raz goes on to argue that they are not, and that, indeed,

> [t]he protection of many of the most cherished civil and political rights in liberal democracies is justified by the fact that they serve the common or general good.... When people are called upon to make substantial sacrifices in the name of one of the fundamental civil and political rights of an individual this is not because in some matters the interest of the individual or the respect due to the individual prevails over the interest of the collectivity or of the majority. It is because by protecting the right of that individual one protects the common good and is thus serving the interest of the majority. (Raz 1992: 135–6)

He contends that the common good often meets the condition of harmony with individual interest, and that if we first agree, echoing Mill, that the protection of individual civil and political rights serves the common good, then we can move to the second, and more controversial, position that the common good served by those rights is, in the majority of cases, more important to individuals than the enjoyment of their own civil and political rights, and therefore that the status that rights enjoy in liberal democracies is due to their contribution to the common good (1992: 136). Raz proceeds to give several examples of cases where the benefits of everyday rights exceeds their benefits to the individual right-holder, and these examples reveal that he and Mill are on the same page with respect to the reciprocity of interests between the individual and society:

> Consider freedom of contract. It is a vital means for assuring people a measure of control over the conduct of their affairs. Its value to individuals depends on protection from duress, deceit, misrepresentation.... [T]he existence of such an environment is a common good. It serves not only those who make contracts. If you doubt this, think of young children. They do not make contracts but they benefit from the fact that they live in a free society in which people

generally have power to control the conduct of their own affairs. (Raz 1992: 136)

This view seems to echo Mill's justifications of rights in that reference is made in the same breath not only to the interest of the right-holder, but to the interest of society as a whole. Mill will most famously make this reciprocal argument about the right to freedom of expression, which I will take up in Chapter 2.

Raz holds that this understanding of the justification of rights from reference to the common good also serves to explain

> [w]hy civil and political rights which are the prize of the official culture of liberal democracies do not enjoy a similar place in the estimation of most ordinary people. Many people judge them by their contribution to their well-being, and it is not much. Their real value is in their contribution to a common liberal culture. That culture serves the interests of members of the community. (Raz 1992: 137)

Having examined both Mill's and Raz's reciprocal interests views of rights, I would like to suggest that such an account ought to be adopted by the egalitarian liberal state for two reasons, both of which are key to the argument of this study. First, reciprocal interests accounts of rights can more easily accommodate a departure from neutrality in cases where rights violations not only affect the interests of the particular affected individuals but also the interests of the community as a whole. Such is the case in instances of cultural oppression – the interests of the minorities are of course infringed upon, but so too are the interests of the society, because presumably we all benefit from a society that treats us respectfully and as equals.

Second, reciprocal interests accounts of rights offer a principled criterion of adjudication – the common good – in hard cases, such as those of hate speech and pornography. In considering whether, for example, pornography ought to be protected as free speech (upholding the rights of the pornographers), or restricted because it interferes with the rights of women (upholding the rights of women), it will prove helpful to have recourse to a third set of interest holders – the society in general. Instead of viewing the issue rather narrowly as a conflict between two sets of rights-holders, it is more fruitful to ask which decision better supports the common good.[6]

In a similar vein to Raz's arguments, Owen Fiss, in *The Irony of Free Speech* (1996), and Cass Sunstein in *Democracy and the Problem of Free*

*Speech* (1995), offer a critique of the dominant liberal viewpoint that rights operate to protect the individual from the harms of the state. However, Fiss and Sunstein look only at the United States' freedom of expression jurisprudence to make this case, and their arguments are thus particularly apposite for themes of this book. Fiss argues that it is a misconception to view the state as always the enemy of freedom of expression. This view is a half-truth, and the other half of this truth can be found in understanding the liberal state as an ally in protecting a collective interest in the democratic process:

> The debates of the past were premised on the view that the state was the natural enemy of freedom. It was the state that was trying to silence the individual speaker, and it was the state that had to be curbed. There is much wisdom to this view, but it represents only a half truth. Surely, the state may be an oppressor, but it may also be a source of freedom.... [T]his view is predicated on a theory of the First Amendment and its guarantee of free speech that emphasizes social, rather than individualistic, values. The freedom the state may be called upon to foster is a public freedom.... The law's intention is to broaden the terms of public discussion as a way of enabling common citizens to become aware of the issues before them.... A distinction is thus drawn between a libertarian and a democratic theory of speech, and it is the latter that impels my inquiry into the ways the state may enhance our freedom. (Fiss 1996: 2–3)

The idea of the state as potentially enhancing our collective freedom by adjudicating its freedom of expression decisions in order to facilitate our collective interest in a robust democratic process is exactly what I am maintaining that an activist egalitarian liberal state ought to do. I will examine the details of Fiss's argument about the freedom of expression jurisprudence in Chapter 7, when I discuss the principles under which an activist egalitarian state may operate. At this point I want only to highlight that Fiss's project is another relevant account of the role of the liberal state that departs from the orthodox liberal reading of the state as the enemy of individual liberty.

Similarly, Sunstein argues (1995: 241) that: 'The American constitutional system is emphatically not designed solely to protect private interests and private rights.... Instead, a large point of the system is to ensure discussion and debate among people who are genuinely different in their perspectives and position.' In other words, the Millian vision of the marketplace of ideas describes a collective interest – and not an individual interest – in a diverse discussion, and the right to freedom of expression is designed to facilitate that collective interest and that discussion, which the framers, along with Mill and Dworkin, saw as an interest crucial to democracy itself.

Unlike Mill and Dworkin, however, Fiss and Sunstein believe that the way to facilitate the common interest in 'marketplace of ideas'-style debates is not necessarily to insist upon state neutrality in the marketplace. In Chapter 7, when I discuss how an activist egalitarian liberal state may work in practice, I will return to Fiss and Sunstein for their insights into the state as a non-neutral facilitator of the marketplace.

## 1.4   Ronald Dworkin: Concern, respect, and rights

Having adopted the reciprocal interests view of the state and individual, and the role of rights within it, it is important to turn now to Dworkin's somewhat contrary account of these topics. Dworkin's egalitarian liberalism provides a framework for understanding the scope of the state's responsibilities to its citizens, articulated primarily in terms of a theory of rights. In developing his egalitarian liberalism, Dworkin first inquires into the meaning of liberalism *per se*. He canvasses a number of traditional liberal positions on political questions, such as the ideas that inequalities of wealth are to be reduced through welfare and other forms of redistribution financed by progressive taxes; the support of racial equality and approval of government intervention to secure it; and the opposition to other forms of collective regulation of individual decisions, such as regulation of the content of political speech and regulation of sexual literature (Dworkin 1986: 185–7). Having catalogued these positions, he then asks whether or not there is a single principle that runs through them. It is often thought that there is not a single principle in these positions, but rather that there is a certain tension revealed within them between the principles of liberty and equality, with equality winning out in liberalism, and liberty winning out in conservatism. In other words, conservatives value liberty centrally and thus oppose welfare schemes, for example, which they view as impinging on the liberty of the taxpayer, while liberals value equality among citizens over liberty for each individual citizen and thus approve of such schemes. Dworkin thinks that such a view is off the mark, because he does not think that liberty is a quantifiable thing that is capable of being independently valued – he argues (1986: 189) that 'the fundamental liberties are important because we value something else that they protect,' namely equality.

Dworkin maintains (1986: 183) that 'a certain conception of equality, which I shall call the liberal conception, is the nerve of liberalism.' What, exactly, is this particular liberal conception of equality? On Dworkin's view, the state's fundamental obligation is to treat its citizens with what he terms 'equal concern and respect,' and from this positive obligation, he grounds his theory of the role of rights. How we are to understand this obligation, and what exactly follows from it, will be of great concern to the argument in this study. Dworkin, in elaborating this notion of equal concern and respect, writes that:

> Government must treat those whom it governs with concern, that is, as human beings who are capable of suffering and frustration, and with respect, that is, as human beings who are capable of forming and acting on intelligent conceptions of how their lives should be lived. Government must not only treat people with concern and respect, but with equal concern and respect. (Dworkin 2005: 272)

Underlying this formulation, though not stated explicitly here, is the idea that this obligation of equal concern and respect means that the government's concern and respect will be equally bestowed upon both majority and minority groups. According to Dworkin, this fundamental right to equal concern and respect might be understood in two importantly different ways:

1. The right to equal treatment, that is, to the same distribution of goods or opportunities as anyone else has or is given.
2. The right to treatment as an equal. This is the right, not to the equal distribution of some good or opportunity, but the right to equal concern and respect in the political decision about how these goods and opportunities are to be distributed.

(Dworkin 1986: 190)

According to Dworkin, the latter, the right to treatment as an equal, is more fundamental than the former, the right to equal treatment. Rights to specific liberties are only recognized when it is shown that the right to treatment as an equal requires that they be (2005: 273). In other words, for Dworkin, the liberal state must guarantee that it takes each citizen's interest into account equally in its decision-making, though doing so is not synonymous with, and need not entail, an equal distribution of resources. In economic controversies, liberals want more of the right to equal treatment than conservatives do, but for both liberals and conservatives, Dworkin maintains, the right to treatment as an equal is constitutive and the right to equal treatment is derivative. He writes:

> Sometimes treating people equally is the only way to treat them as equals; but sometimes not. Suppose a limited amount of emergency relief is available for two equally populous areas injured by floods; treating the citizens of both areas as equals requires giving more aid to the more seriously devastated area rather than splitting the available funds equally. (Dworkin 1986: 190)

In other words, our commitment to treating people as equals may or may not entail the right to equal treatment in a particular case, but whether or not it does depends on the circumstances of that case, rather than on a prior and fundamental commitment to the right to equal treatment.

The important point, though, in all of this, is that Dworkin has recast the debate between liberals and conservatives, and the debate about the nature of liberalism, as one wholly within a core commitment to equality rather than as a debate between liberty and equality. He concludes his discussion (2005: 272) thus:

> We must reject the simple idea that liberalism consists in a distinctive weighing between constitutive principles of equality and liberty. But our discussion of the idea of equality suggests a more fruitful line. I assume that there is a broad agreement within modern politics that the government must treat all its citizens with equal concern and respect.

The shift in emphasis from a debate about the relative weighting of liberty versus equality, to a discussion about the nature of equality itself, is of paramount import for the argument I will advance. Granting Dworkin the idea that liberalism is committed to equality in the sense of the right to treatment as an equal, and that liberties are to be understood as instrumental to that end, rather than potentially inimical to it, takes away the major stumbling block to an activist state – the idea that such a state would violate the liberty of citizens, and is thus anathema for the liberal. As long as the state is activist only in the pursuit of true equality, and the liberties that such a pursuit may violate are liberties that were in fact at odds with equality, there is no problem, according to Dworkin, with their violation.

Dworkin's next task, having dispensed with liberty as a core principle underlying both liberalism or conservatism, is to dispense with another myth that he feels causes liberalism to be misunderstood. This myth revolves around the notion that liberalism is a political theory about state neutrality, rather than about state commitment to equality. He maintains that there are two forms of liberalism – neutrality liberalism and equality liberalism – that have vital differences between them (1986: 205–13). Both argue against the legal enforcement of private morality, and both argue for greater sexual, political, and economic equality, but they disagree over which of these two tenets is primary, and which is derivative. Neutrality liberalism takes as fundamental the idea that government must not take sides on moral issues, and it supports such egalitarian measures as can be justified in accordance with this idea. Equality liberalism, conversely, holds that government's primary obligation is to treat citizens as equals, and insists on moral neutrality only to the degree that is required by egalitarianism (1986: 205).

Dworkin maintains that neutrality liberalism has two defects: first, it is a negative theory based on moral skepticism; and second, it is so narrowly tailored that it merely addresses moral conservatism, rather than also including economic conservatism. As to the first problem, neutrality liberalism is compatible with the view that there is no such thing as 'the good life,' but rather there are only competing, subjective, versions of it. Dworkin wants to leave open the possibility of greater realism about the good, especially since he is a realist about the notion that a society that realizes equal concern and respect towards its citizens is a society that is more truly facilitating the good lives of its citizens than one which does not. Equality liberalism rests on this positive moral position, while neutrality liberalism can operate without subscribing to it.

The second problem for neutrality liberalism, as Dworkin sees it, is that it is too narrowly focused on a hands-off attitude towards state interference in private moral choices of how best to conduct one's life, and as such it is unable to adequately address the problem raised by economic inequalities: whether or not the state ought to intervene to correct for differences in distribution of resources caused by the free operation of the market. Neutrality liberalism, without the positive moral underpinnings of equality liberalism, does not have the theoretical teeth to delve into this matter.

Equality liberalism, on the other hand, is not flawed in this way. It rests on a positive commitment to an egalitarian morality. Equality liberalism insists that the government treat people as equals in the following sense: they must impose no sacrifice or constraint on any citizen in virtue of an argument that the citizen could not accept without abandoning her sense of her equal worth. If individuals are asked to sacrifice their styles of life for the community, they must be able to do so in a way that is consistent with their being treated with equal concern and respect, and there must be some reason advanced as to why they ought to feel that the community that they are being asked to sacrifice for is in fact their community. A citizen can feel a part of the community only if they have some power to shape that community's future. These conditions impose serious restraints on any policy that denies any group of citizens, however small or politically negligible, the equal resources that equal concern would otherwise grant them (1986: 205). Dworkin writes:

> If government pushes people below the level at which they can help shape the community and draw value from it for their own lives, or if it holds out a bright future in which their own children are promised only second-class lives, then it forfeits the only premise on which its conduct might be justified...for society's obligation runs first to its living citizens. (1986: 213)

So Dworkin has made clear that the liberal state's obligation to treat its citizens with equal concern and respect does not entail an equal distribution of resources, but does entail a high degree of participation by the individual in the community, and relies upon their own consent and agreement as to how they are treated relative to others. However, thus far Dworkin's account reveals that the state's role is to perform only those actions consistent with the state's commitment to treating its citizens with equal concern and respect, but Dworkin does not yet have a positive statement as to what this equal concern and respect commitment actually entails.

In this regard, Dworkin says that there are two possible answers to this question of the meaning of equal concern and respect. First, the government is neutral on what constitutes the good life: since people's conceptions of the good life differ, government does not treat them equally if it prefers one conception to another. And secondly, the government cannot be neutral on the question of the good life, because it cannot treat its citizens as equal human beings without a theory of what human beings ought to be: good government means fostering good lives.

Dworkin claims that liberalism picks the former as its constitutive morality, and it is here that neutrality enters back into the Dworkinian picture – not at the primary level of 'neutrality liberalism,' for the reasons just canvassed, but as a means of ensuring that citizens are treated with equal concern and respect. Because people have different conceptions of the good life, the state's job is either to ensure that it promotes all of them equally – or, alternatively, echoing Mill, to provide a background wherein their private proponents may be given equal opportunity to promote their visions themselves. So while Dworkin rejects neutrality as the fundamental underpinning of liberalism in favor of equality as that underpinning, he nevertheless rather quickly returns to an embracing of the notion of neutrality, albeit as a second-order good, insofar as it best promotes equality.

It is worthwhile to pause here to note that thus far Dworkin's account, though innocuous on its face, is already masking some deep tensions in terms of the question of state activism or interventionism in the prevention of harms. Recall that Dworkin claims that concern – one branch of the liberal state's commitment to equality – means that people are the kinds of beings who can feel suffering and frustration. From here, he moves quickly to the idea that *qua* sentient in this way, they are thus worthy of respect, which means that they are to be trusted with the capacity to make their own decisions. What is worthy of note here, I would suggest, is Dworkin's quick move from merely defining concern to this definition's putative entailment of respect, where respect means a hands-off approach to the question of the good life.

This move is questionable in two ways, one more radical than the other. First, and more radically, it is worth asking whether it in fact follows at all from the fact that we are beings capable of suffering and frustration (concern) that we should be left to our own devices (respect) to devise strategies to avoid such suffering and frustration. Second, and less radically, it is worth asking, even granted that there is such an entailment between concern and respect, whether respect is the *only* obligation entailed by concern, or whether there are others.

These are questions of paramount import for the argument of this study. Taking the less radical view, and assuming that there is a connection at least, if not a strict entailment, between concern and respect, I will argue that there is an important further entailment that derives from the idea of concern – namely that when the suffering and frustration that is visited upon a minority by a majority is of such a nature as to be systemic and institutionalized, it is not the case that the minority can merely be treated with Dworkin's hands-off idea of respect. This is because what it means to be a minority frustrated and suffering due to systemic and institutionalized causes is to say that the minority is incapable by its own efforts of remedying the situation, because the traditional channels of remedy are themselves implicated in the very problem; these channels are exactly those institutions which are themselves systemically and institutionally discriminatory.

Given this wrinkle in Dworkin's casting of respect as a hands-off affair between government and citizen, I want to suggest that his quick move from concern to respect is untenable, assuming both that the liberal state sees concern and respect as equally central to its obligations, and that it is serious about treating its citizens equally. I argue that a serious commitment to equality, coupled with an understanding of the fact and mechanics of discrimination, leads to the conclusion that liberalism must depart from its idea of mere hands-off respect in order to remedy such cases. I will argue, further, that Dworkin's rights justification arguments in fact entail this very conclusion, although Dworkin does not seem to see the implication. Part of this project, then, involves reading Dworkin against himself in order to show that a thoroughgoing commitment to the egalitarian principles he articulates necessitates a more interventionist state than he grants. If I am successful in establishing this, a secondary question arises of how to identify these cases – how to know when circumstances are such as to warrant hands-off respect, and when they are such as to warrant state activism. This question will be among the concerns addressed in later chapters.

Returning to Dworkin's liberalism, given that the state's job is to promote each vision of the good life equally, Dworkin claims that the state will find two guiding institutions in effecting its task. For economic decisions, about what goods shall be produced and how they shall be distributed, the economic free market is appropriate; for collective decisions about what conduct shall be prohibited or regulated so that other conduct might be made possible, representative democracy is the best institution. Each provides a more egalitarian distribution than any other general arrangement.

However, Dworkin warns, while these institutions provide a starting point for the state's task of treating its citizens with equal concern and respect, they are not the end of the story. The reason that they are not is that the free market and representative democracy, left alone, cannot produce truly egalitarian outcomes, because people differ not just in terms of preferences, but also in terms of things like talents, leading to unequal distributions under the market economy. Unequal distributions of benefits due to innate talents are unacceptable for the liberal, since differences in talent do not amount to differences in moral worth sufficient to justify such unequal distributions as we have. Given this, the liberal conception of equality thus requires an economic system that allows certain inequalities and not others. Thus, the free market, left unchecked, produces both the permissible (based on preference) and the forbidden (based on talent) inequalities (Dworkin 1986: 197–200).

Therefore, the liberal, to remedy the forbidden inequalities, must introduce some kind of welfare scheme, in order to achieve the best possible practical realization of the demands of equality itself. So the belief in the market economy to generate equal economic distributions based on preferences has to be revised, because preferences aren't the only things that need to be equalized – so too do talents. It is of note at this point that Dworkin seems perfectly comfortable with an activist state to correct for market processes in the case of social welfare. Given this activism, it is worth asking why departures from mere respect are allowable in the economic sphere and not in a broader sphere?

The belief in the democratic process too needs revision, according to Dworkin, because voting does not straightforwardly mean that each person, equally, receives her due concern and respect by equally voicing her opinion. The situation is complicated by the fact that the outcomes of those opinions may end up violating, rather than upholding, equality. This problem arises because of what Dworkin calls 'external preferences' – where a person casts her vote not only according to her own personal preference for her own consumption of resources – such personal preferences are always legitimate, according to Dworkin – but also her secondary preference, or what Dworkin calls an external preference, which is a vote about how resources ought to be consumed or allocated to others. These preferences can frustrate the preferences of minorities in some cases. External preferences, according to Dworkin, always effectively amount to two votes. Thus, they are always an illegitimate and perverse consequence of utilitarianism, for which rights provide the remedy.

Commentators have raised many persuasive objections to the notion of external preferences (see, for example, Hart 1979), but for my purposes Dworkin's broader scheme of understanding rights as checks on utilitarianism in general, rather than on external preferences in particular, is sufficient. Rights may be equally required to ensure equal concern and respect of a minority where their rights are violated by even the internal, merely personal, preferences, of a majority. The point that is worth highlighting is that rights serve a counter-utilitarian function for Dworkin: cases where utilitarian outcomes violate equal concern and respect entail that the state needs to intervene in order to meet its obligation to treat its citizens with equal concern and respect. This intervention is exactly what rights are.

In order to mitigate against the problems of violations of equal concern and respect to minorities caused by utilitarian voting procedures, the liberal needs a scheme of civil rights whose effect will be to determine those political decisions that are antecedently likely to cause such violations, and to remove those decisions from majoritarian political institutions altogether. I will turn to discussing that scheme of rights now, but conclude by noting that the liberal, drawn to the economic market and to political democracy for distinctly egalitarian reasons, finds that these institutions will produce inegalitarian results unless they add to their scheme both welfare to remedy the inequities in the economic sphere, and different sorts of individual rights in the political sphere. Again, it is important for my project of justifying liberal state activism to note that from the outset of Dworkin's articulation of liberalism, which has now become quite mainstream, there are two deep strains of allowable forms of state action in the name of equal concern and respect – welfare and rights.

It will be my contention, in the name of these same goals – concern and respect – that the state needs to remedy cultural oppression in a way that goes deeper than Dworkin's allowable interventions of welfare and the traditional civil rights. I will argue that what it means to live in a society where cultural oppression takes place is to have victims unable to be recipients of respect, in the sense that they cannot, due to the social forces at work in their situations, take advantage of the freedoms and self-determination that the liberal state's stance of respect is supposed to provide. If this is a sound characterization of the operation of cultural oppression, then, I will argue, it leads, in exactly the same way as Dworkin's talents and counter-utilitarian arguments lead, to the conclusion that the state ought to fashion an activist remedy to correct the problem, just as it does in the case of welfare and the case of rights.

My argument is simply that if Dworkin, and egalitarian liberalism more generally, is comfortable with being in the business of fashioning remedies in the case of failures of the state to meet its obligations of equal concern and respect, then the fact of cultural oppression against minorities is simply one more feature of our lives that the egalitarian liberal state must take into account when asking itself the question of whether or not it is meeting its mandate to safeguard its citizens' equality. Seeing that a hands-off policy towards cultural oppression constitutes a failure of its obligations in this regard, it must set about to fashion the appropriate remedy, just as it did, fairly uncontroversially, in the cases of welfare and of civil rights.

It is worth spending some time going through Dworkin's justification of the enactment of civil rights in the egalitarian liberal state, as it will prove to be key to my aims in holding that this very structure of justification in fact leads to the conclusion that the state ought to treat cases of systemic oppression very differently than it does. As already discussed, for Dworkin, rights are to be understood as remedies for the imperfect operation of an unchecked utilitarianism. These rights will function as 'trump cards' held by individuals and serve to check decisions made in consideration of majoritarian aims. The ultimate justification for these rights, as noted, is that they are necessary to protect equal concern and respect, which is how the market economy and political democracy are themselves justified. So, rights are best understood as trumps over some background justification, such as utilitarianism, which is based on a community goal. Utilitarianism, like rights, owes its appeal to its egalitarian cast, but utilitarianism needs tweaking, due to the fact that external preferences are double counted, and hence fails in fact to treat people as equals.

On Dworkin's account of rights, then, we can

> enjoy the institutions of political democracy, which enforce overall or unrefined utilitarianism, and yet protect the fundamental right of citizens to equal concern and respect by prohibiting decisions that seem, antecedently, likely to have been reached by virtue of the external components of the preferences democracy reveals. (Dworkin 2005: 277)

Thus rights are to be understood as offering insurance, or backup, for utilitarian outcomes, rather than acting as replacements for them. On Dworkin's picture, the majority of state decisions will be made by utilitarian calculations, with the caveat of rights-based decisions in areas where the state has determined that some fundamental interests of a minority are unduly likely to be violated if the state did not intervene. The state then intervenes in these cases precisely by invoking a civil right which corresponds with the protection of the endangered minority interest, in order to ensure that that interest is not subject to the vagaries of utilitarian outcomes, given their tendency to distort equality through external preferences.

I would agree that there is a need for the state to intervene in certain cases of unchecked utilitarianism, but Dworkin's characterization of such cases as those where external preferences prevail is insufficient to describe the proper range of relevant cases, for two related reasons: it is too broad in that it grants minorities *per se* a right of moral independence over utilitarians who employ external preferences to discount the way of life of the particular minority group; but stated thusly this right can be used to protect minorities whose lifestyles contravene our egalitarian liberal interest in the promotion of equal concern and respect, or whose lifestyles violate Mill's harm principle. Such minorities may include, but are not limited to: racist organizations, pornographers, smokers, and pedophiles. I will argue that we need to find a theoretical principle that will limit the application of Dworkin's ideas to protect only those minority groups whose protection is consistent with the egalitarian liberal aims of promoting equality and preventing harm. The adoption of the notion of cultural oppression provides just such a theoretical principle.

The second reason for holding that Dworkin's external preferences account of rights is inadequate is Hart's, offered in his 1979 essay 'Between Utility and Rights.' Hart's idea is essentially the inverse of the first criticism offered above, in that there are some lifestyles that contain external preferences which we actively wish to promote, rather than curtail, as they further our egalitarian goals of the fostering of equality and the prevention of harm. For Dworkin, says Hart, those few protected liberties which may not be violated on utilitarian grounds are not justified as 'essentials of human well-being' or by any substantive idea of the good life or individual welfare. What distinguishes liberties that ought to be protected from those that ought not is a procedural rather than a substantive matter based on the content of the particular preference: those liberties where there is an antecedent likelihood that an unrestricted utilitarian calculation of the general interest of a majority vote would likely violate equality by the workings of external preferences will be protected by a right. Hence, the peferred liberties are those such as freedom of speech or sexual relations, which are to rank as rights when we know from our general knowledge of society that they are in danger of being overridden by external preferences in a utilitarian procedure. Thus, according to Hart, Dworkin tries to derive rights to specific liberties from nothing more controversial than the duty of governments to treat their citizens with equal concern and respect.

The problem with the theory for Hart is that it isn't really external preferences *per se* that are problematic, but rather those external preferences that oppose a given freedom, in which case the issue isn't merely procedural, but instead it is tied to the particular content of the particular preference. For example, Hart argues (1979: 94), in the case of liberal heterosexuals who are in favor of granting rights to homosexuals, these external preferences are unproblematic. If this example is correct – and I believe it is – then Dworkin's external preferences idea needs amending. I will argue in later chapters that the appropriate amendment to remedy this problem will come from an analysis in terms of power, as understood by Michel Foucault and others.

If one accepts Hart's and my own criticism, then one denies that the justification for the invocation of rights is a merely procedural matter – rather, it must be understood as substantive. An adequate account of rights, then, requires a substantive rationale through which to determine when a particular majority preference undermines equal concern and respect. By attempting to ground his account in the procedural realm, Dworkin overlooks what in my account is fundamental – namely, the particular cases wherein a historically marginalized group's interests in equal concern and respect are denied. Put another way, Dworkin's failure to satisfactorily ground the justification of rights in the procedural realm is for my purposes a happy failure: it underlines the fact that rights and interests need to be investigated in a deeper, more nuanced way – taking into account not only the narrow interests of the right holders, but also their position in the community and the history of their group's membership in that community.

Dworkin's picture, it has often been pointed out, is adequate only to the extent that one agrees to premise his fundamental right to equality, which is assumed to hold as a guiding moral axiom in both utilitarian and rights-based decisions. The theory is thus vulnerable to the critique that there is no such fundamental right underlying either process – be it utilitarian or rights-based. Such an objection has often been made throughout the rights theory literature, holding that there is indeed a fundamental and primary right to liberty, rather than to equality.[7]

Dworkin argues against this view, and claims not only that the right to equality is more basic than the right to liberty, but more radically that there is no such thing as a right to liberty at all, let alone a primary one. Liberty, as it has been traditionally understood, means the absence of constraints placed by a government upon what a person might do if she wishes. Liberty, on this view, is understood as license, neutral to whatever substantive choices a person might choose to make in virtue of it. Dworkin maintains that to see something this broad as a right, though, is absurd.

According to Dworkin, we can define a right, in basic terms, as something that if it exists, it would be wrong for the government to interfere with, even if interference were in the general interest. In other words, a right is something that survives the passage of any law that the government may make that attempts to undermine it. Defining rights in this way makes clear the absurdity that on this view of rights and of liberty, *any* law is an obstruction of liberty – in Dworkin's famous example, it would be wrong for the government to turn Lexington Avenue into a one-way street, since the restriction on driving in the prohibited direction is indeed a restriction on my liberty. But, of course, it isn't wrong, and it isn't wrong because I don't have a right to liberty in that strong sense.

But what about basic liberties, like freedom of speech? If we try to call them 'basic' because of the quantity of liberty that their restraint violates, this doesn't seem to be an accurate characterization – things like the criminal law violate liberty in a quantitative sense much more greatly than mere traffic laws, without attracting rights controversy. If instead we try to talk about our basic rights as protecting a certain quality of liberty, then we run into the equally intractable problem that any way of explaining different qualities of liberty, as such a distinction would require, will go beyond the bounds of liberty as such, to other values, like equality or dignity, which are what Dworkin thinks are really at stake in the issue of rights justification. He claims that we protect certain liberties – such as freedom of speech and freedom of religion – because we value something that underlies them – not liberty itself, but rather equality of concern and respect. Rights, for Dworkin, represent the liberal state's promise to minorities that their interests will be treated with concern and respect equal to that of the majority.

Dworkin adds (2005: 272) that the particular justification that he has offered of grounding rights in the state's commitment to equal concern and respect is 'only one possible ground for rights.' And indeed he has been criticized for the pragmatism of his justificatory framework – his critics, including Hart, arguing that there ought to be a firmer foundation for rights than as mere correctives for the inadequacies of utilitarianism, because without such a firmer foundation we are left with the odd result that a society with fewer utilitarian failings would have fewer rights. Dworkin, however, does not seem to mind this result, claiming that nothing much is lost in considering rights as merely corrective, rather than fundamental in some deeper sense. For Dworkin, what is fundamental is the state's commitment to equality, and rights are but one way that the state can go about meeting this fundamental commitment:

> We need rights, as a distinct element in political theory, only when some decision that injures some people nevertheless finds prima-facie support in the claim that it will make the community as a whole

better off on some plausible account of where the community's general welfare lies. (Dworkin 1986: 371)

A decision in such a case to opt for the community's general welfare is wrong, Dworkin says, in spite of its apparent merit, because it does not treat the minority population with equal concern and respect.

Another criticism of Dworkin's account is that it doesn't tell us which positive rights we in fact have, but rather only says that if we have a right, it is because the right functions as a protection of an interest which otherwise would be compromised by an unchecked utilitarian-ism. Given that the account proceeds in this way – arguing that if there is a likelihood of violation of equal concern and respect through the operation of utilitarianism, then there ought to be a right granted to preemptively thwart its operation – it is worth noting that for the purpose of arguing that instances of cultural oppression ought to be remedied by the liberal state, casting the problem of cultural oppres-sion against minorities in terms of a malfunction of utilitarianism will meet Dworkin's criteria for when the liberal state ought to intervene with a remedy.

Put another way, since Dworkin's methodology proceeds from viol-ations of equality to rights, the particular rights that we have at any given time must be fluid ones, as they arise and fall away depending on the majority's particular preferences. If rights are fluid in this way, then we can claim a right whenever utilitarian outcomes are such as to threaten an interest to equal concern and respect. If Dworkin wishes to deny a new right, by the same token, he must do so by arguing that our core interest in equal concern and respect is not being threatened by the particular majority preference.

It is noteworthy that this conception of rights sees them as pro-tective of an interest of the right holder – in particular, an interest in equality, rather than in liberty. It is central to my argument that rights be understood as protective of interests, since I will argue that the liberal state has an obligation to protect certain interests, and if rights are protective of interests, then it has an obligation to extend certain rights. However, there has been some debate as to whether the char-acterization of rights as being protective of interests is the most apt description of their role in our political life. In the literature, the view of rights as protecting an interest rather than as protecting a choice of the right holder about how and whether to go about alienating that right against corresponding duty-holders is controversial and unresolved – the choice theory of rights being defended most notably by Hart, and the interest theory being defended by Bentham, Mill, and Raz. The choice theory singles out the right holder in terms of the power she has over the duty in question, and holds that what it is to have a right is to have a choice respected by the law. This degree of power or control over the duty-bearer makes an individual a right-bearer on Hart's account.

However, those holding the interest view maintain that the choice account seems insufficient to describe the relations between rights and duties, because not all rights, the right not to be killed for example, are best understood as alienable in this way. In those cases, we think of the right not as based in power or choice, but as based in some basic human interest, hence the appeal of the interest theory.[8]

For the purposes of this study, I will argue that either account is acceptable, as both make sufficient reference to interests to support the argument for an interventionist state in cases of cultural oppression. The choice theory can be seen to be protective of interests, albeit perhaps less directly, by giving individuals autonomy over the promotion of those interests. As I said earlier, the adoption of the interest theory dovetails quite well with Dworkin's theory of rights as protective of a fundamental interest in equality, rather than as protective of a certain kind of choice or power that one individual has over another. I will argue that viewing rights as protective of interests, under either the interest or the choice theory, can be seen as giving way to a more active, interventionist understanding of the state's role in granting and protecting rights. On Dworkin's view, which sees rights as protective of interests, it is the role of the state to anticipate those issues that might, if left to pure utilitarian calculation, violate an individual's fundamental interest in being treated with equal concern and respect by the state, and to intervene with the enactment and enforcement of a right in such cases, in order to preempt that interest's violation. Given that the interest theory seems to necessitate a more active state role in the guarantee that rights will indeed protect fundamental citizens' interests, it is well suited to my purposes in arguing that the state ought to see cultural oppression as a particular kind of violation of equal concern and respect which it is in the business of actively preventing.

Thus far, then, I have argued that there is a basis in egalitarian liberal theory for an interventionist state, under certain circumstances. Following Dworkin, I argue that these circumstances exist when a decision, left to utilitarianism, would be antecedently likely to violate a minority's interest in equal concern and respect by the government. In such circumstances, the state's job is to remove that decision from the range of decisions allowable by utilitarian procedures by creating a right in order to safeguard that minority's interest. I argued, secondly, that such a view of the role of rights is consistent with the idea of rights as protective of individuals' interests – either their interests in equal concern and respect, as per Dworkin, or their interest in autonomy, as per the choice theory of rights. If that is the case, and rights ought to be understood as protective of individuals' interests, such a characterization is compatible with the notion of an activist state, whose competencies and activities range into the controversial realm of inquiring into fundamental interests and protecting them through rights. So far, then, both theories – rights as safeguards against simple majoritarianism in certain cases, and rights as interests – are compatible with the notion of the activist liberal state.

## 1.5   Conclusion: Towards a framework for an activist state

By examining the theories of Mill, Raz, and Dworkin, I have attempted to offer a picture of the egalitarian liberal state that has conceptual space for state activism to prevent, or at least vitiate, cultural oppression. The egalitarian liberal state finds this space in three ways. First, the state departs from its neutral stance as a liberty-maximizing state in order to prevent harms, as Mill's account allows. This would allow the state to begin to think of cultural oppression as harm, following Mill, substantial enough to violate an interest protected by a right. In Chapter 2, the case for the harm of cultural oppression being substantial enough to constitute a rights violation – of the United States' First and Fourteenth Amendment rights of women and minorities – will be explored. If this case is compelling, then Mill's harm principle will be triggered, and the egalitarian liberal state can contemplate action to remedy this rights violation.

Second, this chapter has attempted, through discussing the work of Raz, Fiss, Sunstein, and Mill, to show not just how rights may be thought of as protecting conflicts between the individual against the state, but how rights are enacted and enforced because they have benefits which extend beyond the individual – extending to protect the common good. This view of rights as protective of the common good will prove beneficial in discussing state activism to prevent cultural oppression, since casting such state action as a benefit to the common good – we benefit as a culture by living in an environment that does not traffic in racist, sexist, or homophobic views – will offset the concern that such state action may come at some expense to the liberty of the speakers of culturally oppressive speech. Though there may indeed be such a cost if the state engages in activism against culturally oppressive speech, that cost should be thought of as offset, and indeed perhaps outweighed, by the benefit to the common good that will come from state activism.

Finally, in addition to seeing allowances within established egalitarian liberal traditions for the state departing from neutrality to prevent certain harms and conceiving of rights as protective of the common, as well as the individual, good, Dworkin's argument that liberalism's fundamental commitment is to treat its citizens with equal concern and respect also forms a crucial piece of the picture, carving out the conceptual space within egalitarian liberalism for state activism to prevent culturally oppressive speech. As the arguments in Chapter 2 will begin to outline, state allowance of unregulated freedom of expression to the speakers of culturally oppressive speech may very well undermine the state's commitment to treating all of its citizens with equal concern and respect, since the concern and respect shown for the speakers comes at the direct expense of the concern and respect due to the targets of the speech – women and minorities. If this is the case, then by Dworkin's own lights, the liberal state must intervene to ensure that it is in fact treating all of its citizens with equal concern and respect.

All three of these strands of liberal theory demonstrate that, against the received view that the liberal state must remain neutral in the marketplace of ideas in order to protect liberty, there are other key tenets of liberalism which must be discussed in order to get a more robust view of the liberal state's commitments. Both Mill and Dworkin implicitly subscribe to the view made explicit by Raz and others that rights are best characterized as protective of interests; however, Mill, Raz, Fiss, and Sunstein, on the one hand, and Dworkin on the other, disagree over who these interest-bearers are – Mill, Raz, Fiss, and Sunstein considering the community at large as among them, and Dworkin rejecting that view.

That dispute notwithstanding, we have, taken together, the idea that state neutrality is not absolute, that rights exist in order to serve the common interest, and that the liberal state is committed to treating all of its citizens with equal concern and respect. These three ideas will form a powerful background to my argument for an activist state to battle cultural oppression. However, notably, neither Mill nor Dworkin has embraced the view that freedom of expression ought to be curtailed, even for these seemingly laudable egalitarian purposes. Since my aim is to carve out a space for an activist liberalism that will be accepted by the egalitarian liberal tradition, Chapters 2 and 3, respectively, will delve into Mill's and Dworkin's positions and attempt to find room in their theories for such activism.

# 2
# Equality, Liberty, and Hard Cases: A Classical View and Contemporary Responses

## 2.1 Introduction

In Chapter 1, I argued that taking three influential tenets of modern liberalism together – Mill's harm principle, Raz's theory of rights as supportive of the common good, and Dworkin's notion of rights as correctives for the limitations of majoritarianism in treating citizens with equal concern and respect – would provide a framework in which to situate an argument for the justification of state intervention in cases of cultural oppression in order to protect equality and liberty.

In Chapter 2, I argue that while the framework articulated in Chapter 1 provides a starting point for the justification of state intervention to promote equality, classical egalitarian liberal theorists have, notably, not gone so far as to endorse active state intervention for the promotion of equality at the direct expense of freedom of expression. It is the aim of this chapter to show why, according to their own insights elsewhere, they should acknowledge a departure from neutrality in these circumstances. John Stuart Mill is the leading classical egalitarian liberal, and thus this chapter explores his views in *On Liberty* as well in *The Subjection of Women*, in order to determine the extent to which they can accommodate an activist egalitarian liberalism. I argue that reading *On Liberty* alongside *The Subjection of Women* yields a more activist Mill.

In order to present this activist Mill in a way that is faithful to his ideas, it is necessary to treat Mill's ideas on the notions of equality, state intervention, and freedom of expression more carefully here. These three ideas are closely linked, in that the issue of state intervention in order to protect equality becomes controversial in liberalism when such an intervention is a curtailment of the freedom of expression of the putative equality violator. Examining the tension between freedom of expression, equality, and state intervention, particularly in the work of Mill in this chapter and in the work of Dworkin in Chapter 3, reveals deep and important reasons why these thinkers have been interpreted as resisting the notion of state intervention in freedom of expression in order to promote equality.

In Chapters 2 and 3, then, I will show that while the framework articulated in Chapter 1 provides a starting point for the justification of state intervention in cases of cultural oppression, neither Mill nor Dworkin seems to go so far as to contemplate active state intervention for the promotion of equality at the direct expense of freedom of expression. Since my argument for intervention aims to be compatible with the egalitarian liberal project, it is my task to show that both Mill and Dworkin ought to, by their own principles, accept it. I will argue here that Mill would in fact be receptive to arguments about cultural oppression, and thus that the popular reading of Mill is in need of revision. I will do this both by calling attention to Mill's arguments in *The Subjection of Women*,[1] as well as by noting the pro-equality implications of his arguments in *On Liberty*. The aim of my arguments will be to support the idea that contemporary interpreters and critics of Mill rely on a misinterpretation of his views, and a more thorough reading of Mill will actually support a pro-equality position more strongly than it supports an unqualified freedom of expression position.

I will argue further, in Chapter 3, that Dworkin, though not receptive to the arguments from systemic discrimination, by his own lights ought to be. In what follows here as well as in Chapter 3, I will present two important criticisms of the views of both Dworkin and Mill offered by feminists and critical race theorists – the silencing and subordination arguments, as they have come to be known. Both of these arguments contend that the harms caused to minorities and women by protected hate speech or pornography generate compelling inconsistencies in liberalism – either in terms of equality or positive liberty in the case of the subordination argument, or in terms of the negative liberty of freedom of expression itself in the silencing argument. Thus, if accepted, these arguments challenge the principles of egalitarian liberalism on its own terms. I will not evaluate the strength of either of these arguments until the later chapters of this book, because I need first to discuss speech act theory and Foucault's ideas of power – the topics of Chapters 4 and 5 – in order to do so. However, once these ideas have been discussed, I will argue that while neither of these arguments are airtight, either singly or in combination, they nonetheless point to an issue that is crucially overlooked in mainstream egalitarian liberal theory: the nature of social power and the need to account for power imbalances when the state is delineating the scope of rights and duties. It is this issue that the later chapters of this work will attempt to come to grips with, using insights from speech act theory and from continental philosophy.

The subordination argument can be cast either as a claim about the interference with the equality rights of the targets of pornography and hate speech, or as an interference with their positive liberties. If, as the argument runs, pornography and hate speech communicate ideas of the inferior moral worth of their targets, then subscription to those ideas by the majority has the result of subordinating the minority. Once subordinated – and the subordination argument will hold that the subordination is enacted in pornography or hate speech – the minority is, by definition, unequal, and will have fewer options – that is, positive liberties – available to them.

The silencing argument claims that the targets of hate speech and pornography have their subsequent attempted rebuttal speech 'silenced' – either because the speech is misinterpreted or not uttered at all – such that protecting the speakers' negative liberty of freedom of expression comes at the direct expense of the negative liberties of the affected targets. These two liberty-based criticisms – the positive liberty arm of the subordination argument and the silencing argument – will be presented in this chapter, after the discussion of Mill's defense of freedom of expression in *On Liberty*, since they can be seen as counter-arguments to his famous instrumental justification for free speech. Since Mill, as a utilitarian, is committed to free speech only insofar as he is convinced that it is indeed the course of action that best maximizes the utility of 'the permanent interests of man as a progressive being,' and since the silencing and subordination arguments question whether such unregulated speech in fact maximizes utility, such questions would need to be taken seriously, and even be accommodated, by Mill.

The second line of argument I will present is an argument from equality – that hate speech and pornography interfere with constitutional commitments to equal protection of the laws. This is the second arm of the subordination argument, and it will be presented at the end of my discussion of Dworkin in Chapter 3, since it seems best targeted towards his presentation of free speech as itself ensuring moral equality. Dworkin, unlike Mill, has had the privilege of responding to this argument against him, and has notably rejected it. I will argue in Chapter 3 that his reasons for rejecting it, however, are at odds with his ostensible commitments to equality, and are thus unacceptable.

Examination of the classical liberal tension between equality, freedom of expression, and state neutrality reveals that the contemporary problem of cultural oppression militates against these classical arguments in a way which compels us to re-examine classical liberal positions in order to meet its challenge. This re-examination reveals an ally in Mill, rather than an opponent, and Chapter 3's discussion of Dworkin's opposition does not seem consistent with the rest of his commitments. Thus, taken together, Chapters 2 and 3 are intended to suggest that there is reason, by liberalism's own lights, to revisit its stance against state intervention in cases of pornography and hate speech.

As noted in Chapter 1, Mill views the right to personal liberty in general as subject to curtailment by the harm principle, should such a curtailment itself maximize utility. However, Mill will go on, famously, to argue that the exercise of our liberty of expression in particular is not to be subject to curtailment by the operation of the harm principle; in other words, the restriction of the right to freedom of expression is deemed in advance to have less utility than allowing the harms to go unremedied. I will examine Mill's reasoning for this position in what follows, but at the outset it is important to note that if his arguments are accepted, it is, at least on its face, a serious setback to my point of view: it becomes difficult to invoke the harm principle as part of a justification for state intervention to prevent cultural oppression, when those interventions will likely take the form of impediments to freedom of expression, which seem to have been explicitly excluded by Mill.

However, this is not fatal to seeing Mill as an ally in an activist state. I will argue that Mill's arguments in *On Liberty* for allowing freedom of expression notwithstanding its harms must be read in concert with his arguments in *The Subjection of Women*, which seem to suggest that Mill was aware of, and concerned to remedy, the harms to women caused by male power in general. If one arm of male power operates through the use of the right to freedom of expression, as the silencing and subordination arguments maintain, then it seems that Mill must be read to be especially concerned about this operation. It is important to remember here that as a utilitarian, Mill cannot be committed to freedom of expression *per se*; rather he is committed to it insofar as it enhances overall utility. The arguments in *On Liberty* are to the effect that freedom of expression promotes the overall utility, but arguments that there are costs of freedom of expression to interests as vital as equality ought to be taken into the equation by Mill, and thus must be taken on board by liberals who follow in his tradition. As Wayne

Sumner succinctly summarizes the scope of Mill's commitments to liberty:

> [Mill]...is not really entitled to assume that the utility calculation will favour liberty equally, or underwrite exactly the same right to liberty, in all 'civilized'countries at all times and under all conditions. Under different social circumstances it is possible for Mill's utilitarian methodology to generate a less absolute principle concerning liberty in the personal sphere. (Sumner 2004: 23)

This is due to the fact that utilitarian cost-benefit analysis must get its data from the actual circumstances of the culture at the time the analysis is performed; as cultures change, so too does the calculation and its dictates. It will be my contention that the present social circumstances of a systemically racist, sexist, and homophobic society are sufficient to tip the delicate utilitarian balance away from liberty in freedom of expression and towards equality through its targeted regulation. Mill certainly saw that a cost-benefit analysis would be the relevant test for determining the appropriate balance between liberty and equality in the service of promoting the general utility, though whether or not he would find today's circumstances sufficient to tip that balance from the one he performed in the writing of *On Liberty* is of course unanswerable. However, Mill's position in *The Subjection of Women* suggests that he may very well favor such a move in such circumstances.

I will maintain that the silencing and subordination arguments' claims about the problematic consequences of certain exercises of the right to freedom of expression, and the arguments that Mill himself raises in *The Subjection of Women*, taken together, are sufficient to demonstrate that Mill would be receptive to a revised reading of his work that would attempt to accommodate the concerns of women and minorities, and that his work indeed is compatible with such revisions. Its compatibility with a changing understanding of the balancing of rights derives in large part from the nature of utilitarianism itself, but one need not sign on to utilitarianism as an overall social theory in order to accept the provisional nature of rights.

As Sumner points out, conceiving of rights as abstract and immutable may easily be seen as an untenable approach, and be instead replaced by a consideration of the way and degree to which rights facilitate the general good. Once one opts for the latter approach, one is endorsing a consequentialist view of the nature of rights. Then, according to Sumner

(2004: 35), and implicitly to Mill, '[w]orking out the right answer for any society will be a complex matter requiring evidence and argument, and will consequently be perpetually open to re-examination and revision.' As Chapters 7 and 8 of this work will demonstrate, and as Sumner notes at length in *The Hateful and the Obscene*, this approach of perpetually revising the scope of rights appears to be in keeping with the Supreme Court of Canada's rights-balancing efforts in its famous *Oakes* test. Keeping in view this commitment to revision, as well as the changing weight of rights, throughout the arguments in these pages will afford a better view of the nature of this project and how its mechanics may better facilitate a more dynamic vision of the egalitarian liberal state.

## 2.2   The role of freedom of expression in Mill's political theory

Understanding the role of freedom of expression in Mill's scheme requires prior discussion of the broad aims of his political theory. At the most general level, Mill's vision of the good society and the good citizen, respectively, places penultimate value on the merits of diversity among people at a societal level, achieved through a cultivation of individuality on a personal level. Such diversity is valuable insofar as it offers us the best chance of achieving Mill's ultimate value: coming to discover the style of life with the most overall utility. He writes:

> It is not by wearing down into uniformity all that is individual in themselves, but by cultivating it and calling it forth, within the limits imposed by the rights and interests of others, that human beings become a noble and beautiful object of contemplation; and as the works partake the character of those who do them, by the same process human life also becomes rich, diversified, and animating, furnishing more abundant aliment to high thoughts and elevating feelings, and strengthening the tie which binds every individual to the race, by making the race infinitely better worth belonging to. In proportion to the development of his individuality, each person becomes more valuable to himself, and is, therefore, capable of being more valuable to others. (Mill 1978: 60)

This passage not only reveals the value Mill places on diversity and individual autonomy, but it also echoes what Mill feels to be the close relationship between the individual and the culture, which was seen in

Chapter 1. Here again, for Mill, benefits to the individual are always tied to benefits to the culture as a whole; these reciprocal benefits reinforce and underline each other, rather than undercut each other, as some liberals, including Dworkin, maintain.

So Mill has these intermediate goals of autonomy and diversity, which are seen as instrumental to the ultimate and ongoing goal of determining the most felicitous style of life. However, Mill is careful to limit the cultivation and expression of autonomy to the point at which its expression interferes with the rights of others: 'Whenever, in short, there is a definite damage, or a definite risk of damage, either to an individual or to the public, the case is taken out of the province of liberty and placed in that of morality or law.'(1978: 80). Short of that, however, Mill is clear that there is important and substantial merit in allowing autonomy to flourish where real harm to others is not an issue, and that there is a strong disutility in not doing so:

> To be held to rigid rules of justice for the sake of others develops the feelings and capacities which have the good of others for their object. But to be restrained in things not affecting their good, by their mere displeasure, develops nothing valuable except such force of character as may unfold itself in resisting the restraint. If acquiesced in, it dulls and blunts the whole nature. To give fair play to the nature of each, it is essential that different persons should be allowed to lead different lives. (Mill 1978: 61)

While Mill does not use the word 'liberty' here explicitly, it is nonetheless clear that his notion of autonomy is closely tied to it; different persons being allowed to lead different lives speaks to the inseparability of autonomy and liberty – we need to be at liberty to cultivate and express our individuality. Once liberty is protected, individuality flourishes; once individuality flourishes, diversity arises; and once diversity arises, we can begin to assess competing visions of the good.

Recalling the discussion in Chapter 1, Mill cashes out his view of the right to individual liberty largely as liberty of self-development – the opportunity to enrich oneself intellectually, ethically, and personally, in such a way as to become a competent judge of the good life. This notion of liberty of self-development, Mill believes, presupposes the notions of liberty of thought and conscience, since it is only if we have the ability to think for ourselves that we may then be able to choose 'our own good in our own way,' which of course is the very point of a free society – that citizens may have different choices of lifestyle available to them and have the agency and the discernment to pick between them.

So, for Mill, the idea of liberty of thought is a crucial precondition for any other liberty – in particular, the liberty of self-development; we can only meaningfully choose what to do and how to live if we have the ability freely to contemplate such choices as educated individuals in a diverse society. He writes:

> As it is useful that while mankind are imperfect there should be different opinions, so is it that there should be different experiments of living; that free scope should be given to varieties of character, short of injury to others; and that the worth of different modes of life should be proved practically, when anyone thinks fit to try them. It is desirable, in short, that in things which do not primarily concern others individuality should assert itself. (1978: 54)

Evident here is the close connection between diversity of opinion and diversity of lifestyle. For Mill, both forms of diversity are to be protected because of our imperfection and evolution as a species – insofar as we have yet to determine the best views and the best lifestyles, all we can do is experiment with as many competing options as possible in order to experientially attempt to address those questions.

Uncontroversially, then, we need liberty of thought and conscience for Mill's scheme of facilitating the determination of the good to get off the ground, but Mill seems to think that freedom of expression follows from freedom of thought. This move from liberty of thought to liberty of expression is a very significant one, in that it goes from the wholly individual realm, where others are not affected, to the social one, where they may be. Once we have entered the public sphere, as Chapter 1 revealed, we need to consider whether the harm principle need be invoked, and of course, in many cases of expression, harm is in fact caused.

As noted earlier, whether or not harm is caused is only a threshold issue for Mill; once we have determined that harm has been caused, we then need to ask whether this harm is caused to an interest significant enough to be considered a right. If and only if that question is answered affirmatively does the harm principle get triggered, and the offending behavior limited. In other words, the harm principle is a necessary, but not a sufficient, condition for the limitation of a right. Mill is of course aware that in holding freedom of expression to be itself a right, and indeed a right that potentially harms others, he must confront the questions raised by the harm principle in delimiting it, but he spends surprisingly little time in *On Liberty* directly addressing the harms of freedom of expression and justifying the allowance of those harms. Rather, his argument is almost entirely targeted towards explicating the utility of freedom of expression and the disutility of suppressing opinions.

Notably, Mill seems almost to go so far as to equate thought itself with expression. He writes that

> [t]here is a sphere of action in which society, as distinguished from the individual, has, if any, only an indirect interest: comprehending all that portion of a person's life and conduct which affects only himself...This, then, is the appropriate region of human liberty. It comprises, first, the inward domain of consciousness, demanding liberty of conscience in the most comprehensive sense, liberty of thought and feeling, absolute freedom of opinion and sentiment on all subjects, practical or speculative, scientific, moral, or theological. The liberty of expressing and publishing opinions may seem to fall under a different principle, since it belongs to that part of the conduct of an individual which concerns other people, but, being almost of as much importance as the liberty of thought itself and resting in great part on the same reasons, is practically inseparable from it. (Mill 1978: 11–12)

This formulation makes clear that Mill sees thought and expression to be so closely connected as to be inseparable, if not conceptually, then at least practically. But what basis does he have for seeing the two as so intimately related? Though he does not make this argument explicitly, it seems that he feels, and I think rightly, that one is not optimally able to form one's own opinions and thoughts if one cannot hear or read the opinions of others. In order to hear or read these opinions, of course, they must have first been expressed freely, so as to be available to guide the thoughts of others. In this sense, then, there is an argument for the idea that freedom of expression is, in a loose sense, *prior* to freedom of thought.

While this seems to be a strong argument for taking the two liberties of thought and expression together, Mill's utilitarian justification for rights, as discussed in Chapter 1, has it that rights are only to be protected as such insofar as they enhance the general utility, or the overall good, of the community. Given that Mill's account justifies the enshrinement of rights by their merit to the general utility, as well as to the particular individual, and that rights in general are limited where that merit is vitiated by certain harms which adversely impact the general utility more than a restriction on the right would, it seems that Mill must be committed to balancing the merit of the exercise of the right to the general utility against the weight of the harm to others that the exercise of the right entails. If this is correct, then Mill ought to be amenable to arguments that claim that disutility in the operation of a right may justify its limitation. This of course would be true for any right, including the right to freedom of expression.

It seems that freedom of thought and freedom of expression each require a separate utilitarian calculation, in light of their different abilities to cause harm. While Mill does not seem to think that either freedom of thought or freedom of expression merit curtailment based on their respective harm versus utility calculation, if he could be shown facts concerning the history and sociology of cultural oppression,[2] it seems that he would need to address these harms, and indeed should welcome the opportunity, since the task of defining the good society is, according to his own view, an ongoing one which can and ought to be revisited in light of new evidence brought to bear on this great experiment.

Notably, in terms of my claim in Chapter 1 that for Mill and Raz, rights are justified by their overall benefit to the common good, Mill's argument for freedom of expression in *On Liberty* turns almost exclusively on the common good afforded by the protection of freedom of expression, rather than on the benefits to the particular individual of such a right. He writes:

> ...[T]he peculiar evil of silencing the expression of an opinion is that it is robbing the human race, posterity as well as the existing generation – those who dissent from the opinion, still more than those who hold it. If the opinion is right, they are deprived of the opportunity of exchanging error for truth; if wrong, they lose, what is almost as great a benefit, the clearer perception and livelier impression of truth produced by its collision with error. (Mill 1978: 16)

Here Mill maintains that the justification of freedom of expression is that diversity of opinion *per se*, whether that opinion is true or false, benefits society as a whole, both presently and in the future, because diversity of opinion alone ensures that truth will eventually unfold. The justification for freedom of expression, then, relies on the location of the utility of freedom of expression to be found in the common good, rather than in the good to the individual speaker or listener, who is understood as an aggregative facet of the common good. As I noted in Chapter 1, Mill's understanding of rights as justified in part by their efficacy in promoting the general utility is useful to my argument for state intervention in cases of cultural oppression, because it is compatible with the view that we must look to the outcome for the community as a whole when we determine the interests that a particular right protects.

Mill's argument above derives its force from the contention that in either of two possible scenarios – that the opinion is true or it is false – the outcome is better by allowing the opinion to be aired, rather than censored. If the opinion is true, the benefit is obvious – we are able to replace our false beliefs with the new true belief. If the opinion is false, we still benefit from the exercise of actively refuting it – such an exercise allows us to sharpen our opinions and to become more intellectually assured of what we already believe.

These two arguments – from the possibility of the truth of an opinion, and from the intellectual merit of deciding between opinions – are among the four main arguments that Mill presents in *On Liberty* in favor of freedom of expression. Mill summarizes these arguments succinctly in Chapter 4: the opinion could turn out to be true; the opinion could contain some portion of the truth; by engaging and debating false opinions, we come to hold our true opinions as more than mere prejudice; and by failing to engage in rigorous and free debate among competing opinions, we lose intellectual vigor, and eventually ideas will lose their very meaning in this slovenly environment.

It is important to note, before examining these arguments in detail, that they have in common an instrumental justification of freedom of expression, and indeed Mill's utilitarianism would seem to dictate that such justifications are the only kind permissible. This is relevant for two reasons. First, as I have already noted, if the argument is instrumental (that is, freedom of expression is valuable because it is the means to a good end), then if it can be shown that the end result is not what was anticipated, there is no conceptual difficulty in adjusting the means. The most effective arguments against Mill take this sort of tack, and the silencing and subordination arguments offered by feminists and critical race theorists take this route. Second, Mill's instrumentalism is in strong contrast to Dworkin, who will argue that freedom of expression is a good in itself (what he calls a 'constitutive' good), though he claims, in my view inaccurately, Mill as an ally in this kind of justification.

I will take this debate up later in Chapter 3, but now I will consider Mill's first two arguments in favor of freedom of expression. Lest we think that we can be sure in advance of the falsity of an opinion, and hence dispense with what Mill thinks is the worthwhile (Mill's third and fourth arguments) exercise of actively refuting it, Mill reminds us that the course of history tells us otherwise:

> We can never be sure that the opinion we are endeavoring to stifle is a false opinion; and if we were sure, stifling it would be an evil still. First, the opinion which it is attempted to suppress by authority may possibly be true. Those who desire to suppress it, of course, deny its truth; but they are not infallible. They have no authority to decide the question for all mankind and exclude every other person from the means of judging...ages are no more infallible than individuals – every age having held many opinions which subsequent ages have deemed not only false but absurd; and it is as certain that many opinions, now general, will be rejected by future ages, as it is that many, once general, are rejected by the present. (Mill 1978: 17)

Mill here again suggests that the benefit of free speech is to society as a whole – present and future – through the benefiting of individuals, and that the course of history has shown that the ideas that we believe and disbelieve change over time, warning us not to be so sure of ourselves that we preemptively dismiss an idea.

Very closely tied to the notion of suppressing an idea because of a mistaken belief in its falsity is the possibility of suppression not due to an innocent mistake as to its truth value, but rather due to a moral judgment about the idea. Mill holds that this kind of moral judgment is ubiquitous and pernicious:

> ...[T]he strongest of all the arguments against the interference of the public with purely personal conduct is that, when it does interfere, the odds are that it interferes wrongly and in the wrong place...In its interferences with personal conduct it is seldom thinking of anything but the enormity of acting or feeling differently from itself; and this standard of judgment, thinly disguised, is held up to mankind as the dictate of religion and philosophy by nine-tenths of all moralists and speculative writers...And it is not difficult to show, by abundant instances, that to extend the bounds of what may be called moral police until it encroaches on the most unquestionably

legitimate liberty of the individual is one of the most universal of all human propensities. (Mill 1978: 81–2)

While this may seem a cynical view of human nature, it seems that the history of censorship has borne out Mill's opinion.[3] In any case, we need not subscribe to Mill's view of human nature – that we can mistakenly and innocently censor, or that we can censor based on narrowly held moral views. Either route is problematic for the simple reason that the effect is the obscuring of what may prove to be the truth.

Mill then begins a second line of argument, to the effect that competing truth claims are rarely wholly true or false, but some mixture of each. Thus, when some opinions are suppressed, we decrease the range of options through which we may be able to sift to find the truth: 'Only through diversity of opinion is there, in the existing state of human intellect, a chance of fair play to all sides of the truth.' (Mill 1978: 46). So, Mill's first and second arguments for freedom of expression appeal to a fairly obvious instrumental justification – the desire to hold true opinions and the belief that freedom of expression facilitates that effort. It is against these two arguments that feminists and critical race theorists launch their silencing and subordination arguments, to the effect that protecting certain kinds of speech, such as hate speech and pornography, actually suppresses other kinds of speech, such that the greatest possible amount of speech, and thus the greatest likelihood at arriving at truth, is not effected. I will turn to these arguments shortly, after considering Mill's third and fourth arguments in favor of freedom of expression.

Mill's third and fourth arguments, on the other hand, appeal to the end of developing critical thinking skills, rather than to the end of holding true beliefs. Since Mill's primary task of determining which style of life is best requires that we hone our critical skills to become competent judges, we are thus aided in our pursuit of the good life by those activities which facilitate critical thinking. Freedom of expression, and its corollary enterprise of sorting true from false as per arguments one and two, facilitates the development of our critical thinking capacity, because:

[w]rong opinions and practices gradually yield to fact and argument; but facts and arguments, to produce any effect on the mind, must be brought before it. Very few facts are able to tell their own story, without comments to bring out their meaning. The whole

strength and value, then, of human judgment depending on the one property, that it can be set right when it is wrong, reliance can be placed on it only when the means of setting it right are kept constantly at hand. In the case of any person whose judgment is really deserving of confidence, how has it become so? Because he has kept his mind open to criticism of his opinions and conduct. Because it has been his practice to listen to all that could be said against him. (Mill 1978: 19)

The idea here is that developing a capacity to receive criticism of one's opinions from others – a capacity only possible through freedom of expression – is a worthwhile undertaking, since it both facilitates the examination of one's opinions and, further, provides the ability to use that discernment, once developed, to choose among competing lifestyle choices – the first aim of Mill's social philosophy.

It is again clear from this formulation that Mill intends to appeal to outcomes in his justification; however, this argument, as opposed to the first and second, proceeds independently of any merit to be gained from the actual content of the ideas that may be expressed; it matters not at all here what the value of the ideas themselves are. Rather, all of the merit is in the process of developing our critical thinking skills. This is important to note because many popular arguments for regulating hate speech and pornography contend that since the ideas expressed in these modes of speech are highly unlikely to be true, is therefore acceptable to dispense with them. However, many of Mill's arguments for freedom of expression, including this one, proceed without reference to the likelihood of the truth of the particular idea.

A corollary to this idea of free expression as supportive of critical thinking is the idea that the *way* that either true or false beliefs are held is relevant to the intellectual health of the believer:

However unwillingly a person who has a strong opinion may admit the possibility that his opinion may be false, he ought to be moved by the consideration that, however true it may be, if it is not fully, frequently, and fearlessly discussed, it will be held as a dead dogma, not a living truth. (Mill 1978: 34)

Here, again, the idea of competent judges plays a crucial role in Mill's arguments. Unless we are the kinds of people who hold beliefs rationally and on the basis of argument, we are ill-equipped to face the many choices of styles of life that confront us in a diverse community. Thus, the rigors of debate among competing beliefs serve not only their direct function of adjudicating between competing views, but also serve the larger function of ensuring that we are competent adjudicators. Mill writes:

> The human faculties of perception, judgment, discriminative feeling, mental activity, and even moral preference are exercised only in making a choice. He who does anything because it is the custom makes no choice. He gains no practice either in discerning or in desiring what is best. The mental and the moral, like the muscular, powers are improved only by being used. (1978: 56)

Thus, according to Mill, there is crucial intellectual merit in the activity of discernment among competing views, and this merit accrues regardless of the truth or falsity of the beliefs being considered.

Finally, without this debate among competing beliefs, there is a sense in which we do not really know or understand the views that we hold:

> He who knows only his own side of the case knows little of that. His reasons may be good, and no one may have been able to refute them. But if he is equally unable to refute the reasons on the opposite side, if he does not so much as know what they are, he has no ground for preferring either opinion. The rational position for him would be suspension of judgment. (1978: 35)

So not only do we hold our judgments as mere opinions when we do not engage in their rigorous examination, but further, we are guilty of irrationality in doing so: without a serious consideration of the competing views, there is no reason to imagine that one's own views are the right ones – we can only make this assessment after thoroughly canvassing the other candidates. Hence, for Mill, without freedom to express competing views, all of our views run the risk of being ineligible candidates for belief, for the reason that they cannot truly be known to be true or false at all.

Such a state of affairs would lead to a dulling of the ideas themselves over time:

> Not only the grounds of the opinion are forgotten in the absence of discussion, but too often the meaning of the opinion itself. The words which convey it cease to suggest ideas, or suggest only a small

portion of those they were originally employed to communicate. Instead of a vivid conception and a living belief, there remain only a few phrases retained by rote; or, if any part, the shell and husk only of the meaning is retained, the finer essence being lost. (1978: 37–8)

When we fall into habits, rather than beliefs, we would then cease to become truly thinking creatures, instead becoming lazy in our intellectual activities: 'Both teachers and learners go to sleep at their post as soon as there is no enemy in the field.... The fatal tendency of mankind to leave off thinking about a thing when it is no longer doubtful is the cause of half their errors.' (1978: 41). So, the risk we face when we neglect freedom of expression again here is based upon the loss of our capacity to judge truth and falsity in general. If we cease to debate the truth or falsity of our beliefs, Mill argues that we will soon hold our opinions, whether true or false, as mere dogma and prejudice.

It is important to note here that *On Liberty*'s characterization of the nature of censorship has been incredibly influential in shaping the subsequent dominant line of liberal thought, both in terms of the traditional liberal fears of the ills of censorship and in terms of the very characterization of the operation of censorship. In terms of the latter, Mill conceives of censorship as occurring by the state, after a (paradigmatically written) utterance has already been uttered. This formulation seems uncontroversial and indeed parallels the nature of 'book banning' practices and jurisprudence, but it is by no means the only, or the most persuasive, characterization of censorship.

If my argument for an activist egalitarian liberal state is to succeed, it must overcome these liberal fears of the evils of state censorship, since part of state activism may involve censorship of one sort or another in order to facilitate equality and a properly functioning marketplace of ideas. In Chapter 6, I argue that the Millian conception of censorship as occurring by the state and after an utterance has been spoken is too limited to capture the full operation of the workings of censorship. The full workings of censorship, importantly, include the way in which speech is censored before it is even uttered, and if this is the case, the liberal fear of censorship is misplaced. I argue in Chapter 6 that censorship in the more robust, post-Millian sense is unavoidable, and thus the liberal state's fears of it are misplaced.

Having now canvassed all four of Mill's arguments for freedom of expression, I will turn briefly to discuss his ideas of the limited circumstances in which such freedom ought to be curtailed. Mill suggests in

*On Liberty* that there are particular circumstances where speech becomes
so close to action as to be governed by the harm principle:

> Even opinions lose their immunity when the circumstances in
> which they are expressed are such as to constitute their expression a
> positive instigation to some mischievous act. An opinion that corn
> dealers are starvers of the poor, or that private property is robbery,
> ought to be unmolested when simply circulated through the press,
> but may justly incur punishment when delivered orally to an
> excited mob assembled before the house of a corn dealer, or when
> handed about among the same mob in the form of a placard....The
> liberty of the individual must be thus far limited: he must not make
> himself a nuisance to other people. But if he refrains from molesting
> others in what concerns them, and merely acts according to his own
> inclination and judgment in things which concern himself, the same
> reasons which show that opinion should be free prove also that he
> should be allowed, without molestation, to carry his opinions into
> practice at his own cost. (1978: 53)

The idea here is that there are some circumstances where freedom of
expression ought to be curtailed because of the likelihood of its inciting
direct and tangible harm – in the above example, the physical harm of
a riot. These circumstantial restrictions are understood as opposed to
content restrictions – it is not the meaning of the expression that is
the source of the restriction, but rather the environment in which the
expression is uttered which gives rise to the restriction. Only when the
context causes injury, rather than the content, is freedom of expression
held to be subject to the harm principle.

Mill does, however, go a step further toward content regulation in a
footnote at the beginning of Chapter 2, where he argues that prosecutions for advocating tyrannicide may be acceptable, but only if such
advocacy then leads to the instigation of the actual crime. Obviously,
the regulation of either the advocacy of tyrannicide or the idea that
corn dealers are starvers of the poor has something to do with the
content of the ideas themselves, or else it would be nonsensical to
claim that they lead in any logical way to certain unacceptable actions
under certain circumstances, but Mill wants to say that the content of
the ideas *alone* is insufficient to merit regulation.

I will conclude this brief survey of the justification of freedom
of expression in *On Liberty* by noting that Mill argues in favor of freedom of expression because of what he takes to be its instrumental

merits, either for the end of holding true beliefs, or the end of developing critical capacities. As a result of this way of arguing, he is vulnerable to arguments which can demonstrate disutilities of freedom of expression which he may have overlooked. Second, freedom of expression is a right that occupies a privileged and almost inviolable place in Mill's theory of rights in that it is not subject, as other rights are, to curtailment by the disutility of its harms, unless it is for reasons of circumstance rather than content. Animating this view is the now orthodox liberal idea that the best remedy for false opinions is not state action, but instead rigorous debate, through which falsity will become exposed to all and be persuasive to none. Or, in other words, the best way to combat false speech is through more speech. This is the view that has animated nearly all of the US free speech jurisprudence of the past century, and is the view of Dworkin, perhaps the most prominent contemporary theorist of liberalism.

## 2.3   Silencing and subordination: The consequences of unregulated freedom of expression

It is precisely this view – that the best way to combat false speech is with rebuttal speech – which the feminist and critical race theory arguments from liberty intend to challenge. The arguments, from both positive (subordination argument) and negative (silencing argument) liberty, is that there is a crucial disutility of unregulated freedom of expression, because the expression that is protected in the cases of pornography and hate speech in fact has the result of reducing the liberty of the oppressed groups that such speech targets, thus thwarting the central liberal goal of maximal liberty consistent with the prevention of harm.

Described another way, the thrust of the subordination and silencing arguments is as follows. Freedom of expression does not always lead to a 'marketplace of ideas,' which many commentators summarize as the utility for which Mill's position argues. Rather, unregulated freedom of expression leads, in cases of culturally oppressive speech, to views of the unequal moral worth of certain groups of citizens, such that those groups are subordinated in society, or their speech is silenced. The act of these groups' silencing or subordination would have the effect of making Mill's marketplace a venue of less than optimal utility for the goal of maximal liberty consistent with the prevention of harm. The subordination and silencing arguments both maintain that unregulated freedom of expression leads to non-maximal liberty as well as failure to prevent harm.

The subordination argument against pornography, advanced by Catharine MacKinnon in *Only Words* (1996), and refined by Rae Langton and Jennifer Hornsby in a series of influential articles, holds that

> [p]ornography *is* the graphic sexually explicit subordination of women, in pictures or words...The claim was not, or not simply, that pornography depicts the subordination of women, or that it has, among its effects, the perpetuation of women's subordination, but that pornography *is* subordination...According to the feminist argument, pornography ranks women as inferior, deprives women of certain powers, and legitimates discrimination against them. (Langton 1998: 262; emphasis as in original)

The idea here is that pornographic representations themselves *are* the subordination of women – they create women's subordinated status in much the same way as does, say, the statement that blacks under apartheid are not allowed to vote, when uttered by the legislature in an apartheid regime.[4] In other words, there is something so powerful about pornography and hate speech that they have the power to actually *enact* subordination – that is, ranking their targets as inferior. In other words, pornography and hate speech do not merely *claim* that their targets are inferior, they actually make it the case that their targets are inferior. This, of course, is saying something stronger than that pornography or hate speech subsequently causes subordination due to the majority's reactions to the speech and their subsequent behavior; here the charge is that the subordination is seen as arising *simultaneously* with the speech itself, and independently of the viewer response to these images. This is quite a strong, and possibly false, claim. Its evaluation requires reference to speech act theory, which I will discuss in Chapter 4 and then use to evaluate the argument.

For now, though, let us assume that the argument is true. The problem, then, in Millian terms, is that there may be a net decrease in liberty to society as a whole in allowing freedom of expression in certain cases, because the protection of the negative liberty interests of the pornographers and hate speakers interferes with the positive liberty interests of the women and minorities whom that speech targets, by subordinating them to the dominant culture, and thus interfering with their range of options in life. The idea here is that this interference is, at least in part, tangible and material: it makes it harder for women and minorities to get the kinds of jobs they want, because employers have mistaken views about their inferiority, caused by the protected speech. It is thus harder to earn the kind of money and thus have the kind of lifestyle they want, for the same reason; and of course it makes their lives harder in terms of mobility, social status, and interpersonal relationships. Such interests are what Isaiah Berlin calls 'positive liberties,' or the liberty to direct and control one's own life:

> The 'positive' sense of the word 'liberty' derives from the wish on the part of the individual to be his own master. I wish my life and decisions to depend on myself, not on external forces of whatever kind. I wish to be the instrument of my own, not of other men's, acts of will. I wish to be a subject, not an object; to be moved by reasons, by conscious purposes, which are my own, not by causes which affect me, as it were, from outside. (Berlin 1968: 131)

The complaints of feminists and critical race theorists in the subordination argument obviously appeal to this notion of liberty; the denial of opportunities to exercise agency because the views of others impede one's choices is a violation of positive liberty, if it is a violation at all.

Such obvious interferences with liberty would of course be of interest to liberals, who would ostensibly want to minimize all obstruction of liberty in the absence of a competing reason not to do so. However, many leading liberals, including Dworkin, are unswayed by the idea that protection of pornography leads to the views of the unequal moral worth of women, and hence violates their positive liberties. It is worth examining Dworkin's reasoning here, because it is relevant, as well, to the argument against unregulated speech from equality, which will be introduced after discussing Dworkin's views. Dworkin argues that, even if we grant the premise that pornography and racist speech has all of the harmful consequences suggested above, the subordination argument is unpersuasive, because

> the point of free speech is precisely to allow ideas to have whatever consequences follow from their dissemination, including undesirable consequences for positive liberty...Freedom of speech, conceived and protected as a fundamental negative liberty, is the core of the choice modern democracies have made, a choice we must now honor in finding our own ways to combat the shaming inequalities women still suffer. (Dworkin 1997: 221)

The premise upon which such an opinion relies is that negative liberty rights are more fundamental to democracy than positive liberty rights, and thus are much more stringently protected. There is a long liberal tradition that holds that this is the case.[5] While it is outside of the scope of this project to examine that view, it is of interest to us for two reasons. First, Dworkin's conclusion above seems intuitively unsettling if we believe that the subordination of women and minorities is a real problem – it does not seem an adequate response to suffering to simply say that such suffering must continue unabated because we have decided to privilege the negative liberty of freedom of expression over all positive liberties. Second, this response will be subject to criticism by critical race theorists and feminists as itself equality-violating and a function of power; the choice to privilege one kind of liberty over another, they will argue, is by no means an innocent or innocuous choice, and it is one with consequences that should be of interest to liberalism generally.

For it to be of interest to Mill in particular, of course, the harm to positive liberty must be sufficiently strong as to warrant protection by a right, and it is unclear whether Mill would be persuaded that the harms to positive liberties such as employment, political influence, and social status are important enough to be considered rights, though his activism on behalf of women's rights seems to suggest that he may be sympathetic to this argument. That question aside, it is nevertheless the case that the subordination argument is somewhat weakened because of its appeal to a set of rights which are understood as being less fundamental than the bedrock negative liberty of freedom of expression.

The silencing argument, however, seems to avoid the weaknesses of the subordination argument by arguing from within the negative liberty of freedom of expression itself. The argument uses Mill's ideas of the utility of diversity of lifestyle and opinion to claim that if we have a society in which the speech of women or minorities is taken out of the debate in advance – because racist or sexist views preclude the targets of the speech from adequately responding to it – then the diversity that Mill thinks is central to the flourishing of society is compromised, because the views and lifestyles that those minorities have to offer to the debate have been discounted in advance by conclusions about their worth conveyed in racist, sexist, or homophobic speech. In other words, Mill's laudable goal of maximizing public discourse is not attained in a marketplace of ideas distorted by the workings of privilege and subordination and their reification in racist, sexist, or homophobic discourse. As critical race theorist Charles R. Lawrence III asserts:

> The reason that racial insults should not fall under protected speech relates to the purpose underlying the first amendment. The purpose

of the first amendment is to foster the greatest amount of speech. Racial insults disserve that purpose. Assaultive racist speech functions as a preemptive strike. The racial invective is experienced as a blow, not a proffered idea, and once the blow is struck, it is unlikely that dialogue will follow. Racial insults are undeserving of first amendment protection because the perpetrator's intention is not to discover truth or initiate dialogue, but to injure the victim. (Lawrence 1993: 68)

Lawrence is implicitly appealing to the instrumentality of Mill's arguments for freedom of expression. If the purposes enumerated by Mill, such as arriving at truth, dialogue, and diversity, are not met, and are in fact thwarted by some speech, then we ought to regulate that speech in the interest of facilitating these purposes. The obvious Millian answer is that insult or injury, as Lawrence here describes them, is insufficient, without further argument, to trigger Mill's criteria for the limitation of a right. Lawrence needs to argue persuasively that the injury is to an interest important enough to be protected by a right, and the passage above fails to enumerate a right that is violated.

In other words, in order to advance an argument against freedom of expression on Millian grounds, one must demonstrate two things: first, that the speech goes against the aims of truth and diversity; and second, that the rights of citizens have been violated through the act of speech. Other critical race theorists have documented at length what, in particular, they mean by the injury that is sustained by the victims of racist speech:

The negative effects of hate messages are real and immediate for the victims. Victims of vicious hate propaganda experience physiological symptoms and emotional distress ranging from fear in the gut to rapid pulse rate and difficulty in breathing, nightmares, posttraumatic stress disorder, hypertension, psychosis, and suicide... Victims are restricted in their personal freedom. To avoid receiving hate messages, victims have to quit jobs, forgo education, leave their homes, avoid certain public places, curtail their own exercise of speech rights, and otherwise modify their behavior and demeanor. (Matsuda 1993: 24)

However, even these harms must still be put in terms of a rights violation on Mill's scheme, and the question is, first, whether these kinds of harms are of a sort which go to a right at all, and if so, to which right in particular.

The two most persuasive attempts to cash out these injuries in terms of a rights violation are as a violation of the right to freedom of expression itself, and as a violation of the right to equal protection of the laws. Of these two, the violation of the right to freedom of expression is more persuasive to egalitarian liberals, because of freedom of expression's centrality to many liberal accounts of rights, including Mill's. Freedom of expression is seen as paramount of all rights for two reasons: because of its centrality to healthy democratic political life, and because it seems to be a prerequisite to freedom of thought itself. While this privileging of freedom of expression over other rights, especially the right to equality, has been problematized by feminists and critical race theorists, it is nevertheless strategically superior to cash out the harms of racist, sexist, or homophobic speech in terms of a violation of the right to freedom of expression: since this is the right that holds such a high place in our theories of rights, its violation in the case of racist, sexist, or homophobic speech demands urgent redress, even according to the tenets of a classical liberalism, such as Mill's. To this end, the silencing argument will attempt to cast the harms of racist, sexist, and homophobic speech as a violation of freedom of expression.

Lawrence continues his discussion (1993: 77) of the harms of racist speech, alluding to the silencing argument:

> [I]t is not just the prevalence and strength of the idea of racism that make the unregulated marketplace of ideas an untenable paradigm for those individuals who seek full and equal personhood for all. The real problem is that the idea of the racial inferiority of nonwhites infects, skews, and disables the operation of a market. It trumps good ideas that contend with it in the market. It is an epidemic that distorts the marketplace of ideas and renders it dysfunctional.

This idea that racist, sexist, or homophobic ideas effectively 'trump' – or 'silence' – the objections that may be raised to them comes closer to getting at the idea that there is a rights violation – either in terms of equality or in terms of freedom of expression – involved in having a racist marketplace; some people's speech, on this view, counts more than other people's speech, which could be cashed out as an equality violation. On another interpretation, 'trump' could mean 'cancel out' or 'silence' the oppositional speech, thereby implying a violation of the right to freedom of expression itself. On either reading, what is important to note is that Mill ought to be receptive to these arguments, if they are true, because they aim, compatibly with Mill's project, at increasing the diversity of the community, which, of course, was one of Mill's chief aims as well.

Moreover, unregulated freedom of expression was held by Mill to be useful only because of its instrumentality in attaining diversity, and thus an argument that diversity can be better attained by some other means is compatible with the ultimate goals of Mill's social philosophy, if not his intermediate goals. Given this, it seems surprising that leading liberals such as Dworkin do not welcome this argument, and I will examine his reasons for this in Chapter 3, after introducing the argument more fully here.

The argument from silencing was advanced by Catharine MacKinnon and others,[6] and it maintains that certain instances of hateful speech directed toward minorities and women preclude an effective response, or counter-speech, from those addressed, thereby denying their right to freedom of expression itself. MacKinnon is not, of course, saying that those addressed literally cannot speak, but rather that their speech will not count towards the debate in the way that the speech of the dominant culture will. The mechanics of this charge have been elaborated by speech act theorists, whose arguments in this regard will be examined in Chapter 4. For now, however, my aim is simply to introduce this argument to show that if successful it, like the subordination argument, is a counter-example to Mill's description of freedom of expression as facilitating a diverse discussion of alternative ways of life without impeding rights. The argument maintains that the constitutional protection of free speech cannot be defended on Millian grounds of facilitating maximal speech and dialogue, because some speech does not facilitate counter-speech or dialogue, but rather thwarts it by effectively denying those addressed their right to freedom of expression. It is important to note that this argument does not necessarily preclude other kinds of defenses of protection of free speech, but it does seem to preclude a Millian defense of free speech as instrumental to diversity. Dworkin will attempt to offer a new kind of justification of protection of hate speech and pornography in an attempt to circumvent this kind of criticism, and I will examine that argument in Chapter 3.

So how, exactly, does culturally oppressive speech silence? Key to making sense of this idea is the insight that the social positions of speakers may be such that some speech does not create an open dialogue or debate, but instead effectively manufactures subject position – in exactly the same way that the subordination argument claims it does – such that telling someone that they are inferior because of their race, gender, or sexuality is not a simple conjecture, rebuttable by evidence to the contrary, but rather, in its very utterance, makes it so. The speech of the powerful so effectively dictates opinions about oppressed groups as to enact or further that oppression, such that minority identity itself is enacted by the content of hateful speech, or women's identities are enacted by the discourse of pornography. The subject thus by such speech will then have their own speech discounted as a result of the inferior subject position formed by the injurious speech. MacKinnon claims:

> In the context of social inequality, so-called speech can be an exercise of power which constructs the social reality in which people live, from objectification to genocide....Together with all its material supports, authoritatively *saying* that someone is inferior is largely how structures of status and differential treatment are demarcated and actualized. Words and images are how people are placed in hierarchies, how social stratification is made to seem inevitable and right, how feelings of inferiority and superiority are engendered, and how indifference to violence against those on the bottom is rationalized and normalized. Social supremacy is made, inside and between people, through making meanings. To unmake it, these meanings and their technologies have to be unmade. (MacKinnon 1996: 30–1; emphasis as in original)

This argument, like the arguments of feminists and critical race theorists generally, begins with the premise that power relations between privileged and subordinated groups are key to understanding the actual workings of social and political interaction. Such an idea, though radical even by the standards of today's egalitarian liberalism, was nonetheless contemplated and embraced by Mill in his *The Subjection of Women*. As David Dyzenhaus suggests, this text, read alongside *On Liberty*, offers a robust understanding of the nature of harm, equality, and autonomy, such that Mill becomes an ally of these contemporary concerns, rather than an opponent of them. I will turn now to a brief summary of Dyzenhaus's position, in order to demonstrate that the popular reading of Mill's *On Liberty* as a text hostile to any consideration of impeding freedom of expression is crude and inaccurate in light of the breadth and sophistication of Mill's concerns.

## 2.4   The Mill of *Subjection*: An early egalitarian activist

While the bulk of *The Subjection of Women* is explicitly concerned with suffrage for women in Mill's Victorian England, the important point for our times is the fact that Mill does not make the mistake of equating the formal equality that would be granted with the attainment of suffrage with substantive, or what he calls 'perfect equality,' that would require much more than mere legal rights. Dyzenhaus notes that Mill views the legally prescribed inequalities between the sexes as the mere formal codification of the actual inequalities of the social relations between men and women and thus Mill would not be likely to make the mistake of thinking that changing the laws would be sufficient to change the social reality that underlies those laws. This distinction between formal legal rights and the reality of the interests they protect as lived on the ground is an important one, because it is exactly the distinction that is made by feminists and critical race theorists in the silencing and subordination arguments. Both arguments grant that the targets of hate speech and pornography still possess their formal rights to liberty – what they question is whether culturally oppressive speech vitiates the formal right. What this distinction points to is the issue of social power, not only at work in the granting of a formal right, but also at work in the way that the right may or may not be exercised on the ground. This question of social power, and what egalitarian liberalism's response to it ought to be, will occupy the latter half of this book.

In *The Subjection of Women*, Mill notes that the underlying social reality of inequality is carried out in the private sphere, which prevents women from forming alliances with each other to overcome their subordination. He further notes that the relationship of power imbalance between the sexes is reinforced and upheld by its apparent naturalness, and thus is given the veneer and supposed legitimacy of a consensual arrangement. To buttress this seeming naturalness, Mill further notes (1997: 14–15) that a morality has developed around the whole arrangement, such that women have come to believe that it is in their nature to 'live for others; make complete abnegations of themselves, and to have not life but in their affections.' This insight is strikingly compatible with many contemporary feminist positions, which recognize that the appearance of consent is by no means the end of the story of oppression and aim to theorize from this recognition.

So Mill's text, then, is notably in keeping with most contemporary feminist analyses of power. What Mill suggests is that the fact that women accept their subordinate role does not mean that these roles are unproblematic. In fact, they are even more problematic by virtue of this supposed 'consent,' because such 'consent' lures one away from considering the roots of oppression underlying the status quo. What is problematic about the inequality of the sexes, according to Mill, is that such inequality necessarily impedes women's autonomous functioning, and such autonomy, on Mill's scheme, is requisite for women to experience for themselves their own conception of the good life.

Dyzenhaus suggests (1992: 540) that insofar as pornography operates under the same insidious veil of consent as does the general relationship between the sexes, it is to be considered as yet another piece of support for the system of domination of women by men, and would thus be objectionable to Mill for the same reasons. Further, because of pornography's confinement to the private sphere, it likewise has the effect of denying women the ability to mount any kind of united opposition to it. Dyzenhaus concludes that Mill's ideas about the subtle manifestations of sex inequality in his *The Subjection of Women* demonstrate that he was well aware of the complexity of the operations of sexism, and the deep harm of gender inequality to the goals of autonomy and liberty.

As Dyzenhaus notes, the radicalism in Mill's position – which is the radicalism that unites him with contemporary feminists in favor of regulation of pornography – is his acknowledgement of the fact that neither consent nor formal equality alone or in combination are sufficient to vitiate inequality. However, this insight seems to be at odds with the utilitarian character of Mill's liberalism – how can we calculate preferences if we are acknowledging that some people's preferences might not be what they seem? Further, once we allow that a regime of systemic inequality such as sexism might operate by skewing preferences, we seem to have opened the floodgates towards paternalism and away from liberalism's hands-off stance regarding inquiring into preferences. There are several passages in *On Liberty* that caution against 'improvement' of others, or inquiring further into people's preferences than their stated ambitions. So the question becomes how to square these passages with the radical strand in *The Subjection of Women*, which notes that there is more to the story than merely taking subjective preferences at face value. Further, the bald claim that taking subjective preferences at face value entails state neutrality is called into question by Mill's position in *Subjection*.

Dyzenhaus suggests (1992: 541–3) that Mill's answer to this paternalism charge is found in his appeal to experience, as opposed to a claim to knowing better than someone else what style of life might be better for them. Instead of thinking in terms of false-consciousness, Mill couches the problem in terms of women's (and men's) limited experience of lifestyles – their possibilities of styles of life have been precluded in advance because of the deep regime of inequality in which they live. Had their possibilities and range of experiences not been so drastically truncated, they might have been able to choose different lifestyles, but as it stands, there was no opportunity to do so, because of the lack of options.

In other words, Mill questions the validity of choices in the absence of sufficient experience. Whether this really escapes the charge of paternalism is doubtful; it seems a mark of paternalism, rather than an escape from it, to claim that the experience of others is provincial. Regardless, the point for the present discussion is that in a spectrum between hands-off utilitarian liberalism on the one side and outright paternalism on the other, *The Subjection of Women* seems to locate Mill towards the paternalism end, and *On Liberty* seems to place him nearer to the hands-off end. This is noteworthy not only because it casts doubt on the popular reading of Mill as the paradigmatic hands-off liberal, but also because of the fact that Mill's more nuanced understanding of choice and consent offered in *The Subjection of Women* seems to put him much more squarely in line with the contemporary feminist position that would regulate certain forms of culturally oppressive speech.

In *The Subjection of Women*, Mill is taking the radical position that we can only really know what our actual preferences are after we have had the opportunity to live free from the limitations of views that our culture perpetuates within us. This is because if our culture subscribes to views that limit women's autonomy, such as the view that it is her nature to serve others, then we cannot use the fact that women appear to want to serve others as having been a choice autonomously made by women. As Dyzenhaus encapsulates:

> In sum, Mill's solution to the puzzle about real and perceived interests and wants is the following. If one's concern is individual autonomy, and if there is reason to suppose that a group's wants were formed under a regime hostile to autonomy, then one cannot appeal to those wants to justify the regime. (Dyzenhaus 1992: 543)

Thus, as long as our priority is autonomy – and the arguments in *On Liberty* are perhaps the best ever written to inspire us to make it such – Mill's claim in *The Subjection of Women* is that in a situation that both denies women autonomy and has developed a sophisticated rhetoric designed to make them believe that autonomy is anathema, women's perceived lack of interest in autonomy cannot be taken at face value, let alone used as support for such a situation.

Thus, it appears that reading *The Subjection of Women* alongside *On Liberty* reveals that Mill is well aware that his concern for autonomy is critically compromised in a society that has insidious mechanisms in place to ensure that half of the population is uninterested in that very ideal. Further, it seems that the Mill of *The Subjection of Women* is obviously interested in remedying this problem, presumably even if the remedy violates his general hands-off posture in *On Liberty*.

If this is indeed the case, then why haven't today's liberals, who claim Mill as their founder, offered nearly as nuanced a view of the problematic nature of autonomy in an oppressive society? Dyzenhaus suggests three reasons for liberal hostility to censoring pornography, and claims that all of them are wrongly imputed to Mill. The first reason is the narrow reading of the harm principle as only applicable to physical harm – since the physical harms of pornography have not been adequately documented by social scientists, the argument goes, this narrow harm principle has not been triggered. The second reason for the liberal reluctance to censor pornography is because of their support for the public/private distinction, which they claim must be upheld in order to preserve the private sphere of autonomy from state interference. Since this sphere must be protected, and since consumption of pornography takes place in private, liberals see no principled reason to invade the hallowed space of the private sphere. Finally, liberals are committed to robust freedom of expression either because they do not believe that speech can cause sufficient harm to justify state action, or because they believe that regulation is more harmful than allowing freedom of expression.

Dyzenhaus suggests that Mill would not have been receptive to the idea of the public/private distinction, since *The Subjection of Women*'s central point is that the inequality of women is perpetuated in the home, in private, and that its location by no means excuses the injustice. Thus, reading *The Subjection of Women* in concert with *On Liberty* reveals two texts which must be taken together to stand for the idea that a liberal society needs to protect liberty in the absence of harm, wherever that liberty is located – in other words, with no allowance for a private sphere that is immune from inquiry.

What, then, of the harm principle? Ought it to be read as narrowly applicable only to physical harm, thus excluding pornography, or ought it to be read more broadly, to include harms beyond the merely physical? Examining *On Liberty* has shown that Mill explicitly states that his concern is with harm to interests sufficiently pressing to be considered rights. Through Dyzenhaus's reading of *The Subjection of Women*, Mill's conception of interests appears to apply to real interests, rather than merely perceived interests, and thus he is comfortable with a certain degree of prescribing what these interests ought to be – the fundamental interest of 'man as a progressive being' refers principally to the interest in autonomy, which is of course an interest which transcends an interest in the merely physical. There seems quite clearly to be no basis in Mill's thought for the notion that the harm principle is applicable only to physical harm. However, even granted that the harm principle seems clearly to be intended by Mill to apply to whatever interest is of sufficient import to justify its being deemed a right, it is still incumbent on those who claim harm to enumerate what right or rights have been violated. The feminist and critical race theory arguments tend to answer this question with reference to either equality or freedom of expression itself, and the upcoming chapters will evaluate to what degree their arguments have been successful.

The final, and most formidable, obstacle in the way of treating Mill as friendly to regulation of culturally oppressive speech is that of course, on its face, *On Liberty* is explicitly a text which is hostile to any form of regulation based on the content of expression. Dyzenhaus suggests that this popular reading of Mill is actually unfaithful to a more nuanced reading of the text, which would, as he puts it (1992: 547), 'permit what we might think of as a liberal censorship policy.' There is no question, Dyzenhaus concedes, that Mill's arguments in Chapter 2 of *On Liberty* are against interferences with liberty that come from outside of the will of the people affected by the decision, even if such interferences are made in what Mill calls a 'spirit of improvement.' In other words, Mill unambiguously insists that interferences with liberty not be imposed upon people, even in some kind of attempt to improve upon the choices they have made.

On its face, Mill's resistance to 'forcing improvements on an unwilling people' seems to characterize quite well the reasons that liberals resist the feminist attempt to regulate pornography. So how could Mill be in favor of regulation of pornography if he resists the spirit of improvement? Dyzenhaus suggests that Mill's desire for freedom of expression coupled with his desire to control a spirit of improvement might be thought of in two ways. The first is the traditional reading, which hopes that freedom of speech might have the effect of curbing the spirit of improvement because through discussion participants will come to expose the 'spirit of improvement' and the denial of liberty that such a spirit represents.

The second way to express the relationship between freedom of expression and the injunction against the spirit of improvement is that free debate may be used to determine 'what coercive action should be taken in order to eradicate oppressive conceptions of the good life; thus permitting, for example, the censorship of pornography' (Dyzenhaus 1992: 547). Dyzenhaus wants to suggest that we can read Mill's injunction against spirits of improvement being imposed upon an unwilling people, and his strong commitment to freedom of expression, as compatible with regulation of culturally oppressive speech if we view his understanding of the operation of the oppression of women in *The Subjection of Women* as taking place in an atmosphere which silences and shapes the desires of women well in advance of admitting them to the discussion, thus effectively denying them meaningful participation in discourse in the first place.

In other words, if the operation of sexism is indeed as Mill suggests in *Subjection*, then the strategy of debate offered in the first reading cannot be used to root out violations of liberty, because women are not in an epistemic position to be able to call attention to their predicament through debate, and thus the oppressive conception of the good life which has women as subservient will not be able to be even discussed, let alone remedied. However, even on the second reading, the same problem arises: who is it who will be there to debate the oppression of women, when the radical point offered in *Subjection* is to the effect that women and men are both unaware of it?

Presumably, there is some faint hope that serious thinkers, such as Mill himself, will be able to see their way through this cultural morass to find a way to critique it. Indeed, the harder it is to see the truth through the deeply held cultural beliefs about inequality, the stronger Mill's case for freedom of expression becomes – if it is rare enough to be able to even perceive the problem of the subjugation of women and minorities, the environment available to express what one has perceived becomes at once more crucial and more fragile. Further, the very depth of the problem also seems to lend support to the idea that we may need a more radical solution to it, such as that offered by the second reading.

Acknowledging, then, that *The Subjection of Women* contemplates this grim scenario of cultural oppression being so deep as to be almost undetectable, it follows that *On Liberty* must too be read as a text which is compatible with, rather than oppositional to, it. Indeed, since *The Subjection of Women* was written after *On Liberty*, it would seem, in the absence of some clear evidence to the contrary, that it is Mill's more mature formulation of the nature of, and remedies for, oppression.

Consistency dictates that we read the two texts in a way which reconciles them, and Dyzenhaus's suggestion is that one plausible way to do this is to see freedom of expression as crucial in attempting to root out oppression through a dialogue about how to stop it, rather than as a means of furthering oppressive – that is, liberty-denying – discourse. This reading requires having a certain faith in humanity's ability to root out its own illiberality, but there is no reason to suppose that Mill did not have such faith. In fact, *On Liberty* has many passages which are almost polemical in their faith in humanity's ability to correct its own wrongs, given the proper environment and conditions for doing so. Of course, it has equally many polemical passages about humanity's inability to correct its own mistakes when in circumstances which are not conducive to such corrections, but it seems that the conclusion to draw from this is not so much a statement about Mill's conception of human nature, but rather a statement about the extreme importance of having the proper circumstances and environment available for debate, because of our susceptibility to being swayed by the climate of our surroundings.

However, even on this reading, it still seems a stretch to see Mill as advocating the somewhat paradoxical idea of having freedom of expression for the sake of forming an agreement among the population in favor of regulation of speech; but perhaps this reading is implausible at least in part because we have been habituated toward the dominant reading of Mill's work as standing for robust freedom of expression in the name of autonomy. Perhaps a stronger reason for supposing that *On Liberty*'s advocating of freedom of expression ought to be read in the way that Dyzenhaus suggests is that it seems more compatible with the overarching goals of Mill's project – the elimination of what, in contemporary terms, I have been calling cultural oppression. It is the elimination of oppression that Mill is most interested in, as his *The Subjection of Women* further testifies to, and he sees freedom of expression as instrumental towards that goal. As I mentioned earlier, there is no reason to suppose that Mill would be hostile to amending anything at all that he advances if it turned out not to be conducive to maximal liberty consistent with the elimination of harm towards others, and the discourses of pornography and hate speech, for reasons that I have begun in this chapter to discuss, may be impediments to liberty.

Dyzenhaus's attempt to read *On Liberty* and *The Subjection of Women* together elucidates that Mill's primary concern in both texts is the overcoming of oppression, both by the state and by the culture at large, and this has the effect of reminding us that this, and not freedom of expression *per se*, is Mill's chief concern. Once Mill's project is resituated in this way, which facilitates a turn to discussing oppression and its various remedies rather than discussing merely the one possible remedy afforded by freedom of expression, we are able to see more clearly how the issues of pornography and hate speech might be compatible with Mill's fundamental interest in liberation from oppression, and thus pose less of a problem for his instrumental interest in freedom of expression.

Further, *The Subjection of Women* of course should be read as a strong endorsement of Mill's commitment to equality. This should be kept firmly in mind, as a reminder that his concern with freedom, so eloquently argued in *On Liberty,* was by no means the only right that he was concerned with. In *Subjection,* he notes that

> the principle which regulates the existing social relations between the two sexes – the legal subordination of one sex to the other – is wrong in itself, and now one of the chief hindrances to human improvement; and that it ought to be replaced by a principle of perfect equality, admitting no power or privilege on the one side, nor disability on the other. (Mill 1997: 1)

Here Mill seems to be returning to his 'permanent interests in man as a progressive being,' which guides his determination of the interests sufficient to be considered rights. Because sex inequality is a hindrance to the cause of human improvement, and sex equality is a boon to it, we ought to be concerned with replacing the former with the latter.

Mill grants that our long-term interests as progressive beings may of course not be immediately apparent to us in the short-term, but that should not deter us from steering a course towards equality:

> Though the truth may not be felt or generally acknowledged for generations to come, the only school of genuine moral sentiment is society between equals. The moral education of mankind has hitherto emanated chiefly from the law of force, and is adapted almost solely to the relations which force creates. In the less advanced states of society, people hardly recognize any relation with their equals.... Existing moralities, accordingly, are mainly fitted to a relation of command and obedience. Yet command and obedience are but unfortunate necessities of human life: society in equality is its normal state. (Mill 1997: 42)

Though of course any attempt to naturalize a particular condition as more innate than any other is controversial at best, nevertheless Mill demands to be read as affirming in the strongest way possible his belief that equality is a necessary condition of morality in general. As he describes it (1997: 96): 'The moral regeneration of mankind will only really commence, when the most fundamental of the social relations is placed under the rule of equal justice, and when human beings learn to cultivate their strongest sympathy with an equal in rights and in cultivation.' Thus equality seems to be a prerequisite not only for our permanent interests as progressive beings, but also for something much more basic: the ability to live under moral laws at all.

In *Subjection*, Mill also seems to be well aware of the fact that though gender equality seems to be an utterly basic requirement for a civilized life in general, pursuing equality in a society accustomed to its opposite is no easy task:

> ...[S]o long as the right of the strong to power over the weak rules in the very heart of society, the attempt to make the equal right of the weak the principle of its outward actions will always be an uphill struggle; for the law of justice, which is also the law of Christianity, will never get possession of men's inmost sentiments; they will be working against it, even when bending to it. (Mill 1997: 82)

This statement would of course be echoed by the feminists and critical race theorists discussed in this chapter, and it seems that Mill is both aware of, and sympathetic to, their concerns.

Also related to the question of whether Mill would be on board with the feminist and critical race theorist critiques of unregulated freedom of expression, the Mill of *Subjection* seems to be quite sophisticated in his understanding of the relationship between rights and power, in a way which is strikingly similar to the tenor of the critique that these contemporary theorists launch. Mill writes of those who think that the achievement of true equality is a simple matter:

> They do not understand the great vitality and durability of institutions which place right on the side of might; how intensely they are clung to; how the good as well as the bad propensities and sentiments of those who have power in their hands, become identified with retaining it; how slowly these bad institutions give way, one at a time, the weakest first. Beginning with those which are least interwoven with the daily habits of life; and how very rarely those who have obtained legal power because they first had physical, have ever

lost their hold of it until the physical power had passed over to the other side. (Mill 1997: 6)

Mill here conceives of power (in this case, physical power) as a precondition for the attainment and origin of a right (in this case, the right of men to control women) in a way which seems to be of a piece with the views of feminists and critical race theorists who contest the ways that rights get demarcated to serve the interests of those who hold social power over the interests of those who do not wield such power.

The arguments in this chapter are intended to suggest that there is reason to consider Mill as an ally within liberalism in the principled opposition to cultural oppression, and as a pioneer in understanding that true liberty and equality are nuanced ideas that require more to actualize than the mere granting of a formal right. In his discussion in *The Subjection of Women* of the radical social conditions that would have to obtain in order for women and men to obtain true equality and liberty, he seems to anticipate contemporary feminist concerns about how imbalances in power between men and women may serve to effectively deny women's liberty.

Further, I have attempted to show here how Mill's concern with freedom of expression in *On Liberty* is compatible with a strategy to maximize equality and autonomy that may regulate freedom of expression. Refocusing attention to Mill's commitment to autonomy and equality reveals how his commitment to freedom of expression should be read as instrumental to those goals of autonomy and equality, rather than an end in itself. If this is correct, then – if freedom of expression can be shown to lack the instrumentality that Mill believes that it has – it follows that the values of equality and autonomy are paramount, and freedom of expression is only valuable insofar as it supports those aims.

This chapter has attempted to read Mill as an ally in the liberal state's active role in remedying cultural oppression, by demonstrating his understanding of the role of social power in impeding the ability of the powerless to achieve autonomy and equality and, through an analysis of *The Subjection of Women,* by demonstrating his primary commitment to equality. Having Mill as an ally goes an important part of the way toward entrenching an interest in rectifying power imbalances within liberalism, but a discussion of Dworkin's views on pornography and hate speech is also necessary to ground my view that liberalism ought to be more interested in addressing power relations than it has been thus far.

# 3
# Equality, Liberty, and Hard Cases: A Contemporary View

## 3.1  Introduction

Contemporary egalitarian liberals – unlike their classical counterparts – have lived through many contentious events where the right to freedom of expression has been tested to its limits: the Skokie, Illinois skinhead marches, hate speech incidents on college campuses, internet pornography and hate speech sites, Holocaust deniers, and cross-burners, to name just a few. Despite this contemporary tumult, freedom of expression has been nearly unanimously affirmed in both the US jurisprudence and philosophical discourse. In what follows, I will examine Ronald Dworkin's influential contemporary justification for freedom of expression, which claims that a thoroughgoing right to freedom of expression is justified by the fact that it guarantees and preserves liberalism's commitment to equality by offering everyone an opportunity to speak, whereas any other policy, such as state regulation, would fail to offer this equal opportunity.

In an interesting contrast to Mill, Dworkin's justification for freedom of expression is based on equality, not liberty, and it is based not on the instrumental reasons for allowing a robust right to freedom of expression, but rather on reasons that Dworkin feels are 'constitutive' features of a democratic society. This justification is by no means immune to criticism, and has indeed been challenged by feminists and critical race theorists who find the cases of pornography and hate speech to be sufficient threats to the freedom of expression and equality of their targets – women and minorities – to warrant limiting freedom of expression in these cases. I will argue that if Dworkin is to take equality as seriously as he claims to, then, by his own lights, he must back away from an unrestricted freedom of expression – which entails a backing away from state neutrality – in light of these distinctly contemporary challenges of the harms of systemic racism, sexism, and homophobia that underlie hate speech and pornography.

The core of Chapters 2 and 3 taken together, then, reveal that the liberal state's focus on neutrality – as endorsed by Dworkin and by the dominant reading of Mill – does not in all cases preserve equality, and that in the cases of pornography and hate speech, it in fact operates to promote oppressive views of women and minorities. Given this, the neutrality requirement ought to be jettisoned in light of our racist and sexist culture, and the liberal state's commitment to equality should instead be championed.

## 3.2  Dworkin on freedom of expression

Dworkin argues that freedom of expression is absolutely crucial to moral agency, and that moral agency is the cornerstone of democratic culture. As moral agents, we should all have an equal opportunity to influence the moral environment of our shared culture. Therefore, to do anything but endorse a bare negative right to freedom of expression for every subject is to violate the state's core commitment to equality. Key to understanding Dworkin's view of the nature of the right to freedom of expression is the distinction he makes between instrumental justifications for freedom of speech, such as Mill's – which famously holds that protecting freedom of expression maximizes utility – and justifications, including his own, which view freedom of speech as a constitutive element of democratic fairness. Dworkin holds that the latter view is in fact the correct view, though he canvasses the history of American jurisprudence and admits (1997: 197–8) that most of the leading decisions have made much greater use of the former. Since the instrumental view is vulnerable to the charge that there is in fact a disutility to its exercise, Dworkin feels that his approach is inherently stronger.

Dworkin does not claim that instrumental justifications for freedom of expression are false, but rather that they fail to capture what really, fundamentally, underlies the right to freedom of expression. The instrumental and constitutive justifications, then, are not mutually exclusive, but the constitutive view is seen by Dworkin to hold even if the instrumental view is proven to be false.

What exactly does Dworkin mean by the constitutive justification for freedom of expression? The constitutive view

> ...supposes that freedom of speech is valuable, not just in virtue of the consequences it has, but because it is an essential and 'constitutive'

feature of a just political society that government treat all its adult members, except those who are incompetent, as responsible moral agents. (1997: 200)

Thus, Dworkin claims (1997: 25–6) that each individual's having a sphere of independent decision-making around moral issues is a precondition of democracy itself, and that freedom of expression is closely tied to facilitating that sphere. The claim is best understood as twofold: for a sustainable democratic culture, it is necessary both that individuals are independent moral agents (or at least have the inherent potential to develop into them), and that government treat them as such. Dworkin goes back and forth between each aspect of the claim, but it is best to consider them each as separate necessary conditions for democracy.

For Dworkin, as a liberal within the egalitarian tradition, the aim of democracy is not merely to facilitate majoritarianism, but rather to facilitate equality. To this end of promoting equality, certain background conditions are required as prerequisites to the effective functioning of democracy, one of which is independent moral agency:

A genuine political community must therefore be a community of independent moral agents. It must not dictate what its citizens think about matters of political or moral or ethical judgment, but must, on the contrary, provide circumstances that encourage them to arrive at beliefs on these matters through their own reflective and finally individual conviction. (Dworkin 1997: 26)

It is uncontroversial to hold that moral independence is a requirement of a democratic culture, at the most simplistic level, simply because freedom of thought seems fundamental to such elementary democratic processes as voting. Further, it is uncontroversial to suppose that freedom of expression is instrumental in facilitating that goal of moral agency.

However, Dworkin means to say something stronger than that – that freedom of expression is not merely instrumental to the goal of moral independence, but indeed constitutive of it. It seems that much more argument and elaboration is needed to make sense of this idea. Certainly it cannot be the case that mere citizenship in a society which protects freedom of expression is sufficient to make every person an independent moral agent. If not, then this raises the question of how much participation in such a culture is necessary to secure moral agency. It seems that it is up to the individual how, if at all, and to what degree, they engage with the ideas presented in a society which protects freedom of expression, and hence, on Dworkin's scheme, up to them how much of a moral agent they in fact are. It is even difficult to think of the relationship between moral agency and freedom of expression as anything but instrumental, although of course it is importantly instrumental.

The second aspect of Dworkin's moral agency necessary conditions, though, requires that government treat its citizens as moral agents, regardless of how or whether the citizenry in fact exercise that agency. Dworkin claims that this treatment amounts, at least in part, to refraining from censorship, particularly in controversial matters of moral or political concern:

> First, morally responsible people insist on making up their own minds about what is good or bad in life or in politics, or what is true and false in matters of justice or faith. Government insults its citizens, and denies their moral responsibility, when it decrees that they cannot be trusted to hear opinions that might persuade them to dangerous or offensive convictions. We retain our dignity, as individuals, only by insisting that no one – no official and no majority – has the right to withhold an opinion from us on the ground that we are not fit to hear and consider it. (Dworkin 1997: 200–1)

So the first requirement of democracy is a certain autonomy of the citizenry in moral decisions – the presumption that citizens are in fact moral agents – and what is necessary in order to meaningfully exercise that autonomy is exposure to different, morally relevant, ideas. It would be vacuous to subscribe to an idea of moral autonomy without also subscribing to the societal conditions, such as exposure to a diversity of ideas, which give such autonomy substance. Hence, it is government's role to facilitate this diversity by protecting speech, thus fulfilling the second part of Dworkin's requirement that government treat citizens as moral agents. This formulation thus closely links freedom of expression with moral agency, both of which, for Dworkin, are necessary conditions of democracy.

Dworkin's second requirement of democratic culture, that government treat its citizens as moral agents, ties freedom of expression in at the level not only of hearing, but also of speaking about, different morally relevant ideas. There are, then, two aspects of freedom of expression – hearing the opinions of others, and disseminating one's own opinions to others – and both are intimately tied to moral agency, which is a prerequisite of democracy. Thus, for Dworkin, freedom of expression is itself effectively a precondition of democracy. Once Dworkin ties treatment as a moral agent to freedom of expression, then a curtailment of freedom of expression becomes an infringement on moral agency, and thus on democracy itself, and consequently cannot be tolerated.

## 3.3   The silencing and subordination arguments, revisited

While this seems a strong argument for allowing free speech in all cases, Dworkin's position is nonetheless vulnerable to criticism by those who find unregulated hate speech and pornography problematic for the moral agency of the women and minorities that such speech targets. It is here that the silencing and subordination arguments will be revisited, this time in light of the concerns they raise about equality, rather than liberty. Again, I will reserve my evaluation as to the persuasiveness of these arguments until Chapter 5, once speech act theory and continental conceptions of social power have been introduced. However, even without those conceptual tools for evaluating these arguments, they are suggestive and persuasive enough on their face to require that Dworkin needs to address them more seriously than he does.

The equality arm of the subordination argument holds that state tolerance of freedom of expression in cases of hate speech and pornography compromises the equality interest of those targeted by racist and sexist speech in favor of protecting the liberty interest of the speakers. In other words, put in terms of the US jurisprudence that Dworkin is primarily addressing, the charge is that the hate speech and pornography decisions privilege the First Amendment rights to freedom of expression of the speakers over the Fourteenth Amendment right to equal protection of the laws of the minorities and women addressed by this speech. The claim is, further, that such a privileging is illegitimate and grounded only in the racist, sexist, and homophobic relations of power operative in our culture, rather than grounded in any legitimate doctrinal reason to privilege the First Amendment over the Fourteenth. As critical race theorist Charles Lawrence III poses the problem:

> We are balancing our concern for the free flow of ideas and the democratic process with our desire for equality.... When we see the potential danger of incursions on the first amendment but do not see existing incursions on the fourteenth amendment, our perceptions have been influenced by an entire belief system that makes us less sensitive to the injury experienced by nonwhites. Unaware,

we have adopted a worldview that takes for granted Black sacrifice. (Lawrence 1993: 72, 82)

Similarly, MacKinnon argues:

The law of equality and the law of freedom of speech are on a collision course in this country. Until this moment, the constitutional doctrine of free speech has developed without taking equality seriously – either the problem of social inequality or the mandate of substantive legal equality.... [T]he First Amendment has grown as if a commitment to speech were no part of a commitment to equality and as if a commitment to equality had no implications for the law of speech.... Understanding that there is a relationship between these two issues – the less speech you have, the more the speech of those who have it keeps you unequal; the more the speech of the dominant is protected, the more dominant they become and the less the subordinated are heard from – is virtually nonexistent. (MacKinnon 1996: 71–3)

The idea behind both of these charges is that hate speech and pornography violate equality because the views that they put forward give rise to unequal opportunities for the minorities and women who are addressed by this speech – if women are treated as sex objects in pornography and the content of hate speech is about the inferiority of whatever minority group is being targeted, then women and minorities go out into a world where those views are prevalent, and their opportunities for advancement are thus hindered accordingly.

Recall also that for MacKinnon, even more strongly, pornography is itself an act of subordination as well as causing further subordination as a result. She writes (1987: 172) that pornography 'institutionalizes the sexuality of male supremacy.... Men treat women as who they see women as being. Pornography constructs who that is.' It is when pornography 'constructs who that is' that it is itself an act of subordination, and it is when women's status is consequently lowered as a result of that construction – in that women are seen either as sex objects, as subservient to men, or as enjoying rape – that pornography causes further subordination down the road. The claim of the subordination argument, then, is that women's status, agency, and positive liberties – all of which boil down to a claim about inequality – are effectively lowered by the very utterance of speech which enacts their subordinate status, and that subordinate status is then furthered by a community which offers women and minorities fewer positive life choices, due to the beliefs spread and accepted by pornography and hate speech.

The claim that pornography and hate speech, at the moment of its very utterance, enact subordination is certainly a strong one. MacKinnon writes (1987: 172) that pornography 'sexualizes rape, battery, sexual harassment, prostitution and child sexual abuse; it thereby celebrates, promotes, authorizes and legitimizes them.' But how can she support this claim? It is here that the work of Rae Langton and Jennifer Hornsby is apposite (see Langton 1993; Langton and Hornsby 1998). Though a full explication of these ideas will be given in Chapter 4, a brief discussion follows here, in order that we may make more sense of Dworkin's response to it.

In trying to explicate and render plausible MacKinnon's claim that pornography itself enacts the subordination of women, Langton and Hornsby apply the apparatus of speech act theory developed by J. L. Austin, arguing that pornography may best be considered an illocutionary speech act, employing Austin's terminology – a speech act that changes the state of affairs in the world at the moment of its utterance, such as saying 'I do' when participating in a legally binding marriage ceremony. While a full explication of these ideas is forthcoming in Chapter 4, in sum I believe that Langton and Hornsby's work offers a compelling theoretical framework to buttress MacKinnon's claim.

The subordination argument holds, then, that if pornography is protected by the First Amendment, pornography violates another competing constitutional value – the Fourteenth Amendment, which guarantees equal protection of the laws for all citizens. If so, the argument continues, then the state's task is to balance the two constitutional values, and since pornography contributes nothing of any importance to political debate, and commitment to equality is a central concern of liberals, the debate should be resolved in favor of equality. Thus, like other instances where speech is regulated due to other compelling and competing interests, such as in the cases of libel and slander, pornographic and hate speech may be justifiably regulated in order to promote equality for women and minorities.

The subordination argument is particularly salient against Dworkin's formulation of the right to freedom of expression, because he views freedom of expression as itself protective of equality, rather than in competition with it. Not only is freedom of expression protective of equality, but further and more profoundly, democracy itself is understood as protective of equality. The whole thrust of Dworkin's conditions of moral membership in a democratic community, which include the right to freedom of expression, is that such conditions are equality preserving (see Dworkin 1997: 25–6).

Thus, the charges of the subordination argument are damaging to Dworkin's justification for freedom of expression because they suggest that freedom of expression cannot in all cases be tied to equality, and that in some cases equality is impeded by the protection of the right to freedom of expression. Hate speech and pornography are inimical to equality, since they subordinate minorities and women and thus offer them unequal opportunities in society – economically, politically, and interpersonally.

The second argument against unregulated freedom of expression – the silencing argument – maintains that the choice to privilege the speaker's dignity and moral agency over the recipients' same interests, by consistently protecting the speech interests of the white, male, majority over the speech interests of oppressed groups, as the US jurisprudence on the topic has repeatedly done, violates the First Amendment rights of women and minorities in favor of those of pornographers and consumers of pornography. If this argument is correct, it establishes the idea that the protection of some speech compromises the speech interests of others. Recall that this argument claims that sexist or racist speech in a sexist and racist culture 'silences' the subsequent speech of women and minorities – either because the chilling effect of the racist or sexist speech is so powerful as to entail that women and minorities will not bother even attempting to rebut it – whether out of fear, disenfranchisement, cynicism, or some combination of each – or that their attempted rebuttals will be wholly ignored, not even heard, or profoundly misunderstood by the dominant culture.

Here again, the work of Langton and Hornsby is illuminating: if women are 'silenced' by pornography, one way to make sense of that claim in spite of the fact that women are of course literally as free to speak as anyone else, is to think of their speech acts under the social conditions of silencing, in Austin's terms again, as infelicitous. Attempted illocutionary speech acts can be said to 'misfire' when the circumstances of their utterance render them not conducive to their being efficacious. One persuasive example that Langton and Hornsby give here is the situation of date rape: when a woman says 'no' to sex, but the man, for whatever reason, hears that as a 'yes.' In such a situation, though the woman has of course spoken, she has been thoroughly misunderstood or ignored – in other words, silenced. Again, while a thorough examination of feminist speech act theory follows in Chapter 4, I believe that this theoretical framework adds the needed back-story behind MacKinnon's claims.

Thus, while of course women and minorities are still technically as free as anyone else to speak, the silencing argument holds that it is the background conditions for their speech, which having been established by the preceding racist or sexist speech are such that any subsequent speech is discounted in advance by the privileged recipients, or not spoken at all by the oppressed speakers. According to these arguments, the speech of the dominant culture so effectively dictates opinions about oppressed groups as to create the oppression of those groups, as the subordination argument has it, and once created, furthers that oppression, as the silencing argument has it. The oppressed – and thus unequal – subjects enacted by such speech will then have their speech discounted as a result of the inferior subject position created by the injurious speech. MacKinnon claims:

> In the context of social inequality, so-called speech can be an exercise of power which constructs the social reality in which people live, from objectification to genocide.... Together with all its material supports, authoritatively *saying* that someone is inferior is largely how structures of status and differential treatment are demarcated and actualized. Words and images are how people are placed in hierarchies, how social stratification is made to seem inevitable and right, how feelings of inferiority and superiority are engendered, and how indifference to violence against those on the bottom is rationalized and normalized. Social supremacy is made, inside and between people, through making meanings. To unmake it, these meanings and their technologies have to be unmade. (MacKinnon 1996: 30–1; emphasis as in original)

This argument, like the arguments of feminists and critical race theorists generally, begins with the premise that power relations between privileged and subordinated groups are key to understanding the actual workings of social and political interaction, and it is this insight that, I will argue, Dworkin fails to contemplate throughout his writings on freedom of expression.

Once the subordinated culture has been oppressed by the speech of the dominant culture, the first step in silencing has been achieved, and the dominant culture is alleviated from the burden of listening to that culture. It is once this has happened that we see more clearly the workings of silencing. Pornography in particular, as opposed to other types of sexist speech, according to MacKinnon, silences women by causing its consumers to miscomprehend the ideas that women intended to express by uttering words in a sexual context:

> When anyone tries to tell what happened, she is told that...[h]er no meant yes.... You learn that language does not belong to you, that you cannot use it to say what you know.... Society is made up of words, whose meanings the powerful control, or try to. (MacKinnon 1996: 4, 5, 10)

Women are stripped of the ability to have their meaning properly heard: though they speak, they are effectively silenced, since they are taken to have said the opposite of what they did, in fact, say.[1]

Seen in this light, the silencing argument can be understood as a charge that the Dworkinian free speech program, enacted in a racist and sexist culture, in effect protects the right to freedom of expression of the dominant culture at the expense of the protection of that same right towards the oppressed cultures. Put in Dworkin's own terms, the silencing argument denies that unregulated freedom of expression allows individuals equal opportunity to speak, and by speaking, influence their culture.

These two arguments – from silencing and from subordination – are independent of each other, and feminists and critical race theorists can and do offer them either as alternatives or in combination. While these arguments are by no means completely above criticism, I believe that they raise an important objection to Dworkin's views about free speech, especially with the theoretical boost offered by Langton and Hornsby. Both of these arguments are of course in stark contrast to Dworkin's view that freedom of expression is necessarily linked to equality, because each points out a particular way that pornography enacts and furthers inequality – the subordination argument by showing how women's status in society is lowered through representations that are degrading to women, and the silencing argument by showing how men's speech is worth more than women's, since women's voices are effectively silenced, especially with respect to speech acts about consent to or refusal of sexual intercourse. We need to investigate further Dworkin's views about these claims in order to see whether he can meet their charges. He has several different arguments against these charges, all of which, I will argue, are inadequate responses to the idea that pornography and hate speech vitiate equality.

Before turning to those arguments, though, let us conclude by noting that the silencing and subordination arguments effect their criticism by granting Dworkin's conception of the link between freedom of expression, moral agency, and democracy itself, and then showing that lack of regulation too denies moral agency and is thus deleterious to democracy. The force of the silencing argument is to grant that freedom of expression is indeed tied to moral agency and then to democracy itself, but to show that given that, the fact that some speech leads to the denial of other speech must itself also entail that moral agency and hence democracy are violated by lack of regulation. The most mild reading of the silencing argument has it that the conclusion is at least a dilemma – essential conditions of democracy are violated both in cases of state regulation of some speech and in some cases of free speech – and a stronger reading has it that democracy is more importantly violated in allowing hate speech than in prohibiting it, because views of the unequal moral worth of citizens are more of an affront to democratic society than is regulation that prohibits such views. Either reading of the silencing argument, however, grants Dworkin's formulation of the relationship between democracy, moral agency, and freedom of expression and reads it against itself by showing that the relationship is violated by allowing unregulated speech, in the cases of hate speech and pornography.

Dworkin's argument for freedom of expression certainly has persuasive rhetorical value. He is all but demanding that we ought to be morally outraged at the very idea of any kind of regulation of speech. It denies our 'dignity,' it claims that we 'cannot be trusted,' it is a 'wrong,' it 'frustrates moral personality,' and it is an 'insult' (Dworkin 1997: 200–1). All of these terms are of course emotionally loaded, and Dworkin seems to rely heavily on that. That said, if indeed there is such a relationship between moral agency, freedom of expression, and democracy, as Dworkin posits, then his argument for freedom of expression is indeed a strong one. However, I want to suggest that it is a strong argument only in less controversial cases of freedom of expression, where harms to oppressed groups from hate speech and pornography do not raise issues about the effects on the freedom of expression and moral agency of the targets arising from the content of the speech in question.

Cases where freedom of expression expresses and furthers views about the unequal moral worth of certain classes of people – women and minorities – such as hate speech and pornography, demonstrate that there cannot be such an easy relationship between freedom of expression and ideas of human dignity and agency. If the content of such speech is doing little or nothing other than disputing the moral agency of women, according to such feminists as MacKinnon, and nothing other than assaulting the dignity of visible minorities, as many critical race theorists hold, then how can there be a necessary connection between freedom of expression, on the one hand, and dignity and moral agency on the other?

In other words, it seems that freedom of expression cannot be *constitutively* tied to dignity and moral agency if in some cases the exercise of freedom of expression denies the dignity and moral agency of its targets. This objection, which owes its inspiration to the arguments of feminists and critical race theorists, seems sufficient to show that there is no reason, without providing further argument against this objection, to believe that there is a constitutive link between freedom of expression and dignity and agency, although there may very well be an instrumental link between these ideas in cases where cultural oppression against women and minorities is not implicated. It seems that Dworkin has not convincingly made his case that there is a constitutive link between freedom of expression and democracy, and the importance of this link being constitutive is hard to overestimate for Dworkin's theory, since he needs to argue constitutively if he is to successfully sidestep any arguments from the disutility of freedom of expression.[2]

## 3.4   Dworkin's response to the subordination and silencing arguments

### 3.4.1   The overall challenge to Dworkin

In discussing Catharine MacKinnon's arguments against constitutional protection of pornography, Dworkin notes (1997: 205) that they are instrumental arguments, and that only by arguing constitutively can they be defeated. Much, then, seems to turn on the question of whether the constitutive argument can get off the ground, and, as I have argued, it cannot, for at least two reasons. First, Dworkin has not established that there is anything other than a strong instrumental link between moral agency and freedom of expression; and second, the arguments from pornography and hate speech, if correct, show that there cannot be a constitutive relationship between freedom of expression and moral agency and dignity if some instances of freedom of expression operate to vitiate both agency and dignity.

Dworkin, then, needs to show that these arguments that pornography and hate speech vitiate dignity and agency ought not to be accepted as they stand; but he makes several statements that show that he fails to appreciate the point of their charges. With reference to racist speech, he writes:

> It is very important that the Supreme Court confirm that the First Amendment protects even such [racist] speech; that it protects, as Holmes said, even speech we loathe. That is crucial for the reason that the constitutive justification of free speech emphasizes: because we are a liberal society committed to individual moral respons-ibility, and *any* censorship on grounds of content is inconsistent with that commitment. (Dworkin 1997: 205)

This just restates the problem. The charge from critical race theorists is that dignity, which Dworkin was happy to equate with moral respons-ibility when it suited his rhetorical purposes, is impaired by the very operation of freedom of expression.

In the case of pornography, Dworkin discusses and disagrees with the Supreme Court of Canada's *Butler* decision that would regulate some pornography containing degrading and dehumanizing depictions of women, because the Court found that such speech constitutes harm not acceptable to a free and democratic society (*R.v. Butler* [1992]1.S.C.R.452). Dworkin writes of *Butler*:

> In a recent decision, the Supreme Court of Canada accepted a dif-ferent instrumental argument for upholding a statute censoring certain forms of pornography.... The Canadian Court conceded that the effect of its ruling was to narrow that constitutional protection, but said that 'the proliferation of materials which seriously offend the values fundamental to our society is a substantial concern which justifies restricting the otherwise full exercise of the freedom of expression.' That is an amazing statement. It is the central, defining, premise of freedom of speech that the offensiveness of ideas, or the challenge they offer to traditional ideas, cannot be a valid reason for censorship; once that premise is abandoned it is difficult to see what free speech means. The Court added that some sexually explicit material harms women because 'materials portraying women as a class as objects for sexual exploitation and abuse have a negative impact on the individual's sense of self-worth and acceptance.' But that kind of harm is so close to mere offensiveness that it cannot count, by itself, as a valid reason for censorship either. Every powerful and controversial idea has a potential negative impact on

someone's self-esteem.... It is obviously inconsistent with respecting citizens as responsible moral agents to dictate what they can read on the basis of some official judgment about what will improve or destroy their characters, or what would cause them to have incorrect views about social matters. (Dworkin 1997: 206–8)

The *Butler* decision stands for the proposition that some pornography may impair the fundamental interests of a democratic society, and is thus subject to state regulation on that basis, so it is no defense against that decision to simply reiterate the importance of society treating its citizens as responsible moral agents. At the very least, Dworkin must acknowledge that there is a standoff between the dignity and moral agency of the speakers and that of the recipients, and then make a compelling further argument for why the agency of the speakers matters more than that of the recipients.

### 3.4.2    Dworkin's response to the subordination argument

Dworkin has three responses to MacKinnon's subordination argument – that pornography subordinates women and thus limits their ability to have equal access to opportunities – and her conclusion that pornography ought to be regulated. First, Dworkin claims that there is a prohibitively slippery slope in entertaining this kind of approach:

> Government could then forbid the graphic or visceral or emotionally charged expression of any opinion or conviction that might reasonably offend a disadvantaged group. It could outlaw performances of *The Merchant of Venice*, or films about professional women who neglect their children, or caricatures or parodies of homosexuals in nightclub routines. Courts would have to balance the value of such expression, as a contribution to public debate or learning, against the damage it might cause to the standing or sensibilities of its targets. (Dworkin 1997: 236)

This, again, simply restates MacKinnon's problem – she *wants* the courts to 'balance the value of such expression...against the damage it might cause to the standing of its targets.' One can at least imagine as plausible the possibility that in such a balancing by thoughtful people with clear criteria for decision-making, *The Merchant of Venice* will pass, and certain kinds of pornography may fail. This is not to suggest that the process of balancing will be at all easy. It indeed may prove to be prohibitively difficult as a practical matter, but this kind of conclusion needs to be arrived at after considered and sincere attempts and debate, rather than at the outset. MacKinnon's point, though, which Dworkin in the above quotation dismisses, is that taking the conflict between the First and Fourteenth Amendments at all seriously would necessarily require some kind of balancing of these interests, and Dworkin's refusal to engage in that balancing calls into question his commitment to equality.

Dworkin admits as much when he writes (1997: 236): 'If we must make the choice between liberty and equality that MacKinnon envisages – if the two constitutional values really are on a collision course – we should have to choose liberty because the alternative would be the despotism of thought-police.' Dworkin's equation of equality with despotic thought police seems a substantial leap. If there were in fact despotic thought police, this would of course be a problem for a liberal society.[3] However, Dworkin needs to show that a careful judiciary – or other body – committed to the equality of women and minorities is in fact a despotic thought police in disguise. It is not obvious that such a careful judiciary, in aiming to uphold democracy's central values of equality, moral agency, and dignity, would necessarily violate those very principles. He has not even come close to establishing that, unless he means to suggest that the very idea of advancing minority equality rights is itself despotic and thought controlling. If so, then in what sense is he committed to equality, moral agency, or democracy at all?

Hence, these arguments against MacKinnon's position seem weak at best. Dworkin's second, and more powerful, response to the subordination argument is that the First and Fourteenth Amendments aren't really opposed at all, and thus that the concerns of feminists and critical race theorists are misguided. Dworkin claims that political equality is preserved through the operation of the First Amendment itself:

> Citizens play a continuing part in politics between elections because informal public debate and argument influences what responsible officials will do. So the First Amendment contributes a great deal to political equality: it insists that just as no one may be excluded from the vote because his opinions are despicable, so no one may be denied the right to speak or write or broadcast because what he will say is too offensive to be heard…. Equality demands that everyone, no matter how eccentric or despicable, have a chance to influence policies as well as elections. Of course it does not follow that government will in the end respect everyone's opinion equally, or that

official decisions will be equally congenial to all groups. Equality demands that everyone's opinion be given a chance for influence, not that anyone's opinion will triumph or even be represented in what government actually does. (Dworkin 1997: 236–7)

The claim here is that an unrestricted First Amendment leads to protection of the Fourteenth Amendment because an unrestricted First Amendment allows each person an *equal* chance to influence the political sphere. This response seems inadequate to the charges of the subordination argument, but before I address that inadequacy, I will present Dworkin's third and final attempted rebuttal to the subordination argument.

According to Dworkin, because pornography has little political merit, it seems immune to his argument above. He thus needs to modify his position slightly in order to claim that the First Amendment, even in cases of pornography, is equality-preserving. He claims that not only should every citizen have an equal chance to influence the political process, but so too should every citizen have an equal chance to influence the moral environment:

Exactly because the moral environment in which we all live is in good part created by others..., the question of who shall have the power to help shape that environment, and how, is of fundamental importance, though it is often neglected in political theory. Only one answer is consistent with the ideals of political equality: that no one may be prevented from influencing the shared moral environment, through his own private choices, tastes, opinions, and example, just because these tastes or opinions disgust those who have the power to shut him up or lock him up...But we cannot count, among the kinds of interests that may be protected in this way, a right not to be insulted or damaged just by the fact that others have hostile or uncongenial tastes.... Recognizing that right would mean denying that some people – those whose tastes these are – have any right to participate in forming the moral environment at all.... In a genuinely egalitarian society, however, those views cannot be locked out, in advance, by criminal or civil law; they must instead be discredited by the disgust, outrage, and ridicule of other people. (Dworkin 1997: 237–8)

Dworkin claims that the only way to preserve our right to *equal* participation in influencing our shared moral environment is through an unregulated First Amendment. To regulate this Amendment in any way would necessarily give some groups an unequal opportunity to speak. However, this seems to straightforwardly beg the question when viewed in light of the charges of the silencing argument. MacKinnon's point in the silencing argument is that *who* is participating in that debate is exactly the question at issue. Her claim is that some speech takes other speech effectively out of the debate, because it is systematically misinterpreted, and in so doing violates the right of all persons to have an equal chance to speak. So, Dworkin is right that equality demands that each person have an equal chance to speak, but the claim of the silencing argument can easily be put as follows: hate speech and pornography effectively deny every person an equal chance to influence government or morality, because those kinds of speech, due to their content, ensure that their target's subsequent speech will be misunderstood and misinterpreted, thus denying the victim the right to speak. If we accept the silencing argument, then Dworkin's idea that the lack of regulation leads to equality fails to be persuasive.

### 3.4.3   Dworkin's response to the silencing argument

Dworkin, however, does not accept the silencing argument. He argues that, according to the silencing argument:

> [i]t is women, not pornographers, who need First Amendment protection, because pornography humiliates or frightens them into silence and conditions men to misunderstand what they say.... Because this argument cites the First Amendment as a reason for banning, not for protecting, pornography, it has the appeal of paradox. But it is premised on an unacceptable proposition: that the right to free speech includes a right to circumstances that encourage one to speak, and a right that others grasp and respect what one means to say. These are obviously not rights that any society can recognize or enforce. Creationists, flat-earthers, and bigots, for example, are ridiculed in many parts of America now; that ridicule undoubtedly dampens the enthusiasm many of them have for speaking out and limits the attention others pay to what they say. Many political and constitutional theorists, it is true, insist that if freedom of speech is to have any value, it must include some right to the opportunity to speak: they say that a society in which only the rich enjoy access to the newspapers, television, or other public media does not accord a genuine right to free speech. But it goes far beyond that to insist that freedom of speech includes not only opportunity to speak to the public but a guarantee

of a sympathetic or even competent understanding of what one says. (Dworkin 1997: 232)

Dworkin's objection here derives much of its rhetorical force from its occlusion of the issue of social power that is so central to the silencing argument, and indeed all of the arguments against the refusal to regulate hate speech and pornography. Though Dworkin is certainly not oblivious to the notion of social power elsewhere in his writing, he does not address it in his remarks here. Creationists, flat-earthers, and bigots are minority groups precisely *because* the views they espouse have already been tested, debated, investigated, and empirically rejected through a fair democratic discussion process. In other words, their views are ridiculed for *legitimate* reasons, according to the Millian account of free speech as a search for truth.

This is crucially not the case, however, for the views of minorities and women, and the reason that their views are ridiculed and dismissed has everything to do with the illegitimate power that dominant groups are able to exercise upon historically disadvantaged groups, discounting their views for reasons that have absolutely nothing to do with their merit as ideas. Interestingly and inexplicably, Dworkin seems to understand that power is important in discussing the scope of freedom of expression, because he grants, above, that it is a defensible position to maintain that access to the press is importantly impeded by economic concerns. Why would this concern be any different in principle than the concern that other people's views are discounted, or not given airtime, not because of economic factors, but rather because of racist or sexist prejudice?

The issue underlying both of these important impediments to the exercise of free speech is that of social power, and that issue seems to be all but denied outright by most liberal accounts of freedom of expression, including, notably, Dworkin's. As Dworkin maintains above, free speech includes nothing else but the bare negative liberty for any subject to speak without direct impediment by the state. It is this bare bones account of free speech that all of the feminist and critical race theory arguments object to in one way or another, claiming alternatively that the marketplace of ideas is not a neutral space, as Dworkin and Mill would have it, but is instead corrupted by racism and sexism which serve to deny the ideas of minorities and women in advance. It is only through an analysis of the concept of social power, to which I will turn in Chapters 4 and 5, that we can redress these shortcomings of the marketplace. Without it, we are led to views as inadequate as those offered above by Dworkin.

The charge of the silencing and subordination arguments, as we have seen, is that free speech cannot be constitutively tied to morality – in the case of the subordination argument because the speech enacts the unequal moral worth of its subjects, and in the case of the silencing argument, because the effective deprivation of the speech of women and minorities must give them lower moral status by Dworkin's own lights. Dworkin's response to these charges – in the case of the subordination argument, that unregulated freedom of expression itself ensures equality – does not beg the question directly, since he is claiming, effectively, that there is no need for the subordination argument. However, his response still crucially misses the point of these arguments. Dworkin is saying that there is no conflict between the First and Fourteenth Amendments, because an unrestricted First Amendment leads unproblematically to the upholding of the Fourteenth Amendment's equal protection clause. However, the charge of the subordination argument is exactly the opposite – unregulated freedom of expression applied systematically in favor of the hate speaker and the pornographer denies minorities and women the equal protection of the laws. In other words, protecting pornography gives rise to the silencing argument – privileging the freedom of expression interests of the speaker over the freedom of expression interests of the minority is an immoral and unjustified reification of the status quo of the powerful, at the expense of the relatively powerless. Dworkin's point above is only persuasive if it is convincing that pornographers are the minorities whose interests are genuinely in need of protection. However, such a response occludes the feminist and critical race theorists' point that pornography and hate speech are the voice of majority hegemonic power, and thus the privileging of their interests over the interests of minorities is yet another instance of these operations of power working to oppress, rather than vindicate, minority interests.

It seems, then, that Dworkin's attempts to justify freedom of expression as constitutive of moral agency, and as protective of equality, do not effectively meet the charges offered against these justifications by feminists and critical race theorists. The silencing and subordination arguments from feminists and critical race theorists – which call into question whether unregulated freedom of expression in fact promotes liberty and equality – have raised important challenges to Dworkin's scheme, suggesting that there is room to criticize orthodox liberal justifications of free speech. Thus it seems that the problem of harm to women and minorities from hate speech and pornography remains unaddressed in Dworkin's attempt to dismiss it. If the arguments I have been presenting are persuasive, then these concerns about crucial liberties and equalities are the very concerns that Dworkin's theory must genuinely address.

What these first three chapters have attempted to show is that there is conceptual space within egalitarian liberal theory for the departure from state neutrality in order to regulate culturally oppressive speech and the rights violations – cast either in terms of equality or in terms of liberty – to which such speech gives rise. Chapter 1 attempted to show that there are significant strains of egalitarian liberal thought that lend themselves to a conception of an activist state that regulates cultural oppression in the name of equality: Mill's harm principle, Raz's conception of rights as serving the common interest, and Dworkin's conception that the function of the egalitarian liberal state is not to protect a liberty right, but rather to treat all of its citizens with equal concern and respect. Subsequently, Chapters 2 and 3 attempted to examine why other strands of Mill, as the leading classical egalitarian liberal, and Dworkin, as the leading contemporary egalitarian liberal, have not gone so far as to regulate freedom of expression for the activist state.

What this examination has shown, I believe, is that in the case of Mill, reading *On Liberty* alongside *The Subjection of Women* reveals him to be more sympathetic to the issue of cultural oppression than reading *On Liberty* alone would suggest. In the case of Dworkin, however, we have seen that the centrality of equal concern and respect does not seem consistently applied to the question of hate speech and pornography; by his own lights, Dworkin should depart from his commitment to state neutrality in order to protect his own stated central concern – the liberal state's treatment of all its citizens with equal concern and respect.

At the end of these three chapters, then, we are left with the conceptual space for the liberal state to embrace an activist position, with the understanding that such a position would come at the expense of its presumed neutrality in the marketplace of ideas. I say 'presumed neutrality' because the subordination and silencing arguments call into question the idea that there really is any such neutrality – the state is always promoting (by legalizing) some speech at the expense of other speech, according to the silencing argument, or promoting (by legalizing) some speech at the expense of either positive liberty or equality. What this criticism raises is the issue of state power, and how that issue goes notably unaddressed in liberal philosophy and jurisprudence. It is this issue which will become central in the remaining chapters. First, the issue of the power of the state as disproportionately applied to certain groups over others, as the silencing and subordination arguments suggest, will be addressed. The flip side of this is if the state takes this criticism on board, and then departs from its neutral stance in order to protect equality against the harms of culturally oppressive speech, how we can be sure that its activism is rightly directed – that is, directed truly to protecting equality, as opposed to its own, or some other, interest. This question is also one regarding state power, and its resolution is key to allaying the traditional liberal concerns with abuse of such power.

In order to properly address both sides of this issue of state power – the unconscious state unwittingly acting to promote the rights of the majority over those of the minority, and the conscious, activist state taking steps to ensure that equality is preserved, at the expense of neutrality – we need to take a much closer look at the nature and role of the liberal state. This closer look, achieved through an examination of the nature of state speech and through continental theories of social power, will reveal a state that is always already implicated in power, and thus necessarily in need of a revised understanding of its role. It is to this question of state power and state speech that I now turn.

# 4

# Power and Politics: Speech Acts and Freedom of Expression

## 4.1 Introduction

Thus far, I have argued that there is conceptual space within egalitarian liberalism to accommodate an activist state in the service of regulating culturally oppressive speech. In Chapters 2 and 3, I argued that the criticisms of the traditional liberal justifications for unregulated freedom of expression brought by feminists and critical race theorists in the silencing and subordination arguments demonstrated the lack of attention paid to power relations by egalitarian liberal theory. The discussion in this chapter will show – using the framework of speech act theory developed by J. L. Austin – that while there are significant problems with the silencing and subordination arguments as they stand, in particular their conclusion that the speech of pornographers and hate speakers is powerful enough to silence and subordinate, they nevertheless make what I think is a fundamental point – that liberal thinking about the allocation and delineation of rights leaves something crucial about power undiscussed, and that speech act theory provides a very helpful framework for finally discussing the relationship between language and power that the silencing and subordination arguments have only gestured at.

I argue, further, that these concerns about power are not fundamentally at odds with egalitarian liberalism, but instead ought to be taken on board by it. By liberalism's own commitments, there is an obligation owed by the state to pay attention to power, for at least two reasons, both of which are intimated in the silencing and subordination arguments. First, these arguments suggest that a state which is oblivious to the implications of rights allocations on power relations may itself give rise to rights violations – in the cases of pornography and hate speech, either in terms of equality or in terms of freedom of expression – and the state has a clear and uncontroversial obligation to prevent such violations, insofar as it is uncontoversially committed to upholding the rights of all of its citizens equally. In other words, this first point is that a state which is not aware of its own power may unwittingly neglect its obligations to its citizens.

Second, the discussion in Chapters 2 and 3 aimed to show that the silencing and subordination arguments either implicitly or explicitly make use of the notion of power in claiming that there is an obligation to protect women and minorities from the harms of speech in certain situations. They claim that the social situation of minorities and women is importantly disanalogous to the social situation of the dominant culture, and that because of this, there is reason – grounded either in equality or in liberty – to protect minorities and women from the rights violations that may be caused by the dominant culture's exercise of its freedom of expression rights. However, egalitarian liberalism has, to date, not acknowledged the importance of the discrepancy in power experienced by minorities and women, and has thus decided these hard cases of freedom of expression in what appears on its face to be an abstract and formal manner, which has produced results which, by the liberal principles I outlined in Chapter 1, ought to be considered unjust.

I will hold, along with the feminist and critical race theorists advancing the silencing and subordination arguments, that this abstract and formal manner serves to conceal the relations of power which are in fact operative in the state's leading judicial decisions regarding constitutional protection for hate speech and pornography. In other words, this second point concerns the obligation of the state to remedy imbalances in power as between groups of citizens, again in order to treat all its citizens with equal concern and respect.

It is the aim of this chapter to begin to explicate more fully the idea of power operative in these critiques, and to show how a certain understanding of the nature of power makes sense of the charges advanced by the silencing and subordination arguments. In order to begin to address the issue of state power being pointed to in the silencing and subordination arguments, I need first to introduce the conceptual framework of speech act theory as pioneered by J. L. Austin in his seminal *How to Do Things with Words*, since this will facilitate the development of a more robust vocabulary for discussion of the relationship between speech and power. Austin's book, while introducing the idea that some speech is best considered as action – that is, in its very utterance, speech changes states of affairs in the world, rather than merely reporting upon states of affairs in the world – nevertheless does not fully consider the political implications of why and how some speech comes to be best considered as action and other speech does not.

To begin to answer this question, I will then introduce Foucault's notion of power framework in Chapter 5, which will complete the framework necessary for my argument that state speech as exemplified in rights enactment and limitation will be seen to be the paradigmatic instance of powerful, rather than neutral, speech acts that the egalitarian liberal state has got to consciously be aware of, and self-regulate, in order to ensure that it indeed treats its citizens with equal concern and respect.

It is important at this point to introduce speech act theory, not only because the most sophisticated versions of the silencing and subordination arguments use it as their conceptual framework to discuss the relationship between speech and power, and I need to be able to address those arguments effectively, but further, and more importantly, speech act theory will form a key element of my argument for the necessity of examining state power and state speech, as opposed to examining the particular speech of pornographers and hate speakers, as the silencing and subordination arguments would have it. I will argue that the import of speech act theory for our purposes is – like Foucault's understanding of power – in its reconceptualization of the role of the state, rather than in an explication of the power involved in the actions of pornographers and hate speakers individually. I will argue, in Chapter 5, that speech act theory is more fruitfully applied to the state's speech act of rights deployment than it is to the actions of hate speakers and pornographers.

I argue that the theorists discussed in this chapter lay a fruitful foundation for understanding the role of the state in the operation of power in general, and in rights justification and operation in particular. These theorists provide the groundwork for understanding how state power functions with respect to the enactment of rights, thus providing the tools for developing a framework which takes this power into account when thinking about rights, rather than ignoring it as contemporary egalitarian liberalism seems to do.

Further, such a framework will enable us to determine whether a particular state enactment or limitation of a right either undermines or facilitates equality. Put another way, an increase in equality through the deployment of a right, for instance, is best considered as a readjusting of power relationships, such that the balance of power is shifted to reflect the fact that those with less power now have more. Thus, this power-conscious egalitarian liberalism can be characterized as the effort to ensure that power relations move toward equitable positions, rather than away from them. In Chapter 8, an examination of the leading judicial decisions in the US, Canada, and the UK will enable a determination of this question.

How it is that under some circumstances, some kinds of utterances – what Austin terms 'performatives' – have the effect of simultaneously enacting a new state of affairs in the world, rather than merely reporting on existing states of affairs, is Austin's chief concern in *How to Do Things with Words* (1975; first edition published 1961), and it is mine as well, insofar as the answer to this question serves to elucidate the operation of state power as it is performatively exercised in the state's speech act of rights enactment or curtailment. I will argue that in describing the circumstances under which performatives 'do something,' Austin is implicitly invoking the notion of power.

I will argue, with Butler, whose work will be discussed in Chapter 6, that power is what is efficacious in making a performative work or not work, and that the Austinian analysis of speech acts, enhanced by a Foucauldian/Butlerian understanding of social power, makes sense of the role of state power in the creation and limitation of rights, more than – as feminist speech act theorists such as Rae Langton and Jennifer Hornsby maintain – it makes sense of the silencing argument's notion that women's speech acts fail to effect the performative of refusal in certain circumstances. If the enactment and limitation of rights can be understood as performative gestures, then the state apparatuses that allow those gestures to have the efficacy that they do can be better understood and thus ultimately put to better use in the service of promoting equality. Analyzing state power in terms of speech act theory will help to elucidate the conclusion that I suggested, but did not elaborate on, at the end of Chapter 3 – that the silencing and subordination arguments garner their strength through the notion that *the state* is overlooking the operation of its own power at work in its decisions about the scope of rights. This notion of *state* power operating through the state's decisions can be contrasted to the idea that *individuals* such as pornographers or hate speakers function as the locus of power. When we incorporate the insights of speech act theory, the state emerges as a much more plausible performative actor than do pornographers or hate speakers.

Of course, the aim of all of this is to try to provide tools for an improved egalitarian liberalism, rather than to argue against that tradition. This is not to say that in all cases a move toward equality is necessarily warranted – there may in some cases be other rights or other interests which compel us to forgo our concern with equality in order to protect these interests instead. However, in keeping with Dworkin's conception of egalitarian liberalism, it would seem that these cases would be exceptions to the general principle that the fundamental obligation of the liberal state is to treat its citizens with equal concern and respect.

I will first discuss speech act theory, as elaborated by J. L. Austin in *How to Do Things with Words*, and show how his theory has been taken up by feminists and critical race theorists in the more sophisticated formulations of the silencing and subordination arguments, such as those offered by Rae Langton and Jennifer Hornsby. Especially in its contemporary feminist guise, speech act theory implicitly makes use of the idea of power. Since this is the case, I will attempt to read Austin and his interpreters alongside the Foucauldian understanding of power developed in Chapter 5. In the course of this analysis, my aim is to show that there are compelling reasons within egalitarian liberalism for an acknowledgement and accommodation of the Foucauldian idea of power relations, as well as for the insights of speech act theory. The effect of this accommodation, however, is to problematize the issue of the role of the state as a powerful speech actor with respect to its function in rights enactment and limitation. Throughout this discussion, I want to argue that rights themselves should be viewed as speech acts exercising power, and to show how such an understanding of rights can yield a more nuanced view of the role of the state in furthering and producing power, as well as produce more fair results in cases that turn on the notion of equality, such as the hard cases of hate speech and pornography.

## 4.2   Doing things with words: J. L. Austin's speech act theory

In his seminal *How to Do Things with Words*, Austin describes what he feels are crucial differences between three kinds of speech acts: locutionary, perlocutionary, and illocutionary. Locutionary utterances simply describe states of affairs in the world. These are the most common types of speech acts, and we often think of them as indeed the only kinds. Our commonsense assumption is that words have a second-order relationship to events, in that words merely describe acts after the fact, rather than participate in them. Locutionary utterances are these second-order utterances, and Austin is content to leave his discussion of them at that. The central point of the book, however, is to claim, in contrast to the commonsense view, that there are two other kinds of utterances – per-locutionary and illocutionary, both of which *cause* conditions to change in the world as a result of their utterance, rather than merely report on the conditions of the world. In other words, he claims that some utter-ances have a first-order relationship to events – that in doing some-thing, the speaker is in fact creating a new state of affairs in the world.

Perlocutionary utterances create effects in the world not simultane-ously with their utterance, but after the recipient or listener performs a mental act which concludes with her taking up a different stance or position than she occupied before the utterance. An example of such a speech act is a sentence which insults someone, such that the recipient of the insult's position in the world moves from being a person who is not insulted to being a person who is insulted. According to Austin, such a movement does not occur simultaneously with the utterance, and requires both a subsequent temporal as well as a mental shift to occur within the recipient in order for the requisite change in the state of affairs in the world to be effected. However, even though the effect of the speech upon the new state of affairs is not simultaneous, it is nevertheless the case, according to Austin, that perlocutionary speech acts have a first-order relationship to events in the world – they parti-cipate in the creation of events, rather than merely report on them.

It is the third type of speech act, however, which will occupy the bulk of Austin's and my concerns. These are speech acts where the change of state of affairs in the world is effected simultaneously with the utterance, and the change is not dependent on a mental shift in the recipient, but rather only on the proper circumstances of the utter-ance, as well the comprehension of the listener, such that if these circumstances obtain, the change in the world is immediate. He calls such utterances 'performative' or 'illocutionary.' Well-known examples of performative utterances include saying 'I do' when one is marrying; christening a ship when one has been authorized to do so; and calling balls and strikes at a baseball game when one is an umpire. According to Austin, in contrast to locutionary sentences, performatives do not describe or report, and are not usefully thought of in terms of their truth value. Rather than thinking of performatives in terms of truth values, Austin feels that they should be thought of as actions. A perfor-mative sentence, for Austin, *does* something, rather than *reports* some-thing. This distinction between sentences which do and sentences which report has been widely accepted, and seems intuitively correct when considering Austin's examples – there is undoubtedly a qual-itative difference between saying 'I do' at a wedding and saying 'the grass is green' to someone who asks what color the grass is. Therefore, I will be adopting Austin's distinction between locutionary and illocutionary sentences in what follows.

How, then, do performatives do their work of doing things, rather than merely describing them? Austin makes clear that the role of the speaker and the circumstances of the utterance are the two keys to effective performatives. He writes:

> [I]t is always necessary that the circumstances in which the words are uttered should be in some way, or ways, appropriate, and it is very commonly necessary that either the speaker himself or other persons should also perform certain other actions, whether 'physical' or 'mental' actions or even acts of uttering further words. Thus for naming the ship, it is essential that I should be the person appointed to name her. (Austin 1975: 8)

These necessary background conditions for effective performatives are what Austin calls 'conventions,' and the persons performing the utterance must be the proper persons as per the convention, or else the transaction will fail to effect the illocutionary function that it intends – that is, the state of affairs in the world will not change as a result of the utterance. Austin refers to those performatives that fail to be effective because of the circumstances of their utterance as 'infelicitous.' In such cases, the utterance fails because the conventions that would have ensured its success were not present. Conversely, performatives which succeed in changing states of affairs are deemed 'felicitous.'

Performatives can be wholly or partially infelicitous under the following circumstances: when the listener fails to comprehend the utterance, when there is no convention, when the convention is invoked in inappropriate circumstances, or when the convention is invoked by inappropriate people. Conversely, what makes a performative efficacious is that its 'felicity conditions' have been met, as opposed to a descriptive sentence being made true by virtue of its correspondence with the states of affairs in the world. Austin is interested, then, not simply in the words of a statement, but in the totality of the context in which that statement is uttered:

> In order to explain what can go wrong with statements we cannot just concentrate on the proposition involved as has been done traditionally. We must consider the total situation in which the utterance is issued – the total speech-act – if we are to see the parallel

between statements and performative utterances, and how each can go wrong. (Austin 1975: 52)

So Austin is interrogating the entirety of a speech situation in order to ascertain why it is that some speech acts fail to effect what it is that they intend to perform, while others succeed.

He believes that there are several ways to account for the failure of performatives. The first has to do with the comprehension – or what Austin calls 'uptake' of the listener about what was intended by the utterance: 'Generally the effect amounts to bringing about the understanding of the meaning and of the force of the locution. So the performance of an illocutionary act involves the securing of uptake.' (1975: 177). One aspect, then, of the success or failure of the speech act depends on the listener – how they respond to what has been performed, or at least whether they have adequate cognition of the meaning of the utterance, is crucial to resolving the issue of whether the speech act has in fact been felicitous.

Another aspect of the success or failure of a performative is whether it is uttered in keeping with the conventions under which such utterances have been deemed appropriate: 'Strictly speaking, there cannot be an illocutionary act unless the means employed are conventional.' (1975: 119). This criterion refers not only to the speaker or the listener, but also to the overall circumstances surrounding the utterance, such that '[t]he truth or falsity of a statement depends not merely on the meanings of words but on what act you were performing in what circumstances' (1975: 145). For example, conventionality is demonstrated through voicing the phrase 'I do,' which is inefficacious in marrying unless the speaker is, immediately prior to the utterance, unmarried, and unless the phrase is uttered in the presence of a qualified officiator. As another example, the phrase 'strike three' is infelicitous in calling the batter out unless the person uttering it is acknowledged as a sanctioned umpire.

It is Austin's project to investigate these circumstances and background conditions in order to interrogate what he calls 'the total speech situation'; Austin claims (1975: 148) that 'The total speech act in the total speech situation is the only actual phenomenon which, in the last resort, we are engaged in elucidating.' So Austin's view of language is thus quite radical, in that it goes beyond questions of the meanings of words on paper, and looks instead toward the world of concrete and social facts in an effort to discern the overall workings of language within social life.

Austin's project has important implications for discussing freedom of expression both with respect to how to evaluate the harms of pornography and hate speech – that is, through considering the overall social circumstances of the utterance, rather than merely considering the words used – as well as on the issue of how to understand the state speech at work in rights enactment and limitation which legitimates porno-graphy and hate speech as valid forms of expression. These issues are implicitly illuminated as issues of power, and it is my task in this chapter and the next to attempt to say more about power, in the hope of finding a way to accommodate the insights of its major theorists – Foucault and Butler – within egalitarian liberal theory.

Austin does not address the issue of power directly, and he considers his analysis in *How to Do Things with Words* to be descriptive – rather than normative or political. Nevertheless, his work has been adopted by thinkers such as Butler and Langton, who see political and nor-mative implications of his work. The politics implicit in Austin's ana-lysis are revealed when he discusses the various types of illocutionary speech acts and the different kinds of actions that they perform. He describes five subcategories of performatives:

> We may say that the verdictive is an exercise of judgment, the exer-citive is an assertion of influence or exercising of power, the com-missive is an assuming of an obligation or declaring of an intention, the behabitive is the adopting of an attitude, and the expositive is the clarifying of reasons, arguments, and communications. (Austin 1975: 163)

The precise differences among these five categories are not important for our purposes, but the crucial idea here is not only that there are a number of ways to effect a performative, depending on the circumstances of the utterance and its intended outcome, but also that all of these differently nuanced performatives are each, to one degree or another, dependent upon the notion of power – 'an exercise of judgment,' 'an assertion of influence or exercising of power,' and 'declaring an intention' all implic-itly or explicitly reference an assertion of power by the speaker. However, since Austin himself does not explicate what he means by the word 'power' to describe these situations, and since I have yet to define it, I will move to a discussion of Foucault in the next chapter, whose insights in this area will be adopted. For now, though, what is important to note is that all of these five subcategories of performative utterance are dependent upon the speaker being the proper person to perform the utterance, and how a person comes to be deemed proper for the purposes of performing the speech act seems usefully construed as a function of authority or power.

## 4.3   Silencing, subordination, and speech acts

Having given a brief summary of Austin's classic account of speech acts, I will now turn to consider one influential feminist attempt to ground the silencing and subordination arguments in speech act theory – that expressed by Rae Langton and Jennifer Hornsby in a series of influential articles (see Langton 1993, 1999; Langton and Hornsby 1998). In 'Speech Acts and Unspeakable Acts' (1993), Langton aims to show that the subordination and silencing arguments – in particular, those developed by Catharine MacKinnon – are strengthened through the apparatus of speech act theory. Langton deals only with arguments for the regulation of pornography, but her reasoning is equally applicable to arguments for the regulation of hate speech. She claims that pornography might fruitfully be thought of as an illocutionary speech act, which causes either or both subordination and silencing in its very delivery. As an illocutionary speech act, it is to be considered, at least *prima facie*, as comparable to such uncontroversial illocutionary acts as marrying and naming ships. That pornography belongs alongside these other illocutionary activities is by no means obvious, and the bulk of Langton's efforts are directed towards establishing that pornography ought to be considered illocutionary and felicitous even though it departs from these paradigm cases in many respects.

Langton begins the task of applying the Austinian account of illocutionary acts to pornography by noting that the force of illocutionary acts are determined by felicity conditions which, as the preceding discussion has shown, have something to do with social context; they are best understood as conventions, combined with the speaker's intent. Langton notes further that some kinds of illocutionary acts require for their efficacy that the speaker be in a certain position of authority in order for the act to work as planned. Langton calls these 'authoritative illocutions': actions whose felicity conditions require the speaker to be occupying a position of authority in the relevant domain: for example, being a judge when issuing a sentence.

Given this structure of the background conditions for effective illocutionary acts, the question arises as to how one can know what the illocutionary force of an utterance is, when it is not a paradigm case like marrying, in which everyone knows what the felicity conditions are, who can meet them, and when they have been met. Langton argues that it is most plausible to suppose that some felicity conditions were met in the case of pornography, and that they were sufficient to secure the illocutionary efficacy of the action, since, by hypothesis, the silencing and subordination arguments maintain that the acts in question are of the authoritative sort, so making sense of this claim requires the supposition that pornographers are in fact in a position of authority sufficient to secure the illocutionary effects feminists are claiming. Langton, correctly, thinks much of the debate turns on this question of whether pornographers are in fact the voice of the dominant culture, or whether they are instead more fruitfully thought of as a minority in need of protection against moralistic state persecution. The answer to this question is key to determining whether pornography in fact subordinates or silences. Everything, for this analysis then, turns on whether pornography is in fact authoritative and that enough felicity conditions are satisfied to secure subordination or silencing.

Langton begins her discussion of this crucial question of pornographers' authority by noting that even if an illocution is sufficiently authoritative to yield certain results, there is nevertheless a limit to the extent to which saying something is so can make it so – for example, according to Langton, the Catholic Church's saying that homosexuality is an objective disorder does indeed subordinate the homosexual, but it is less clear that it makes it the case that the subordinated person does indeed have an objective disorder. That said, that women are subordinated by certain illocutions is sufficient to warrant concern, even though it may not be the case that such subordination means that women really are inferior to men.

However, Langton notes, for some authoritative illocutions (for example, 'You're fired,' when said by the boss), saying so does indeed make it so. These are what Austin calls exercitives. But for other kinds of speech acts, which Austin calls verdictives, such as an umpire saying, 'You're out,' this isn't quite as clear-cut. There is still the fact of the matter of whether the ball was in fact inside or outside of the strike zone, regardless of what the umpire called. It is in both the exercitive and verdictive senses that Langton thinks that pornography may work to subordinate women. She maintains that subordinating speech constructs reality by legitimating and making permissible certain ways of acting, in part by representing them as ordinary and normal. The speech of the powerful purports to describe the world, but it is really disguising the fact that it is creating important aspects of the world by virtue of the power that such speech has. For example, say that pornography typically represents women as enjoying certain sexual acts more than others. And say that in fact, prior to the publication of the pornographic images, this is not the case. However, if pornography has the power to effect illocutionary speech, it will become the case first that male consumers of pornography will be able to authoritatively order that these acts be performed, and second that women will come to see themselves as having, and perhaps even wanting, to perform them.

In other words, authoritative verdictives have illocutionary effects on the normative beliefs of their consumers – pornography operates, in part, by legitimating false beliefs. In turn, when these false beliefs are turned into the speech of the powerful consumers of pornography – because males in a misogynist culture are by definition powerful – they have the illocutionary effect of in fact subordinating the women about whom the speech makes claims by requiring them to perform acts that, prior to the influence of pornography, they had no interest in performing.

At this point, it is worth exploring the notion of causality at play in the scenario that I have just sketched. A great deal turns conceptually on fixing the harm of pornography and hate speech as illocutionary in nature. If the effects of pornography are held to be causal in a traditional probabilistic sense – where a factor (C) is a cause of an effect (E) if, and only if, the presence of C raises the incidence of E for a large population and raises the probability of E for an individual case when all factors other than the presence or absence of C are held constant[1] – then whether pornography causes these effects on women would be subject to the usual scrutiny of social science, and could be established by recourse to the traditional studies showing whether a causal link was statistically significant. There have been numerous such studies over the past thirty years with respect to the question of whether pornography causes the effect of sexual violence and they notably have failed to produce a conclusive determination that that there is any such causal connection, at least between non-violent pornography and sexual violence.[2]

However, sexual violence is of course only one of the effects that pornography may cause. The idea I have been considering throughout this study is the notion that pornography and hate speech contribute to the inequality of women and minorities through the ability of these media to subordinate and silence them. Such a hypothesis is intrinsically less amenable to social scientific testing, due to the fact that there are a myriad of causes of inequality in our culture, and it would be extremely difficult, though not impossible in principle, to isolate pornography or hate speech from any of the other causes in order to determine its particular causal role. However, envisioning the harm of inequality in terms of the traditional causal framework outlined above leaves it empirically testable in principle, in the sense that the cause – pornography or hate speech – is seen as antecedent and is instrumental to a subsequent harmful effect – such as subordination or silencing – such that if the cause were removed, the incidence of the effect of inequality would be lessened.

In contrast, the illocutionary hypothesis, while still a causal hypothesis, is nonetheless causal in a way that veers significantly away from the traditional model of causality and would tend to preclude in principle its confirmation or falsification by traditional social science methodology, due to the near simultaneity of cause and effect that it posits. Some would see this as a disingenuous sidestepping of the requirement that any theory about an empirical state of affairs should be subjected to scientific scrutiny. Others believe that it finally clearly defines the societal harms caused by pornography, a characterization which has long eluded adequate characterization by the social science models. While nothing for my purposes turns on either position, since I will not conclude by endorsing pornography or hate speech as either illocutionary nor otherwise causally effective in the subordination of women or minorities, it is still important to place the illocutionary hypothesis within this debate about pornography's relationship to empirical evidence, to better see its strengths and weaknesses.

Langton maintains, I think correctly, that actors who are different from and lesser in authority than the state can sometimes subordinate nonetheless; the question is only when and under what circumstances. Langton answers this by saying that when either the local perceived legitimacy or the local efficacy of the utterance is sufficient, subordination is effected. Put this way, she seems to think it plausible that given our own social conditions of living in a historically and systemically sexist, racist, and homophobic society, such local perceived legitimacy may indeed be in effect such that the dominant culture has the power, through pornography, hate speech, and other means, to legitimate certain behavior towards and by women and minorities.

Even granting all of this, however, the conclusion of regulation of speech still does not follow. One way that such a conclusion may be avoided is through the traditional liberal answer to problems of this kind – if women can fight this oppressive speech with speech of their own which argues against it, the correct position will win out in the end due to free debate on both sides. However, the very force of the silencing argument, in combination with the subordination argument, is to suggest that women cannot simply combat speech which subordinates with more speech, since the very point of the silencing argument is to deny the force or possibility of their speech.

Langton thus turns her attention to the silencing argument, anticipating that speech act theory will be illuminating here as well. She contends that if it is indeed the case that some speech is best construed as action, as per speech act theory's hypothesis, then 'silence' is not to be thought of strictly as literal silence, but more broadly construed as any manifestation of the failure to act; pornography prevents women from doing things with their words. Langton contends, quite uncontroversially in light of Austin's analysis, that performing speech acts is a mark of political power, and failing to perform a speech act that one would otherwise like to perform is a real mark of powerlessness.

In other words, if having authority in the relevant domain is sufficient to perform a speech act, then having no authority in the relevant domain is sufficient to fail to perform a speech act, or to have what Langton calls 'illocutionary disablement.' Examples of illocutionary disablement include a homosexual attempting to marry in jurisdictions where marriage is restricted to heterosexual couples, or a black person in South Africa during apartheid attempting to vote. Langton contends that these acts are literally unspeakable, not just disobedient.

This idea of illocutionary disablement is rooted in Austin's conception of conventions as requisite for felicitous speech acts: felicity conditions are fixed by conventions, and one important way that conventions are set is through prior speech acts. Some speech determines the kinds of speech there can be in the future, so, therefore, some speech can silence, not just by ordering, but by defining the parameters of accepted speech. In other words, the speech acts of men in pornography can themselves be understood as establishing a convention wherein the speech of women is systematically misconstrued by men. According to Langton, we may be said to have situations of illocutionary disablement in cases such as where a woman's 'no' indicating declining to participate in sexual activity is not understood, just like Donald Davidson's example in *Inquiries Into Truth and Interpretation* (2001: 270) of the actor on stage yelling 'fire' for real – the locution and intention are there, but the uptake is not secured for the listener, and the speech act thus misfires.

If conventions are set by the prior speech acts of authoritative speakers, the interesting point for our purposes is that this implicates the speech acts of the state as much as it implicates the speech acts of the pornographers or the hate speakers. I will consider the speech acts of the state in more detail in Chapters 5 and 6, but for now I simply wish to highlight that this idea of speech acts as potentially restrictive of further speech creates a three-tiered structure of power: first, the state's power as the primary – and uncontroversially authoritative – creator of the limits of acceptable speech becomes the first site of illocutionary power; second, the individual speakers who then speak the speech thus enacted and legitimated by the state are themselves created by the power of the state in delimiting their speech; further, these individuals may themselves exercise power over others, if Langton's hypothesis about the mechanics of the silencing and subordination arguments is correct.

It appears, at all of these levels, that there may be some kinds of structural constraints on the speech of women and minorities. Certain felicity conditions are not being met for the woman who tries to say 'no,' and so the question becomes who is it who establishes these felicity conditions. In paradigm cases such as marrying, the felicity conditions were set, uncontroversially, by prior speech acts in the law, but in the case of pornography (and the same holds for hate speech), Langton is forced to make the implausible claim that the felicity conditions are in fact set by the pornographers. According to Langton and MacKinnon, the consequence of pornography is that no matter what a woman says, the only thing she can in fact do with her words is consent. If this is the case, then a woman's authority over her own body is compromised through pornography. Thus, if pornography sets up the rules for the speech acts of sex – if pornography is the speech that determines the kind of subsequent speech there can be – then, Langton concludes, it is exercitive speech in Austin's sense, for it is in the class of speech that confers and removes rights and powers.

All of this seems acceptable as far as it goes, but the premise concerning pornography's authority is of course empirical, and has yet to be convincingly established by Langton or other feminists, and seems quite dubious on its face. I want to suggest that pornographers and hate speakers do not have this authority, at least not directly. Rather, I will contend, it is *the state* that has the straightforward authority to enact felicitous speech acts, and it does so by creating legislation or judicial decisions concerning, *inter alia*, the constitutional protection of hate speech and pornography. To the extent that these decisions have protected hate speech and pornography, they have given the hate speakers and pornographers whatever limited authority they do have, but much more important than this limited authority is the very public authoritative speech act of the state that says that such speakers and their speech are endorsed by the state itself. This idea and its far-reaching consequences will be further developed and interrogated in the next chapter.

Another critical question that Langton's analysis leaves open is whether pornography's silencing, even granting that it does in fact silence, gives rise to a violation of the First Amendment rights of its targets. Even if Langton shows that pornography may prevent women from doing certain things with words, this does not necessarily mean that pornography runs afoul of the First Amendment because of this. So the question, then, is: Does the free speech that the First Amendment protects include free illocution? Langton and Hornsby want to answer 'yes' in their article 'Free Speech and Illocution' (1998) and they claim Mill as their ally here. Their suggestion is that a good justification of the right to free speech is the right to do certain illocutionary things, though they do not attempt to prove it. While Langton and Hornsby have not demonstrated that the First Amendment includes the right to illocution, they want to suggest that such an interpretation makes the most sense of the importance of free speech.

As discussed in Chapter 3, Dworkin notably rejects the idea of illocution as protected speech, arguing that such a conception departs from what he feels is the fundamental notion that freedom of expression is a negative liberty. Protecting illocution – or protecting the idea that listeners will understand what is being said – would require that free speech be construed as a positive liberty, as others not only have to refrain from impeding the speech, but also learn how to listen better, so as to enable the attempted performatives to meet their felicity conditions. Such an undertaking would move freedom of expression into the positive liberty sphere, because of the active involvement required. While such a positive conception of liberty may indeed be desirable, it is outside of the scope of this project to argue for such a conclusion, as my aim is to show that state regulation of some speech is acceptable within the tenets of liberals of Dworkin's ilk, who view freedom of expression as a strictly negative liberty.

However, even granting the quite controversial idea that the right to freedom of expression protects illocution, Langton and Hornsby run into a further problem in that they cannot maintain that any illocution at all should be constitutionally protected, because if they did, then pornographic illocutions would have to be defended as well. Thus, they only defend the illocution of refusal, not the illocution of subordination. Langton writes:

> If there are conflicts between freedoms to speak – if the free speech of men silences the free speech of women – then there is a choice about which speech is to be protected. If there is a conflict between

freedom to perform illocutions of subordination and illocutions of refusal – it just might be that refusal matters more. (Langton 1998: 276)

There is an intuitive appeal in this kind of sentiment, and while it may seem that the appeal depends upon agreeing with the feminist position, I want to maintain that there is in fact a more general and important reason why such a position is appealing.

Langton's remark derives its appeal from its gesturing towards power relations. She is saying that given the nature of the interests and the relative power of the groups, justice requires that we favor the interest in refusal of the subordinated group over the interest in subordinating by the dominant group. This suggestion provides an excellent segue to turn to Foucault's work on the issue of power, in an attempt to show how it, in conjunction with speech act theory, may illuminate the issues that feminists and critical race theorists seem to be implicitly employing.

The discussion in the past chapter has demonstrated how power and speech are intimately related, even if they are not related in exactly the way that Langton and Hornsby want to maintain. However, there is still a lot which remains to be said about the nature of power, which I will turn to in Chapter 5. To conclude, though, what the preceding discussion has revealed is that the relationship between speech and power – gestured to in the silencing and subordination arguments – nevertheless leads away from their conclusion that this relationship culminates in the power of the speakers of pornography and hate speech. Rather, as we have begun to see, the relationship of speech to power leads to the more plausible, but more radical, conclusion that this relationship in fact culminates in the state, whose speech acts in enacting laws and deciding the scope of those laws in its judicial decisions is unequivocally powerful.

This conclusion, which I will spend the rest of the book elaborating and defending, has far-reaching implications, particularly regarding the end of the egalitarian ideal of state neutrality in the marketplace of ideas. The discussion of speech act theory in this chapter has suggested that the undercurrent in the silencing and subordination arguments – that the liberal's lauding of state neutrality in freedom of expression cases operates to conceal and to further power imbalances – in fact holds great truth. Given this, the state is not and cannot ever be neutral. It is always exercising its power in the speech acts taking place in its judicial decisions. If this is the case, egalitarian liberals can, without violating their other key commitment to equal concern and respect, abandon their claims to neutrality. Indeed, they ought to, because the claim to neutrality is in fact pernicious and allows for rights violations to go unnoticed by the state.

Taking speech act theory on board in this argument shows how the state is always already implicated in power relations, and is thus never neutral. While this is in some ways a radical reconceptualization of the state from that of traditional liberalism's idea of state neutrality, I want to argue that it is not incompatible with the fundamental tenets of liberalism, and indeed can provide for a more robust, and ultimately more just, conception of the state. However, there is still much elaboration needed on the nature of state power, and I will turn now to a discussion of the leading theories of state power, which will come from outside of the liberal tradition and from contemporary continental political theorists. It is my contention that these theorists, while not usually invoked in liberal debates, can offer a much more nuanced view of the role of state power, and one which liberals would be well served to accept if the liberal state is to be successful in undoing the harms of cultural oppression. Given that, I will turn in Chapters 5 and 6 to a discussion of Foucault's and Butler's conception of state power.

# 5
# Foucault: Power, Discourse, and the State

## 5.1   Foucault and the nature of power

Michel Foucault's insights into the nature and mechanisms of power have been among the most persuasive and influential of the last century, though his account has been almost universally overlooked in debates about liberalism. Foucault's exclusion from the discourse may be owed partly to the fact of his own hostility toward liberalism, and partly to the fact that analytic and continental philosophy have a long history of antagonism and thus a propensity to talk past each other. One of my chief aims in this book is to show how the insights into the relationship between power and speech of continental thinkers, such as Foucault, can inform current debates in analytic liberal philosophy, particularly those debates about the scope and limits of egalitarianism. The first three chapters of this book discussed those liberal debates, with particular emphasis on the North American debates over pornography and hate speech. The discussion of speech act theory in the previous chapter, Foucault in this one, and Judith Butler in the next, will finish laying the foundation of the continental positions, which I hope will inform the debates addressed in the first half of the book.

Foucault's theory of power is central to my account not only because its influence demands that it be addressed in any discussion of power and politics, but because he makes the crucial point that power is not a matter of obvious physical coercive force by the state, but is more subtly operative through language. The connection between power and language was made by Austin in the preceding chapter, but Foucault takes this point a pivotal step further in arguing that it is not through language *per se*, but rather through discourse – particular organized bodies of knowledge – that power operates. This point underlines my contention that the body of jurisprudence itself, combined with the academic body of work surrounding it, is a discourse in the Foucauldian sense, and as such an important site of power. Even further, the discourse surrounding freedom of expression in particular operates at a meta-level, on a Foucauldian reading, since it governs the scope and limits of all further discourse.

It is the idea of discourse as a function of power that the liberal discussion – through its claims to state neutrality – denies. I will argue that Foucault's contention that discourse is anything other than neutral, coupled with Butler's novel arguments about the nature of censorship that I will introduce in the next chapter, decisively entails that the liberal idea of state neutrality is false and must be abandoned. Once the state abandons neutrality, the way is paved for an activist egalitarian liberal state to take shape, since all that impeded the latter was the idea that any speech or resources provided by the state for the protection of women and minorities would be a violation of its central commitment to neutrality. If neutrality never existed, as the arguments of Foucault and Butler have it, then of course this obstacle disappears. However, in order to be able to advance this chain of reasoning convincingly, I must in this chapter address those parts of Foucault's account that are less compatible with this view – namely, that Foucault, famously, did not view state power as central to his account. I will attempt to show that while this is the case, it does not undercut my use of Foucault in the context of my argument that state discourse is a vital instrument of power.

Foucault's account of power is counterintuitive to commonsense accounts of power that would understand it as top-down – concentrated in the hands of the political elite, centrally concerned with physical force or the threat of such force, and repressive to the masses. Instead, for Foucault, power is diffuse, decentralized, and creative, as much as it is repressive. Foucault's account is particularly noteworthy for my discussion of the hard cases of freedom of expression, such as pornography and hate speech. Foucault maintains that the chief creative functioning of power occurs through discourse, and I will show through an examination of what he means by these terms – power and discourse – that like Austin, Foucault implicates the state, rather than the individual, in discourse production.

The conclusion that we must turn to the state to analyze its power and rethink its stance on neutrality, however, has not been accepted by Judith Butler, in her book on freedom of expression, *Excitable Speech* (1997). Since Butler is working in the Foucauldian tradition, and addresses the silencing and subordination arguments directly, it is important to examine her arguments. In *Excitable Speech* she concludes that individual speakers sometimes hold the power to perform efficacious and novel speech acts, and that this power alone – without reference to the state – is sufficient to ground a liberatory politics. However, as I will demonstrate in Chapter 6, an adequate liberatory politics must also include an interrogation of state power. I will show how she and Foucault – although at times against their own understanding of their work – combined with the speech act theorists examined in Chapter 4, lead to a reconceptualization of the state as a very powerful speech actor. If egalitarian liberalism can incorporate this conception of the state – and I will argue in Chapters 7 and 8 that it can and it ought to – then liberals will finally be in a position to end their insistence on a futile conception of neutrality, and to take up, fully and fruitfully, their commitment to treat all citizens with equal concern and respect by acting to end cultural oppression.

The silencing and subordination arguments, while raising important issues of power imbalances between speakers and the targets of their speech, nevertheless make use of an idea of power that does not square entirely with the Foucauldian picture. The silencing and subordination arguments either locate the site of power in the individual pornographer or hate speaker, which thus far seems implausible, or, seemingly more plausibly, they gesture towards the idea that the state is the obvious site of omnipotent and thoroughgoing power, which it wields in favor of majority interests, and against women and minorities. In either case, these formulations are at odds with Foucault's understanding of the operation of power, which maintains that power is not located centrally either in individuals or in the state. Thus, a central question for the remainder of this book will be to resolve the state's role in the operation of power – on the one hand, incorporating the important insight of the silencing and subordination arguments holding that liberal accounts of rights elide what ought to be central issues of state power, while, on the other hand, maintaining a faithfulness to what I feel is Foucault's more nuanced and more insightful understanding of power as decentralized.

While Foucault wants to maintain that power is not concentrated in the hands of the state, the account of speech act theory given in Chapter 4 has suggested that the role of the state is more central, perhaps, than Foucault imagined. If the state's speech acts are by definition authoritative, as I have argued follows from Austin, then this gives the state a lot more power in its speech acts than private actors, or non-state institutions, have, at least on the surface. I will aim in this chapter to combine Foucault's insights about power and discourse, including state power and state discourse, with the insights of speech act theory and the silencing and subordination arguments. The result shows, following Foucault, that while the state is not the only important site of power, nevertheless, in legal discourse – as the silencing and subordination arguments gesture towards but do not flesh out – the state's discursive power is seminal and unacknowledged in liberal theory in general, and in the discourse surrounding freedom of expression in particular. Indeed, the discourse around freedom of expression takes its place at the pinnacle of the state discourses because it sets the rules for all further discourse – which speech will be allowed and which speech disallowed, both by individuals and by the state itself. Thus, the unexamined effects of the power embedded in the freedom of expression discourse are particularly pernicious. The silencing and subordination arguments point to this perniciousness but leave major theoretical gaps regarding the unexamined effects of the state's discursive power.

Key to my understanding of power is Foucault's insight – also adopted by Foucault's contemporary intellectual heir, Judith Butler – that power runs through discourse, rather than through individuals. This conception of power challenges the notion of power, offered in the silencing and subordination arguments, as being centered in individuals – and it persuasively demonstrates that the latter arguments should not be accepted as they stand. At the same time that Foucault and Butler demonstrate the limitations of the silencing and subordination arguments' understanding of power, Foucault and Butler also indicate, albeit to some degree unwittingly, that a more nuanced understanding of power leads to an inquiry into state power. While Foucault and Butler do not themselves undertake this inquiry in their own work, I will attempt to begin it, in Chapters 7 and 8, especially with reference to how we should understand the role of state power and state speech in cases of hate speech and pornography – cases that reveal the workings of unexamined state power operating at the margins of freedom of expression discourse. This is the extent to which I feel my account departs from a Foucauldian account, and I will attempt to show in this chapter that while this is indeed a departure, it is nevertheless not a pernicious one.

After defining Foucault's notion of power in detail in Section 5.2 below, I will aim later in this chapter to make three points about the implications of Foucault's position with respect to the nature and role of the liberal state. First, Foucault's comments about the state are supportive of my claim that state speech is a primary locus of power, even given that his understanding of power is not state-centered. Second, I will argue that Foucault's conception of power as located in discourse not only strengthens the claims of speech act theorists such as Austin, who maintains that speech is not only a function of power, but also provides a way to understand both the nature of the body of jurisprudence surrounding freedom of expression as well as the resistance to that discourse. The latter, I will argue, is exemplified in the silencing and subordination arguments. Finally, I will argue that Foucault's conception of power as residing in discourse, rather than in individuals, decisively turns the issue of responsibility for pornography and hate speech away from the individual speaker and towards the state. After making these three points, I conclude that together they entail that the liberal myth of state neutrality must be abandoned, as it functions only to conceal state power. This concealment of state power results in exactly the effects that proponents of the silencing and subordination arguments maintain, even if the mechanisms by which those effects are achieved are not entirely consistent with the proponents' accounts.

Taking the first three chapters of this book as establishing the proposition that there is conceptual space within egalitarian liberalism for an activist state, and taking the second three chapters as demonstrating that there is a relationship between state speech and state power that has not been fully explored by liberal theory, I will be able to turn in Chapters 7 and 8 to argue for an activist egalitarian liberal state that seeks to end cultural oppression in order to meet its core commitment of treating each citizen with equal concern and respect.

## 5.2   Discourse and counter-discourse

For Foucault, power is the overarching idea through which to understand all human enterprise. More specifically, he claims that power – operating through discourse – is responsible for the creation of human subjects as we have come to know them. In this formulation we begin to see how power is understood by Foucault as *productive* of subjects, rather than merely repressive of them:

> The notion of repression is quite inadequate for capturing what is precisely the productive aspect of power. In defining the effects of power as repression, one adopts a purely juridical conception of such power; one identifies power with a law which says no; power is taken above all as carrying the force of prohibition. Now I believe that this is a wholly negative, narrow, skeletal conception of power,

one which has been curiously widespread. If power were never any-thing but repressive, if it never did anything but to say no, do you really think one would be brought to obey it? What makes power hold good, what makes it accepted, is simply the fact that it doesn't only weigh on us as a force that says no, but that it traverses and produces things, it induces pleasure, forms knowledge, produces dis-course. It needs to be considered as a productive network which runs through the whole social body, much more than as a negative instance whose function is repression. (Foucault 1984a: 61)

Two ideas emerge here: that Foucault identifies merely repressive power with law and juridical discourse (a formulation that I will discuss at much greater length later in this chapter), and that in opposition to this, he sees power as not only occasionally productive and creative, but rather as fundamentally so. It is the 'yes' of power that makes power enticing and thus self-perpetuating.

So what, exactly, is this 'yes'? The central 'yes' is the formation of subjects through power. But in what sense can we say that subjects are formed through power? Foucault famously maintains that power oper-ates centrally through the production of discourse – organized bodies of knowledge – and discourses create human subjects as we have come to know them. One paradigmatic example would be the discourse of psychiatry, which began in the nineteenth century. Through that organ-ized body of knowledge, we derive such subjects as the hysteric, the narcissist, and others thus labeled by their mental disorders. These kinds of people were *produced* by the discourse of psychiatry and could not be said to exist without that discourse, according to Foucault. He writes:

In any society, there are manifold relations of power which per-meate, characterize and constitute the social body, and these rela-tions of power cannot themselves be established, consolidated nor implemented without the production, accumulation, circulation and functioning of a discourse. There can be no possible exercise of power without a certain economy of discourses of truth which oper-ates through and on the basis of this association. We are subjected to the production of truth through power and we cannot exercise power except through the production of truth. (Foucault 1980a: 83)

For Foucault, then, power is operationalized through discourse, and dis-course is a necessary and crucial condition of power. Even more radically, for Foucault, truth itself is produced by discourse, which means that it is produced by power. The idea of truth as produced by power is radically at odds with commonsense ideas of truth, which see truth as that which liberates us from power. For Foucault, instead, truth is a function of power and keeps its actual workings in disguise. Foucault's question, then, is not only what the discourses of truth teach us, but, more profoundly, how they create us and rule us. Thus, a thorough interrogation of power involves interrogation of discourse, and to interrogate discourse is to reveal the myths, disguised as truths, that we have taken up as key aspects of our very identities.

What we accept as truth, then, for Foucault, is thoroughgoingly a matter of power and politics, as it plays out in discourses. Foucault employs war imagery again in this regard (1984a: 74): 'It's a battle about the status of truth and the economic and political role it plays.' This war imagery is apt because for Foucault, power necessarily produces resistance, and since power operates through discourse, resistance to power, too, operates through discourse. Foucault calls these resistant discourses 'counter-discourses,' and he feels that it is very important to examine and bring to light these counter-discourses, lest the more dominant discourses be seen uncritically as truth.

Foucault calls the methodology for identifying resistance to power 'genealogy.' His idea here is to uncover the discourses that have been hidden by the workings of the dominant power structure, thus shifting the relations of power by exposing the dominant discourse *as discourse*, rather than as truth in an objective sense. He describes the notion this way:

> Let us give the term genealogy to the union of erudite knowledge and local memories which allows us to establish a historical knowledge of struggles and to make use of this knowledge tactically today.... What it really does is to entertain the claims to attention of local, discontinuous, disqualified, illegitimate knowledges against the claims of a unitary body of theory which would filter, hierarchize and order them in the name of some true knowledge and some arbitrary idea of what constitutes a science and its objects. (Foucault 1980a: 83)

The idea at play here is that these local, underground, or subverted knowledges, if uncovered by the genealogical process, would provide a counter-force to hegemonic and unilateral streams of power, exposing them as fraudulent in their claims to universality and primacy. Foucault claims that the dominant discourses are those asserting their own scientific status, and he maintains that the revolutionary aspect of the genea-logical project is in its ability to challenge these notions:

> It is really against the effects of the power of a discourse that is con-sidered to be scientific that the genealogy must wage its struggle.... By comparison, then, and in contrast to the various projects which aim to inscribe knowledges in the hierarchical order of power associ-ated with science, a genealogy should be seen as a kind of attempt to emancipate historical knowledges from that subjection, to render them, that is, capable of opposition and of struggle against the coer-cion of a theoretical, unitary, formal and scientific discourse. (Foucault 1980a: 84–5)

It is here that the core of Foucault's liberatory politics is revealed – he wants to undertake the genealogical enterprise because he wants the relations of power to be tipped differently from how they have been thus far.

These ideas of genealogy, counter-discourse, and resistance are very important for my purposes. I want to argue that there ought to be attention paid to the 'local knowledge' of the lived experiences of sexism, racism, and homophobia. This type of lived experience – of being silenced and of being subordinated as a consequence of racism, sexism, and homophobia – is exactly what the feminists and critical race theorists who have advanced the silencing and subordination arguments aim to reveal. The authors of these arguments attempt to express a revolt against the dominant discourse maintaining that law is a science and that rights are being distributed in an egalitarian fashion. Foucault, it seems, would concur with the silencing and subordination arguments being considered counter-discourse, given his description of the genealogical project:

> It is through revolt that subjectivity...introduces itself into history and gives it the breath of life.... One does not have to maintain that these confused voices sound better than the others and express the ultimate truth.... It is sufficient that they exist and they have against them so much which is set up to silence them.... [I]t is due to such voices that the time of men does not have the form of an evolution, but precisely that of a history. (Foucault 1981a: 8)

For Foucault, the very fact that the silencing and subordination argu-ments exist and offer different and opposing points of view to the dom-inant discourse is itself revolutionary, and it is revolutionary regardless of whether we ultimately accept those arguments in their entirety as they stand.

For my purpose of trying to offer a more tenable reading of the claims behind the silencing and subordination arguments, it will prove useful to consider the freedom of expression literature – both the jurisprudence and the philosophical arguments presenting theoretical support for that jurisprudence – as part of this apparatus of truth/power. This literature is hence problematic at least for being not what it appears on its face, and rather, for being yet another conduit of power. This is what I think the proponents of the silencing and subordination arguments meant to suggest in claiming that the state privileges the discourse of the dominant culture in its pornography and hate speech decisions, while still proclaiming its own neutrality.

Foucault calls these formative or dominant discourses 'the human sciences' – the humanities and social science disciplines – and he claims that they are each a function of power:

> [W]hat struck me, in observing the human sciences, was that the development of all these branches of knowledge can in no way be dissociated from the exercise of power.... Generally speaking, the fact that societies can become the object of scientific observation, that human behavior became, from a certain point on, a problem to be analyzed and resolved, all that is bound up, I believe, with mechanisms of power – which, at a given moment, indeed, analyzed that object (society, man, etc) and presented it as a problem to be resolved. So the birth of the human sciences goes hand in hand with the installation of new mechanisms of power. (Foucault 1988a: 106)

If human behavior at a certain point became a problem to be analyzed and resolved, and thus the human sciences arose to tackle this project, it is difficult to see how law should not be included with these discourses and perhaps be chief among them, since law is obviously regulative of human behavior. Laws – both prohibitive and permissive – define the scope of our conduct, and the scope of our conduct is exactly what interests Foucault when he speaks about power as productive of subjects. Further, law is heavily reliant on the human sciences to produce evidence for its decisions and policies, and, reciprocally, such reliance becomes an important piece of the power of these sciences, giving them more power by virtue of the legitimacy conferred upon them by their adoption into legal decisions. Such a relationship would seem to make law the human science *par excellence*, in its capacity as the arbiter of the other human sciences.

If this is correct, and law is indeed a powerful discourse within the human sciences, then why does Foucault explicitly characterize his project as deeper than what he calls 'juridical' – meaning those forms of power produced by the state in order to prohibit certain behavior? The most obvious example of juridical power in Foucault's sense of the term is the criminal law, since of course it is the function of the criminal law to prohibit certain kinds of behavior and impose sanctions to back those prohibitions. However, contrary to Foucault's rather circumscribed understanding, law can more plausibly be seen as both productive and repressive in that laws are permissive as well as prohibitive. A permissive law about a particular behavior, such as marriage, can importantly be said to be productive of that behavior. That Foucault relies on such a narrow view of the law so as not to recognize this point is, in my view, a significant weakness of his account. I believe that my account, which reads Foucault more expansively, offers a more faithful account of the nature of law, while at the same time illuminating Foucault's portrayal of how the law operates as a conduit of power.

## 5.3   Power, the state, and the law

As I have noted, the idea of power as delocalized, and running throughout the entire social body, is contrary to commonsense understandings of the notion of power, which would locate it paradigmatically in the state. Foucault, famously, resists this idea (1984a: 63): 'What we need...is a political philosophy that isn't erected around the problem of sovereignty, nor therefore around the problems of law and prohibition. We need to cut off the king's head.' For Foucault, focusing the issue of power around statehood, law, or prohibition implies that power is localized in the state, fixed through law, and repressive through prohibition. Foucault strongly resists all three of these ideas because, as I have shown, he sees power as the dynamic producer of truth and discourse, in all its varied forms, and thus neither fixed, repressive, nor localized.

My project, however, needs to make use of the idea of state power on at least three fronts: state power as manifest in the upholding of hate speech and pornography as protected speech under the First Amendment; state power as manifest in the line of cases that privilege the First Amendment over the Fourteenth Amendment; and the enactment and limitation of rights in general as state speech acts, which as such are paradigmatically powerful. Each of these three sets of speech acts requires the power of the state to produce and to regulate the discourse around freedom of expression, understood, as I have argued, as a master discourse controlling all other discourses. Because state power plays such a central role in my argument, further exploration of Foucault's understanding of the way in which power is manifest in the state is required if my account is to be faithful to the Foucauldian corpus as a whole. This further exploration will reveal that my understanding of state power is legitimate on Foucauldian terms, even though many parts of his *ouvre* would seem to be at odds with such a reading.

He sets out his understanding of the nature of power and the state as follows:

> To pose the problem in terms of the state means to continue posing it in terms of sovereign and sovereignty, that is to say, in terms of law. If one describes all these phenomena of power as dependent on the state apparatus, this means grasping them as essentially repressive: the army as a power of death, police and justice as punitive instances, etc. I don't want to say that the state isn't important; what I want to say is that relations of power, and hence the analysis that must be made of them, necessarily extend beyond the limits of the state. In two senses: first of all because the state, for all the omnipotence of its apparatuses, is far from being able to occupy the whole field of actual power relations, and further because the state can only operate on the basis of other, already existing power relations. The state is superstructural in relation to a whole series of power networks that invest the body, sexuality, the family, kinship, knowledge, technology, and so forth. (Foucault 1984a: 64)

Here Foucault certainly affirms that the state is an important site of the operations of power, but he denies that it is prior or central to the functioning of power in all of its guises. Rather, the state is posterior to other forms of power that must be operative in order for the state to exist in the first place. Thus the state cannot be entirely efficacious in establishing and regulating all operations of power.

That said, Foucault of course acknowledges the state's obvious and important role in the unfolding and manufacture of power, especially in its function of formalizing power relations through law. I want to maintain that law is among our most powerful discourses; Foucault's writing supports my claim, even though he does not focus particularly on law. In a 1971 essay entitled 'The Order of Discourse,' Foucault asserts that the truth of law is not to be deemed a source of power on its own, but rather seen in a larger context in order that we may fully understand it: '[I]t is as if even the word of the law could no longer be authorized, in our society, except by a discourse of truth.' (1981b [1971]: 55) Understanding the discourse of law means recognizing it as a part of a regime of discourses that authorize what is to be taken as truth. Law thus conceived is precisely what I am attempting to advocate: law, and state discourse generally, is by no means the neutral, interest-blind matter that mainstream analytic political philosophy or philosophy of law want to maintain. It is instead always embedded with power – the power of producing the knowledge that we take to be truth, and the power of endowing with legitimacy and rights some individuals and institutions and not others.

Perhaps more than any other discourse in the human sciences, law in particular has its claim to truth built into it: its rules are self-validating and its effect on our behavior instantly binding. Foucault coins an apt term for the close relationship between law and the powerful discourse it manifests: the 'juridico-discursive.'[1] The law is, consistently with our commonsense understanding, 'laid down' in discourse. Phrasing this insight in the language of this book's previous chapter, then, law produces felicitous illocutionary speech acts.

Even further, Foucault notes, law, alongside science, is a privileged source of truth: 'It's the characteristic of our Western societies that the language of power is law, not magic, religion, or anything else.' (1980b: 201). So though Foucault does not focus on law, but rather on the more decentralized locations of power, such as schools, prisons, and the military, it is nevertheless clearly the case that he grants law's discursive efficacy in the production of truth.

All of this is perfectly consistent with my account of state speech acts as being embedded with power. Indeed, once we adopt Foucault's notion that power runs principally through discourse, my account is strengthened by the understanding of jurisprudence as a discursive production. However, Foucault is notably uninterested in the law as a site for his research, and if the account of Foucault offered here is a faithful one, it thus becomes important to inquire *why* he is so uninterested. Foucault's focus is on discipline – briefly, techniques of controlling individual bodies and beliefs – and he believes that discipline occurs most interestingly in sites that are removed, to some degree or another, from the law – places such as schools, prisons, and psychiatric hospitals. Thus these places, and not law, become the sites he investigates. Foucault writes (1980a: 102): 'We must eschew the model of Leviathan in the study of power. We must escape from the limited field of juridical sovereignty and state institutions, and instead base our analysis of power on the study of the techniques and tactics of domination.' Foucault is correct in maintaining that the law alone would be an insufficient site of investigation into the techniques and tactics of domination, but I maintain that even granting him this point does not deny that the law is particularly efficacious in becoming a paradigmatically sovereign site of power, out of which techniques of discipline are developed.

The preceding discussion has shown that Foucault acknowledges this relationship between law and discipline. Sporadically he writes less of a dichotomy between law and discipline, and of more of a continuum between them:

> I do not mean to say that law fades into the background or that institutions of justice tend to disappear, but rather that the law operates more and more as a norm, and the judicial institution is increasingly incorporated into a continuum of apparatuses (medical, administrative, and so on) whose functions are for the most part regulatory. (Foucault 1980d: 144)

Again, this formulation concurs with my account of the state – in its judicial function – as an efficacious speech actor whose actions create one of the most powerful discourses we have, even while day-to-day discipline functions through apparatuses to some degree removed from the state.

Foucault's model appears to suggest an undertaking of a two-tiered analysis of power – first, power in its more formal guise, which is played out in the discourses of law and rights, and secondly, power manifesting as the result of that first formal understanding, which Foucault describes as the discourses of 'knowledge' or 'truth.' Thus, the formal establishment of power in law and rights facilitates the operation of power in the discourses of truth. Such a formulation is highly compatible with my understanding of the role of law as central in the web of power, even if not originary in that web.

Foucault's discussion of 'right' and 'rights' is often ambiguous. Frequently, he seems to conflate the two terms; sometimes 'right' means the divine right – or authority – of the sovereign, and sometimes it evokes the notion of rights, namely interests deemed worthy enough to be protected by the state, to employ Mill's formulation. It is worth distinguishing these two very different ideas, even if Foucault at times does not. Perhaps Foucault does not distinguish the two terms because he wants to point out, rather cynically, the great extent to which rights, in the latter sense, are tied to the discourse of sovereignty, or right.

Foucault acknowledges that the egalitarian discourse of state-sanctioned rights of course exists as the dominant discourse, but that underlying that discourse is the highly inegalitarian discourse of discipline, or what he calls 'micro-power':

> Historically, the process by which the bourgeoisie became in the course of the eighteenth century the politically dominant class was masked by the establishment of an explicit, coded and formally egalitarian juridical framework, made possible by the organization of a parliamentary, representative regime. But the development and generalization of disciplinary mechanisms constituted the other, dark side of these processes. The general juridical form that guaranteed a system of rights that were egalitarian in principle was supported by these tiny, everyday, physical mechanisms, by all those systems of micro-power that are essentially non-egalitarian and asymmetrical that we call the disciplines.... The real, corporeal disciplines constituted the foundation of the formal, juridical liberties. (Foucault 1977: 222)

For Foucault, there is a counterintuitive relationship between law and the disciplines – it is the disciplines that are 'the foundation of the formal, juridical liberties.' Seeing the relationship between law and discipline in this way explains why Foucault is reluctant to focus on the juridical aspect of this relationship, but the direction of causality is not at all obvious.

For my purposes, however, the question of causality can be left open. What is interesting is that Foucault is certainly not in thrall to the concept of rights, in marked contrast to liberal discourse's focus on them. In Foucault's view, the discourse of rights only serves to mask the inegalitarian mechanisms of power that exist 'on the underside of the law' (1977: 223). It is this lack of respect for rights as the only – and thoroughly authoritative – discourse, to which proponents of the silencing and subordination arguments at times allude. Such proponents are discontented with the mainstream liberal idea that because women and minorities have the same formal rights as other citizens, equality exists, and no further state measures are called for to secure its realization. Such proponents would find an ally in Foucault, who feels similarly:

> Liberty is a practice.... The liberty of men is never assured by the institutions of law that are intended to guarantee them. This is why

almost all of these laws and institutions are quite capable of being turned around. Not because they are ambiguous, but simply because 'liberty' is what must be exercised.... I think it can never be inherent in the structure of things to guarantee the exercise of freedom. The guarantee of freedom is freedom. (Foucault 1984b: 245)

For Foucault and for the proponents of the subordination and silencing arguments – contrary to mainstream liberal discourse – merely granting formal rights is insufficient to guarantee actual liberties on the ground, and this is where I think mainstream liberalism has much to learn from both Foucault's work and the subordination and silencing arguments. I believe, and will argue in Chapters 7 and 8, that these insights are not at all antithetical to the liberal state's core commitment to treating its citizens with equal concern and respect. Indeed, these oft-diverging viewpoints can inform each other.

However, there is one crucial respect in which Foucault and liberalism are at odds, and that concerns state neutrality. The notion of power running through discourse and producing what we take to be truth would preclude neutrality at every level. The state is a discourse producer, and as such it is always implicated in power relations, rather than being somehow exempt from them, as liberal discourse would suggest. My claim – that Foucault's analysis of power ought to lead to the end of insistence on liberal neutrality – will be further reinforced in the next chapter, when I examine Butler's persuasive arguments that state speech necessarily regulates discourse – in other words, that the liberal state is always already guilty of its own worst fear: censorship. Neither Foucault's account of power, nor Butler's account of censorship, ought to be taken as devastating to liberal discourse. I will maintain in Chapter 7 that these insights are not antithetical to liberalism's core commitment – insofar as its core commitment is seen as the treatment of all citizens with equal concern and respect – and can be accommodated by an enlightened egalitarian activist liberal state.

## 5.4   The silencing and subordination arguments, revisited

Having examined Foucault's notion of power as diffuse and operative through discourse, it is time to bring these insights to bear on the silencing and subordination arguments, as well as on the charges of culturally oppressive speech that the arguments have brought to light. Analysis of Foucault's *ouvre* has at least these important implications for these arguments. First, his insistence on the historicity of subjects will prove to echo and buttress the concerns of the proponents of the silencing and subordination arguments. Second, Foucault's idea of power as decentralized and not centered in the individual subject will challenge the idea, advanced by most proponents of the silencing and subordination arguments, that power resides in the individual pornographer or hate speaker. Finally, Foucault's ideas of genealogy and counter-discourse will reinforce the silencing and subordination arguments' point that the discourses about silencing and subordination offered by women and minorities are fruitfully understood as counter-discourses. I explore each of these implications in this section.

First, with respect to historicity, Foucault's conception of discourse explodes the very idea of neutrality even further than have the speech acts theorists canvassed in Chapter 4. Instead of positing ahistorical subjects who live amid the backdrop of a neutral state, as liberalism would have it, we have instead a very different formulation:

> The history which bears and determines us has the form of a war rather than that of a language; relations of power, not relations of meaning. History has no 'meaning,' which is not to say that it is absurd or incoherent. On the contrary, it is intelligible and should be susceptible to analysis down to the smallest detail – but this in accordance with the intelligibility of struggles, of strategies and tactics. Neither the dialectic, as logic of contradictions, nor semiotics, as the structure of communication, can account for the intrinsic intelligibility of conflicts. (Foucault 1984a: 56)

Foucault here affirms the intelligibility of history and its efficacy in forming human subjects, and claims that the key to comprehending the unfolding of human history is to focus on, and illuminate, the history of power relations. Understanding what is meant by the idea that history 'bears and determines us' goes far towards appreciating an important idea that liberalism has failed to take into account, which is the notion of an historical, rather than an ahistorical, subject. The idea of an historical subject implicitly lies behind the silencing and subordination arguments, and we can see this when returning to these arguments in light of Foucault's understanding of power and discourse.

Foucault's critique of the ahistoricity of subjects is an important part of what critical race theorists identify as crucial to understanding the nature of the injustice in leading hate speech decisions, such as the 1992 United States Supreme Court decision in *R.A.V. v. City of St. Paul*,[2] which allowed the white plaintiffs to burn a cross on the lawn of a black family on First Amendment grounds. Foucault's understanding of power as producing particular kinds of subjects, depending on the historical situation, and the discourses operative in that situation, can perhaps best be seen by way of the compelling example that is the decision in *R.A.V.* The best way, I believe, to make sense of the judgment in *R.A.V.* is to say that the Court decided to protect this speech by decontextualizing the history of cross burning, and by portraying the cross-burners as an unpopular minority whose speech the Court must defend against the state's power of censorship. The majority opinion, written by Justice Scalia, illustrates the results of ignoring the historicity of power relations while deciding whose interests deserve state protection. This demonstrates the legal system's gross inadequacies in upholding the rights of a minority group. As critical race theorist Mari Matsuda poses the problem:

> In effect, the opinion proceeds as though we know nothing about the origins of the practice of cross burning or about the meaning that a burning cross carries both for those who use it and those whom it terrorizes. What we do learn from the opinion is that cross burning is not a 'majority preference' and that the ordinance [which would have not protected the speech] reflects inappropriate 'special hostility' against 'particular biases.' The cross burners are portrayed as an unpopular minority that the Supreme Court must defend against the power of the state.... The reality of ongoing racism and exclusion is erased and bigotry is redefined as majoritarian condemnation of racist views. The powerful impact of the burning cross – the assault, the terror – is also inverted. The power is replaced in the hands of those who oppose racism. The powerful antiracists have captured the state and will use the state to oppress powerless racists. (Matsuda and Lawrence 1993: 135)

In light of the preceding discussion of Foucault's understanding of power and historicity, it becomes clear that *R.A.V.* was wrongly decided, and taking Matsuda's and Foucault's comments together, we can begin to see why. What is wrong with the decision in *R.A.V.* is mainstream liberalism's failure to account for the operation of power and historicity in its decisions of when to apply and how to define rights. The decision was, instead, governed by the Court's ahistorical – in other words, fictional – discussion of the power relations between black and white people. Foucault's insistence on historically constituted subjects adds further weight to the viewpoint of critical race theorists that fully understanding a hate speech situation means understanding the historicity of the utterance. Critical race theorists contend that the liberal state is guilty of insisting that its subjects are ahistorical. Perhaps the state's insistence on ahistoricity signals a blind attempt to ensure the vaunted goal of neutrality: if the state pretends that all citizens are homogenous and applies blanket policies to everyone, then the state will have met its neutrality requirements.

However, the conflation of neutrality with ahistoricity does not seem to be a necessary move; certainly we can conceive of situations where the liberal state could recognize the historicity of its subjects, and right historical wrongs, without violating neutrality. For instance, the Canadian state could, and indeed did, compensate its First Nations citizens who suffered physical and sexual abuse in the state's residential schools for over a half century without making any claims about preferring the First Nations'conception of the good life over any other competing conception. This example demonstrates that the liberal state need not be committed to the ahistoricity of its subjects in order to maintain neutrality. When historicity is overlooked by legislators and judges, as is often the case, dangerous decisions, such as that in *R.A.V.*, can result.

Not only does Foucault see history as determinative of subjects, but he also suggests that history is itself the history of power. If this is the case, then it follows that power is to be understood as existing prior to selfhood. Foucault wants to claim that power is the primary and formative element of human life and experience, and this claim entails subscribing to the quite radical notion of subjects as effects, rather than creators, of power. He writes:

> The individual is not to be conceived as a sort of elementary nucleus...on which power comes to fasten.... In fact, it is already one of the prime effects of power that certain bodies, certain gestures, certain discourses, certain desires, come to be identified and constituted as individuals. (Foucault 1980a: 98)

Thus, individuals cease to be the primary locales of power and instead become mere functions of it. This has devastating implications for the silencing and subordination arguments to the extent that these arguments make use of the idea of the hate speakers and pornographers as themselves the instruments of power exerted upon powerless minorities and women. A Foucauldian analysis would resist such a view, since it makes individuals too central and obvious a site of power to account plausibly for power's diffuse and decentralized operations.

As was shown earlier in this chapter, Foucault argues that the dominant mode for thinking about power, which he often calls 'sovereign power,' is inadequate. Oppression is thus not what the silencing and subordination arguments define it as being – a global constraint that one person, or one group, exercises over another. Foucault feels that such a construction must be false, both because the subject is not the extreme of power's exercise and because power is not merely repressive but fundamentally creative as well. For Foucault, the shift from thinking about subjects as having power, to thinking about a set of practices in which power is actualized in the practices' effects, signals a departure from the conceptual model of sovereignty that dominates thinking on politics and law.

The discussion in this chapter has revealed that Foucault understands the relationship between power and the state to be more complicated than it initially appears, but that his understanding of the individual in relation to power is simpler. For Foucault, the individual is very clearly not the primary site of power, and individuals are not understood as bearers of power, but rather the very creation of subjects is itself a function of power. Subjects are certainly an important part of the operation of power, for Foucault, but they are not located at the apex of power.

However, even though the silencing and subordination arguments cannot be accepted as they stand, given that they rely on an untenable account of power in the individual subject, these arguments serve another very important function on a Foucauldian understanding, bringing to light a counter-discourse in which women and minorities express their frustration at having been silenced and subordinated by the dominant discourse. Before the authors of the silencing and subordination arguments published these ideas, this discourse was even more underground than it is today. At present, as a result of the discourse surrounding the silencing and subordination arguments, there exists a flourishing academic and jurisprudential discourse influenced by these arguments' overarching concern: that liberalism's rights discourse operates to obscure the power relations embedded in the allocation and delineation of rights. This is a powerful idea that, as I maintain, leads to the undermining of liberalism's neutral pretensions. Such an undermining, I will hold in Chapters 7 and 8, signals not the end of liberalism but rather an opportunity for a reinvigorated and self-consciously powerful liberal state that would be – for the first time – equipped with the resources to understand its own power and wield it in the interests of advancing equality.

## 5.5 Conclusion

This chapter has aimed to make three points about Foucault that demonstrate how his theory about the nature of power is relevant to the discussion of whether and how the liberal state should actively work to end cultural oppression in order to treat its citizens with equal concern and respect.

First, Foucault's notion of power as operative through discourse greatly strengthens my case that speech and power are intimately linked. Having demonstrated that, we can no longer return to the liberal myth that the state's speech is outside of power; the idea of state neutrality in the marketplace of ideas is finally laid to rest by Foucault's theory. In the next chapter, I will begin to explore a further reason, offered by Judith Butler, why the liberal claim to neutrality is fatally flawed. In contrast to one of the chief reasons offered by liberals for state neutrality – the avoidance of censorship by the state – Butler contends that censorship operates quite differently from how liberals envision it does, and that this difference again implicates the state in non-neutrality, as well as showing, from another angle, how neutrality is impossible in principle. Again, my critique of state neutrality, informed by the arguments of Foucault and Butler, is not meant to be hostile to liberalism. I will argue in Chapters 7 and 8 that the liberal state, untethered from the bonds of its claims to neutrality, will be able to speak freely – for the first time – in the service of equality.

Second, Foucault's claims about the nature of state power, while not central to his account, are nonetheless supportive of my central claim that state power in the form of juridical discourse needs to be both admitted by the liberal state and interrogated by the state if we are to realize finally the central liberal goal of the treatment of all citizens with equal concern and respect. Without such an admission, the discourse around freedom of expression operates, as I have shown throughout these pages, as an extremely powerful and dangerous discourse that dictates the terms of subsequent discourse. Since the freedom of expression discourse operates at a meta-level among discourses, getting to the root of its workings is key to the goal of enhancing the opportunities for equality in the liberal state.

Finally, examining Foucault's account of power, discourse, and genealogy reveals that, contrary to some formulations of the silencing and subordination arguments, individual citizens such as pornographers and hate speakers do not wield enough power to effect successful illocutionary speech acts. That said, the voices of women and minorities, coalescing in the silencing and subordination arguments themselves, may in fact be powerful enough to constitute a genealogy or counter-discourse to the mainstream discourse that has rights distribution as an egalitarian and neutral allocation.

# 6
# Censorship and Silencing

## 6.1 Introduction: Post-sovereign speakers in a post-sovereign state

In her book *Excitable Speech*, Judith Butler attempts to take on board Foucault's idea of post-sovereign power and meld it with the ideas of performative speech acts and Derrida's idea of citationality to create what she calls 'a politics of the performative.' Butler proposes that the combination of post-sovereignty and speech act theory affords, for perhaps the first time in history, the possibility that a previously disempowered speaker can resignify a previously injurious speech act.

If she is correct, this offers a powerful challenge to my view that the liberal state needs to be engaged in its own speech on behalf of the disempowered (that is, the silenced or subordinated) speakers, since, according to Butler, such speakers are not disempowered after all. I will argue that Butler's attempt to ground a liberatory politics out of the bare fact of post-sovereignty is ultimately unsuccessful because post-sovereignty, even when combined, as she has it, with speech act theory and Derrida's idea of citationality, can in no way guarantee the efficacy of the disempowered speaker's ability to resignify speech. At most, the marketplace of ideas is more egalitarian on Butler's account than it is for the proponents of the silencing and subordination arguments, or on Foucault's and Austin's accounts, but it is not egalitarian enough to provide sufficient opportunities for speech acts that will guarantee that the state's treatment all of its citizens with equal concern and respect. Thus, state intervention is still vitally needed to meet this demand.

That said, Butler's account does offer a very interesting, and I think correct, view of the nature of censorship. Many liberal thinkers have defended what I contend is the obfuscating and deeply problematic

139

idea of state neutrality because of the fear that in the absence of neutrality, censorship would result. This is far from an implausible worry, and indeed, as Chapter 2 has demonstrated, stems from as canonical and influential a thinker as J. S. Mill. Butler's view will cast very serious doubt on this orthodox liberal view, and in so doing, I will argue, she provides the decisive argument against the need for, and the desirability or possibility of, state neutrality.

In what follows in this chapter, then, I will first take up Butler's politics of the performative and show that it does not achieve the level of protection for historically disempowered speakers that an egalitarian liberal state would need to provide to all of its citizens. However, Butler's account of censorship does provide a very powerful idea of the nature of censorship and one that implicates the state at such a primary level that state avoidance of censorship is untenable. Butler's account demonstrates the futility of the classical liberal objective of state neutrality.

## 6.2   Excitable speech: Judith Butler's politics of performativity

In her book *Excitable Speech*, Judith Butler offers a novel take on the freedom of expression debate that is informed by Foucault, Derrida, and speech act theory. In introducing the issue of state power as manifested in state speech acts, she says (1997: 62): 'It will be necessary to distinguish between those kinds of violence that are the necessary conditions of the binding character of legal language, and those kinds which exploit that very necessity in order to redouble that injury in the service of injustice.' In other words, while state speech is of necessity powerful, it remains imperative to make the distinction between benign and pernicious state speech. Making this distinction, through examining state judicial discourse, will be the concern of Chapters 7 and 8. Butler's account offers a good starting point for this inquiry.

I suggest that the authoritative nature of state speech is paradigmatically realized in its decisions to enact and to limit rights, and that this power and authority is problematically ignored in mainstream liberal accounts of the state, where the state is seen as the neutral arbiter of competing private interests. Foucault's analysis of the nature of power, discourse, and the state demonstrates that the liberal view is not only naïve but dangerously false. It is dangerous, I believe, because such a misleading view of state action (or more aptly, non-action) serves to elide the power of the state and obscure its real operations. Butler's point above – regarding the issue of state power as manifested through state speech acts – is that it is worthwhile to determine which state actions in particular make use of this eliding of the operation of power in order to further injustice, and which instead are simply powerful *qua* state action. Not only is this distinction worthwhile, but it is crucial if the state is going to fulfil its commitment to treating all of its citizens with equal concern and respect.

Butler claims that we understandably want accountability for racist, sexist, and homophobic speech, and so the liberal state posits a subject to bear that responsibility. The problem with positing a subject to bear responsibility is that such a subject is a mere grammatical fiction, according to the Foucauldian tradition, in which Butler situates herself. Subjecthood in what Butler, following Foucault, calls the 'juridical' sense does not exist in reality because the view of subjects as agents of power rather than as instruments of it is, as I have shown in the previous chapter, false. For Butler, ignoring the fact that sovereign or juridical subjectivity of private subjects is a legal fiction – which liberal discourse insists on ignoring – stalls the analysis of how discourse (legal, pornographic, or otherwise) produces injury, by taking the subject and the spoken action as the uncontroversial point of departure for the analysis, rather than as the subject of the analysis itself (1997: 47).

According to Butler, proponents of the silencing and subordination arguments make precisely this mistake – they assume that power resides in the speakers of hate speech and pornography, then conclude that the responsibility must simply lie with these speakers as well. These assumptions operate according to a commonsense view of power, what Butler and Foucault call the 'sovereign' sense, in which the subject's power is assumed to be as thoroughgoing as that of the sovereign. However, this view has been shown to be simplistic on the Foucauldian account.

Contrary to the silencing and subordination arguments, Butler argues that the power of racist, sexist, and homophobic utterances does not derive from the speakers' independent power and social standing. Butler stands with Foucault and Derrida in understanding, rather, that the power derives from the citationality and historicity of the actual words uttered. She maintains that it is only because racist epithets, for example, have a particular history in a painful racist past that they are able to inflict the injury that they do. Racial slurs have their painful effects to an important degree because they recall times when the racist label was literally fatal; pornography has its painful effects because of times when women had even less protection from rape than they have presently. This seems an important insight, and an insight that relocates the question of the efficacy of racist, sexist, and homophobic speech back towards the speech and the speech situation – as per Austin – rather than towards the individual speaker.

Butler's resituating the power of speech acts in language and history has important and far-reaching ramifications for my discussion. First, it suggests that policies that entail strictly individual liability for racist or sexist utterances fail to address the real chain of responsibility at play in such utterances. This evokes the Foucauldian idea that a juridical notion of subjecthood and responsibility is inadequate to the task of a proper understanding of speech acts and power. While it is tempting here to mobilize our familiar assignments of blame and responsibility, Butler makes it clear that to do so would perpetuate a fiction, causing us to fail to grasp what is truly at stake. Instead, if the power of a speech act derives from historicity of language itself, language's power exceeds merely that particular iteration and draws its force instead from the history of its meanings. Veering away from the perspective of the silencing and subordination arguments, Butler proposes another way to view hate speech and pornography, a view that she feels incorporates the best of Austin and Foucault.

Butler's account relies on the insights of Derrida as well as the above thinkers, in particular his view that the meaning of utterances fundamentally cannot be determined in advance of the utterance by the speaker herself. Derrida points out the necessary indeterminacies of language, a project that would, if successful, serve to demonstrate precisely why the speaker is not, and can never be, sovereign. While a full account of Derrida's argument would take us too far afield, a discussion of his notion of citationality will provide the relevant aspects of his account that Butler employs.

## 6.3   Speech, citationality, and the politics of the performative

Derrida introduces his arguments about the citationality of language as evidence of its mutability and its indeterminacy. He writes:

> Every sign, linguistic or nonlinguistic, spoken or written, in a small or large unit, can be cited, put between quotation marks; in so doing it can break with every given context, engendering an infinity of new contexts in a manner which is absolutely illimitable. This does not imply that the mark is valid outside of a context, but on the contrary that there are only contexts without any center or absolute anchoring. (Derrida 1988: 12)

In other words, the ability to cite a sign is an ability to recontextualize it, and the ability to do this is limitless. Because of the power of citationality to reconfigure the meaning of the sign for any new con-text, Derrida thinks that the citationality of signs establishes language's indeterminacy of meaning, rather than continuity of meaning as had been previously assumed in other theories.

Derrida sees citationality as heralding the end of thinking about lan-guage in terms of fixed meanings, and maintains that Austin's account of speech acts opens the door to this new way of thinking by eliminat-ing the view that language merely reports states of affairs in the world, and thus has meanings that are fixed insofar as they must correspond to these states of affairs (Derrida 1988: 13). Since the performative is by definition about creating its own, brand-new state of affairs, it cannot be thought of simply as a tool for describing a world already given to us, as merely locutionary sentences are understood.

However, Austin's view isn't radical enough, according to Derrida, because it presupposes the efficacy of the speaker's intent in deter-mining meaning, rather than interrogating that very efficacy. In dis-cussing the speaker's intent in uttering a performative, Austin simply assumes that there is an obvious correspondence between such intent and the deciphering of the content of the performative. Such a picture is altogether too tidy for Derrida, as it disallows for the existence of the radical discontinuity of meaning that he insists is to be found in all communication, including performative communication.

Where Derrida uses the notion of citationality primarily to demonstrate an absence of the speaker's total control over the meaning and context of the performative, Butler takes this result a step further and shows that there are deep political consequences for this fact. Derrida's account demonstrates that we do not have total control over the meaning of our speech acts, due to their citational nature, and Butler goes one step further to argue that this 'out of controlness' of our speech means that there is a possibility to reformulate the meaning of a speech act through its very citationality, and reformulate the meaning to be more politically favorable to the interests of the speaker.

Butler begins *Excitable Speech* by adopting Foucault's insights that lan-guage is intimately tied to the creation of subjecthood. She notes that perhaps the reason why words can indeed wound, as the proponents of the silencing and subordination arguments maintain, is that we are linguistic beings, created by language. We are called into being through language, and following Foucault, the identity that we acquire through language has everything to do with the discourse that makes such an identity meaningful, which in turn has everything to do with power.

Butler concurs with Derrida's claim that no term or statement can function performatively without its accumulated historicity. Butler claims, for example, that this is how racist injury works. The speaker who utters a racist slur is citing the slur, and the injury is due to the recollection of times throughout that minority's history when use of that phrase had explicitly deadly consequences. So far, then, Butler has not departed to any great extent from the other thinkers I have been considering with respect to hate speech.

Butler truly departs from all of the thinkers on speech acts and power I have thus far examined when she determines that Derrida's notion of citationality has liberatory potential – potential that she thinks suggests that the state regulation of hateful speech is as unnecessary as it is wrongheaded, and that subjects themselves should instead employ what she calls 'counter-speech' as a way of positively transforming these Derridean gaps in language's meaning.

Butler maintains that the nature of language as – importantly – out of the speaker's control means that words do not necessarily have to wound, because speech can have a future not dependent on the words themselves or the speaker's intention. There is, then, a possibility of a resignifying, liberatory counter-speech, which recasts previously injurious language in a liberatory vein. To this end, she invokes Derrida's idea of the citational nature of speech and argues that because speech indeed can be cited, and hence be given a new context and meaning, we can resignify words that once wounded in order to deny them their ability to hurt us. For Butler, classic examples of this operation in action include the gay community's resignifying of the formerly injurious words 'fag' or 'queer,' and the black hip-hop community's resignifying of such slurs as 'nigger.'

Butler follows the Foucauldian idea that the contemporary political situation is 'post-sovereign,' meaning that we cannot look to a single source of uncontested political power, to a single person or body whose command is absolute. The post-sovereign age heralds the beginning of the diffuse and decentralized power that was Foucault's project to interrogate. Since power is no longer embodied in individuals in the way that it was in the time of sovereign power, Butler maintains, speech acts are no longer capable of wielding the force that they were once able to claim. Once we untether the speech act from the sovereign subject, which Butler's account of the nature of speech effects, we can begin to theorize about the possibility of counter-speech that holds the potential for liberation from cultural oppression.

Butler, then, wants to question the view that hate speech or pornography enacts subordination or silencing with power that would be sovereign in its efficacy. She doubts that hate speech or pornography really are as felicitous as they appear on the implicitly sovereign account of speech acts that the authors of the silencing and subordination arguments posit. On Matsuda's account, according to Butler (1977: 18), hate speech is the linguistic re-articulation of social subordination and thus reproduces the status quo of power relations. As opposed to this retrograde sovereign account of the efficacy of the speech act, Butler wants to argue that, just as gender norms are dependent upon their daily re-enactment in order to be continued (as Butler maintained in *Gender Trouble*), so too the social structure of power that speech acts effect and reinforce is dependent upon such speech acts' regular enunciation for that social order's continuation.[1]

It is here that Butler believes she has pinpointed a fissure in the chain of efficacy – or sovereignty, to use her term – where such reification can be undermined. She contends that if this system of power, along with the oppression that it produces and to which proponents of the silencing and subordination arguments object, needs constant re-enactment in order to be effective, then

> [i]t is at the site of enunciation that the question of its continuity is to be posed.... As an invocation, hate speech is an act that recalls prior acts, requiring future repetitions to endure. Is there a repetition that might disjoin the speech-act from its supporting conventions such that its repetition confounds rather than consolidates its injurious effects? (Butler 1997: 19–20)

Butler wants to answer 'yes' to this rhetorical question. She believes that this affirmative answer is implicitly supported by Austin because on his account, the speech act proceeds at least in part by way of convention or ritual. Because of the malleability of convention – and because of our contemporary post-sovereign condition – the speaker gains an opportunity to break with the convention, cite the previously injurious speech, and resignify its meaning.

One of the acts in which power clearly functions is that of naming, as Althusser famously noted (Althusser 1971), and the name is understood as 'having a historicity, a way that it carries with it internally, all of the history and contexts of the past use of the name. Racism works through this operation.' (Butler 1997: 36). This is exactly what the proponents of the silencing and subordination arguments point out. However, for Butler, it is only half the truth, and it is the other half that primarily interests her. She claims that this repetition of injurious historical phrases is how trauma, history, and memory are repeated, but also our way to break with this chain of historicity.

Butler maintains that because speech is to an important degree out of the subject's control, the subject's sovereignty and agency are eroded to a significant degree. Thus, individuals speak with something less than sovereign force, which if true entails that they have less than full agency with respect to their speech acts (Butler 1997: 39). This harks back to the notion that it misses the mark to imagine the responsibility for hate speech and pornography as lying in the hands of the individual speakers. When we examine hate speech and pornography, we ought always to consider the extent to which we can legitimately focus our attention on the offenders rather than on the state, whose speech is in fact sovereign and whose performatives are always felicitous. Butler grants the felicity of the state's speech, but she doubts that we can look to the state to remedy the injustice that hate speech and pornography may produce. Whether the state may be an appropriate place to look for reforms in the name of equality is the topic of Chapters 7 and 8.

Instead of looking to the state, Butler insists on a local, individual, and performative remedy for the injustice produced by oppressive speech, through exploiting the lack of sovereignty involved in the speech acts of private speakers:

> These terms we never really choose are the occasion for something we might still call agency, the repetition of an originary subordination for another purpose, one whose future is partially open.... Understanding performativity as a renewable action without clear origin or end suggests that speech is finally constrained neither by its specific speaker nor its originating context. Not only defined by social context, such speech is also marked by its capacity to break with context. Thus, performativity has its own social temporality in which it remains enabled precisely by the contexts from which it breaks. (Butler 1997: 38–40)

Butler urges that we, as individuals, find the liberatory potential to resignify injurious speech through the post-sovereign absences that characterize contemporary communication, as remarked upon by Foucault and Derrida.

However, I maintain that Butler wants it both ways – she wants to say both that presumably authoritative speakers are not in fact authoritative, and that presumably disempowered speakers are in fact empowered. But this does not seem intuitively true, especially when we examine the lived experience of the attempted speech acts of historically disempowered groups. Surely if speech is out of control, then this must be true for both the oppressed and the oppressors. Surely if speech has liberatory potential in its re-signifiability, then that power exists for oppressors to resignify injuriously as well. If this is the case – and I cannot see how it could be otherwise – Butler's account fails to guarantee that Dworkin's criterion of egalitarianism – that the state treat all of its citizens with equal concern and respect – will be met. Of course, Butler is not writing within the liberal tradition, so this criticism does not pose a direct problem to her. Nonetheless, the limitations of Butler's account pose a very serious problem for anyone who wishes to have a politics of genuine equality, in any tradition – liberal or otherwise. While Butler is correct to note that there are indeed 'fissures' in language, these fissures are by no means guarantees of efficacious speech acts, and it is hard to see why we should settle for anything less.

Though Butler is correct to point out that a speech act can go both ways – either as oppressive or as resignificatory – such an admission must be taken to its ultimate, and ambiguous, conclusion: speech is out of control in ways that may be either injurious or liberatory. But such a conclusion is not very reassuring for a society committed to treating its citizens with equal concern and respect and committed to elimination of cultural oppression. I insist that we need to go to where speech can be reliably efficacious and sovereign – to the state – if we are really committed to using the power of speech to restore the enactment of these principles in contemporary egalitarian liberal society.

While I think that Butler is ultimately overstating the strength of her conclusions, nevertheless the insight that speech acts have liberatory as well as oppressive potential is a useful one. Its implications for the silencing and subordination arguments should be quite straightforward. To the extent that these arguments rely on thinking of the actors themselves as those who hold the power to wound, *qua* powerful majority, Butler would say that they are mistaken.

Not only are the silencing and subordination arguments guilty of a misguided view of individual agency, so too, and more importantly, is all of liberal theory. Butler writes:

> One ought to be in a position to utter words in such a way that the meaning of those words coincides with the intention with which they are uttered, and that the performative dimension of that uttering works to support and further that intended meaning…. Presupposed by this conception of the utterance is a normative view of a person with the ability and power to exercise speech in a straightforward

way. This is conceived by Langton as essential to the operation and agency of a rights-bearing person. (Butler 1997: 84)

Here Butler raises quite a serious challenge to some of the most basic tenets of liberalism – in that she is claiming that the autonomy and agency that liberalism posits is dubious – if speech is not as sovereign as thinkers like the proponents of the silencing and subordination arguments maintain. She claims that their accounts of pornography '...exploit a certain notion of liberal sovereignty to further [their] own aims, insisting that consent always and only constitutes the subject' (1997: 85). A serious question that I will address in Chapters 7 and 8 is whether or not Butler's concerns can be met by liberalism, or whether they are hostile to its very foundation. I will argue that these concerns can, and must, be met by an activist egalitarian liberal state.

In *Excitable Speech*, Butler makes a great deal of the idea that speech's being out of control should be considered liberatory, in that it contains resignificatory possibilities for the speaker. Because we are living in a post-sovereign age, according to Butler, speech is not the stable and authoritative force it once was, but rather it is marked by its ability to be reconfigured in ways that are new and heretofore unspeakable. While I agree with Butler about this new-found potential for dynamic and resignificatory speech, she fails to discuss the all-important question of which speakers – and at what times, and under what circumstances – can perform a resignificatory, or for that matter even an illocutionary, speech act. It is this question that I will now address, and the discussion in the preceding two chapters and this one has made clear that our answer will be found through reference to the power relations present when a speaker speaks. While this power is indeed not nearly as strong as sovereign in the individual case, and while power is more fluid and diffuse than it has been in the past, it is still due to power's functioning that one is either able or unable to effect the speech acts that one wishes to effect. If this is the case, and speech acts still are a function of power, then we should think of resignificatory speech acts neither as available to all nor as necessarily truly revolutionary, in that they may reify, rather than question, the very power structure that has oppressed us. If resignificatory or illocutionary speech acts are a function of power, as the preceding two chapters and this one have demonstrated they are, then the best characterization of the resignificatory or illocutionary act is that through such, a person or group has been granted more power than she or it had held previously, rather than that person's or group's speech having called the very framework of power into question.

The real site of power to interrogate with respect to these questions is the state in its speech acts concerning freedom of expression. What Austin, Foucault, and Butler make clear is the idea that speech is never neutral and has everything to do with power. Closely related to this is the notion that the state is not innocent in its own speech. We can, given the ideas of the theorists canvassed in these last three chapters, view the freedom of expression discourse as itself an operation of power – and perhaps the most powerful of all performative speech – in that it is the discourse which sets the limits for all future discourse. The theories I've investigated in the two preceding chapters and this one change the classical liberal story of freedom of expression by making explicit the fact of power and its pervasive operation, where liberal accounts occlude them. The real force of this insight is evident in what follows here, where I will conclude, in opposition to the classical liberal account, that 'subjects' aren't acted upon through 'censorship' in quite the way that liberals imagine, and that this has important consequences for thinking about the freedom of expression debate.

Thus far, I've attempted to lay the groundwork for theorizing quite differently about the role of the liberal state in hard cases of freedom of expression. What I have been arguing is the result of Austin's, Foucault's, and Butler's accounts is that it is not individual actors (for example, pornographers or hate speakers) who should be at the focus of the freedom of expression debate, but rather the state itself. The state is of central importance when it issues an authoritative speech act, as through such it grants or denies rights in general, and more specifically it delimits the right to freedom of expression. It is the latter state role that has the largest impact on the scope of subsequent discourse.

Such a shift in focus leads us away from the whole problem of whether the state ought to censor private actors involved in free speech. We ask instead whether the state itself, now conscious of its role in the web of power relations, should delimit a particular right differently in order to promote equality. Of course, this still leaves open the possibility that this latter question will still yield results that are interpretable as censorship according to the classical liberal account, the most influential example of which is Mill's *On Liberty*, which I examined at length in Chapter 2. To address these Millian concerns, I will discuss a novel analysis of censorship offered by Judith Butler and Fred Schauer, which holds that censorship operates quite differently than the classical liberal account has thus far imagined.

## 6.4   Censorship reconsidered

The schema I've sketched so far, which implicates state power in the creation and remedying of cultural oppression, certainly seems much more plausible than the bald formulation of pornographers and hate speakers as the wielders of power. In adopting this schema, however, I must address the issues that such an account raises in terms of state power and agency, and the nature of censorship. First, it should be noted that my formulation provides that individuals are not the only, or even the primary, wielders of power, but also, and as importantly, are constrained by state power. As Foucault insisted, power is not only restrictive but also, and more importantly, productive, and this is just what Butler's formulation suggests. The subjects produced by the 'don't ask, don't tell' policy of the United States military re gays in uniform, for example, she suggests, are importantly censored before they ever speak (restricted), but are also given a new identity (produced) as a particular kind of homosexual, namely, one who is forced to deny that sexuality.

One very important implication of this formulation is that censorship does not, and indeed cannot, operate in anything like the way that classical Millian liberal accounts suppose – that is, contrary to Mill's account, subjects are not potentially censored by the state after speaking or after forming an intention to speak. They are 'censored,' if the term even makes any sense, well before they start to speak, and they are censored by repressive discourse itself, much of which is state driven. On the classical liberal conception of censorship, 'censorship is an act of external interference with the internally generated communicative, expressive, artistic, or informational preferences of some agent' (Schauer 1998: 150). This view takes for granted the traditional liberal account of subjectivity, where a subject is uncontroversially endowed, or deemed to be endowed, with the privacy and autonomy to formulate her own preferences, thoughts, and feelings. This picture takes the distinction between the internal – the realm of the agent – and the external – the realm of the other, usually the state – for granted. On the other hand, a Foucauldian account, including Butler's, would problematize this distinction: if subjects are a production of power that is to some degree external to them, it would follow that there is no sharp distinction between the private, autonomous subject and the external world, composed of forces that act upon such subjects.

According to the 'new' censorship to which Butler and Schauer subscribe, however, it is a serious mistake to think of interior expressive or communicative forces of subjects as prior to or immune from external influence. Instead, external forces of censorship come into play at the level of preference formation, not simply at the level of 'preference frustration,' the latter being what Schauer identifies as the moment of censorship on the traditional picture. Since the preferences of subjects are at least in part determined externally – through cultural pressures, through the nature of language itself as a system of constraints on what is speakable, through artistic discourse defining the limits of what is art, as well as through state speech – it becomes reasonable to think of these antecedent limiting events as themselves a part of censorship, and indeed a more crucial part, than the 'subsequent' censorship of the classical Millian liberal view. As Schauer describes it:

> [O]ur communicative existence is dependent on the rules, conventions, and understandings over which we as individual communicators have only the smallest amount of control.... With our communicative capacities so much out of our control, the idea of communicative preferences as overwhelmingly endogenous seems strained, and that makes the idea of identifying censorship with the exogenous seem equally strained. Without an idea of the internal there seems little point in talking about the external, and without the idea of the external, the idea of censorship seems fragile. (Schauer 1998: 159)

Given that this 'new' censorship picture maintains that censorship is occurring both necessarily and prior to the speaker's formulation of the intent to speak, Schauer concludes that the phrase 'censorship' is not useful as a descriptive category of an act, but is useful, rather, as an ascriptive category stating a conclusion about which *kinds* of censorship we find objectionable.

The further details of Schauer's view are not particularly important for my purposes, but what is important is that subscribing to this view – which seems quite intuitively plausible, the more we examine how rule-based systems like language and social convention operate in forming our preferences – entails that the classical liberal view of censorship, as external and after the fact, as well as the classical liberal view of individual agency, as presumptively autonomous, are inadequate descriptions of both the operation of subjects and the operation of censorship. This inadequacy provides a crucial step in arguing for state regulation of certain forms of speech in the name of equal concern and respect, since one can no longer convincingly argue that such regulation is anathema to the liberal state, as it appears, on Schauer's analysis, to occur necessarily and at the behest of the state, among other sources.

Butler accepts Schauer's distinction between external and internal censorship, though she terms the former 'explicit' and the latter 'implicit.' Butler is much more interested in the implicit form, as the explicit form sees power as merely repressive, rather than productive, and sees the subject as having complete control over her speech, at least up until the moment of explicit censorship, both of which are unacceptable on a Foucauldian or Derridean framework. Regarding implicit censorship, which she later calls 'foreclosure' in order to call attention to the fact that it is unclear whether we should be using the word 'censorship' for this kind of operation at all, Butler says that it

> ...refers to implicit operations of power that rule out in unspoken ways what will remain unspeakable. In such cases, no explicit regulation is needed in which to articulate this constraint, and the operation of implicit censorship suggests that there are powerful operations of censorship that are not based in explicit state policy or regulation. (Butler 1998: 249)

So far, this formulation is akin to Schauer's in that it affirms the idea that we ought to examine the work done by the censorship that takes place well before the subject actually speaks. However, Butler does not take this insight in the direction that Schauer does – towards reconfiguring the concept of censorship altogether and engaging in an inquiry about why some forms of censorship are more egregious than others.

Instead, Butler uses this insight to form the basis of her notion of resignificatory, liberatory, counter-speech. Since foreclosure must paradoxically speak the unspeakable utterance in order for that utterance's unspeakability to be effected – a law must name the speech it wants to prohibit – and since the power that forecloses speech is post-sovereign, and hence incomplete, there is room carved out for resignificatory counter-speech, since both of these facts leave fissures in both the speakability and the power of the forbidden utterance.

Another important implication of this thinking about speech acts that foreclose or restrict subsequent speech is that it forces us to see the freedom of expression literature – both the jurisprudence and the academic discourse – as having, of necessity, a triple meaning. First, we have the meaning of the words taken at face value, including the force they convey due to the circumstances of their utterance. Second, words can be understood as part of the apparatus of truth/power, over and above their literal meaning. For example, if there were a court decision that favored giving hate speakers the right to burn a cross on a black family's lawn, to cite the earlier example of *R. A. V. v. City of St. Paul*, we would on the one hand say that this decision does just that, but on another level we would implicate this decision as part of state-sponsored speech that gives more power to hate speakers – who, *qua* white, are members of the dominant group – than it does to minorities. Moreover, the decision projects state power behind the idea that speech recalling the racist violence of an earlier era is by no means unspeakable, thereby offering encouragement for more similar utterances in the future.

Third, Butler's notion of implicit censorship or foreclosure has the consequence that the speech in *R. A. V.*, for example, names the speech act of cross- burning as permissible and thereby defines the scope of future speech acts both by individuals and by the state. The decision in *R. A. V.*, for example, defines the scope of the state's future speech acts insofar as the decision, *qua* precedent, operates as restrictive speech for future judicial state speech acts. It also defines the scope of individuals' future speech acts in that legal decisions operate to delimit the range of state-sanctioned and state-prohibited actions, and thus to delimit the range of acceptable and unacceptable individual behavior. The classical liberal accounts only acknowledge the first of these three levels. I am arguing that the liberal state would be well served to acknowledge the other two, as doing so would allow the state to reflect on its own speech, with all its implications, and come to be able to ask the question of whether any particular state speech act furthers or hinders the liberal state's goal of treating all its citizens with equal concern and respect.

Acknowledging these three levels of the operation of speech means that a large number of texts that were heretofore unchallengeable – due to their utterance by parties who were considered to be beyond scrutiny, and due to the fact that we were habituated, prior to speech act theory and Foucauldian power analysis, to look only at one level of the meaning of utterances – have suddenly become problematized. In my view, scrutinizing discourse through the lens of all three levels of speech would be a welcome change – and one that we can make within the confines of the liberal state.

A further implication of this triple meaning of texts is that not only must we interrogate texts from the 'top' of power – such as texts by the state and by academics – but further, this understanding of text as power will enable us to focus on a heretofore hidden set of discourses, those which Foucault terms 'counter-discourse,' the texts of the relatively powerless. If we are interested in a post-sovereign understanding of power, one seeking to expose the discourse of the powerful as powerful, and one seeking to reveal the hidden discourses of the less powerful, then we must look to both state and counter-discourses to do this. In the case of the discourse of the powerful, the method is to deconstruct the hidden power beneath the text; in the case of the discourse of the powerless, the task is first to find the texts, and then to show how they speak of a reality that was denied by the discourse of the powerful. For our purposes, then, we can see the silencing and subordination discourses as instances of the discourse of the powerless, and their recounting of the lived experiences of sexism and racism as something that the discourse of the powerful elides.

Yet another implication of this way of viewing the state as a key producer of the dominant discourse is that though the state is never to be seen as neutral, due to its relationship to the workings of power, we can nevertheless distinguish between instances when the state's enactments are in excess of its legitimate power and when they are not. When we look at the jurisprudence surrounding hate speech and pornography in Chapter 8, this will become one key indicator as to whether the state's judicial pronouncements reflect the exercise of state power to the detriment of the state's commitment to equal concern and respect for its citizens – or to the furtherance of it.

## 6.5   Conclusion

In other words, I am interested in what might be termed 'post-sovereign liberalism.' The idea here is that, given the state's implication in power relations, there is still, nonetheless, room for a self-conscious state to take on the process of self-correction. The process would include consideration of when the state has spoken and wielded its power in ways that cause silencing and subordination and when it has not, as well as conscious attempts by the state to monitor and achieve its commitment to equal concern and respect for its citizens. There is every reason to imagine that this process is possible in principle, and there is even evidence that some liberal states, such as Canada, may be on their way to enacting it, as I will examine in Chapter 8.

What I want to know is simply when power is operating in the service of equality and when it is not. Given this, my focus on the state becomes quite reasonable, especially in light of the degree to which a focus on the individual appears to be untenable. The discussion of state power offered thus far, as well as the critique of traditional notions of censorship, have served to call into question the legitimacy of the liberal state in refusing an activist role.

Before concluding, it is crucial to note that while I believe that the 'new censorship' articulated by Schauer and Butler is correctly observed – and gives the lie to the naïve liberal idea of censorship as existing strictly after ideas have been formed and speech expressing those ideas has been uttered – it is nevertheless still evident that censorship in the liberal sense clearly exists and that the liberal state is still justified in being concerned about it. In other words, there is no contradiction between implicit and explicit censorship – both can and do operate alongside each other. This point has been elided by Butler and Schauer, but it is important for my purposes, since my project is not at all to dismantle liberalism's core commitments but rather to show that the insights of continental theories of power and language can help to resolve puzzles in the issue of freedom of expression.

That said, Mill's concerns in *On Liberty* remain valid, even in light of the new censorship, but they become only half of the story. The other half of the story entails that if implicit censorship exists – and it appears, given the workings of language and power that I have articulated over the last three chapters, that it does – then liberals have more to worry about in terms of their response to censorship – state neutrality in the marketplace of ideas – and less to worry about in terms of their responsibility for censorship itself. What I mean by the state having less to worry about in terms of its own responsibility for censorship is not that the state does not cause censorship, but rather that it *unavoidably* causes censorship in the implicit sense. This implicit causation is evident particularly in the state's freedom of expression decisions: the role of these decisions is to delimit the scope of future discourse, and this act of delimitation has now been revealed as censorship in the form of foreclosure. If this is correct, the question becomes: What follows in terms of the state's responses or remedies for this?

I want to suggest that if the state is always already implicated in implicit censorship, then its preoccupation with explicit censorship, and in particular with its remedy for explicit censorship – neutrality – should abate. While explicit censorship remains a live problem that the liberal state should take pains to avoid, as Mill suggests, I want to argue that if the unavoidable fact of implicit censorship is occurring all the time and alongside the mere potentiality for explicit censorship, then the state's remedy for explicit censorship – neutrality – makes no sense in light of this interplay between implicit and explicit censorship. This is because the fact of implicit censorship entails that the state is never neutral, even in principle. The state must always speak – and in particular, speak with respect to freedom of expression cases. In the very act of speaking, the state loses its neutrality and becomes implicated in the workings of power and implicit censorship.

If this is the case, then the state is never neutral, and so the effort to maintain neutrality in order to remedy the possibility of explicit censorship is futile. I believe that this is a crucial point for the liberal state to acknowledge and transcend. Once the liberal state no longer feels bound to the idea of neutrality, which a Foucauldian analysis of power, together with the points made by the new censorship theorists, have demonstrated is impossible anyway, the state can then use its admitted and now fully self-conscious non-neutrality in order to speak in ways that further its commitment to treating its citizens with equal concern and respect.

# 7
# The Liberal State Reconceived: Advocacy and Jurisprudence in the Service of Equality

## 7.1  Introduction

Thus far I have argued that the liberal state ought to depart from its neutral stance in order to uphold its core commitment of treating its citizens with equal concern and respect, and that the liberal state can be relied upon to remedy its own failures to protect this core commitment. I will now discuss how this may be achieved in practice by examining, in this chapter, academic literature on activist states, and in the next chapter, how Canada and the European Union effectively model this activist, non-neutral, liberal state through their hate speech and obscenity jurisprudence.

A central prerequisite to establishing that an activist liberal state is feasible is demonstrating that a shift in understanding of the nature of rights is possible. I have argued that such a shift – from viewing rights as ends in themselves and protective of the individual, to seeing rights as instrumental and protective of the group – is not only possible, but of a piece with the thinking of the founding and leading liberal thinkers I have canvassed in the first three chapters of this work. A return to the spirit of their work will help solve the problem I have identified in Chapters 2 and 3: that the United States' constitutional protection of hate speech and pornography violates the core commitment of egalitarian liberalism because such protection entails that all citizens are not, in fact, being treated with equal concern and respect by the state. Further discussion of that problem in Chapters 4 and 5 suggested that its resolution may lie in an interrogation of the nature of speech itself; such an investigation reveals a relationship between speech and the social power of the speaker that is overlooked in mainstream liberal discourse. The idea of speech as always implicated in power relations entails that it is state speech at the level of *adjudicating* hate speech and pornography cases, rather than hate speech and pornography themselves, that ought to be of paramount concern when we consider the state's commitment to treatment of all of its citizens with equal concern and respect. I believe that this insight is not at all a threat to liberalism but rather an opportunity for the egalitarian liberal state finally to depart from neutrality and use its power to work for equality.

My idea of an activist liberal state requires both that the state come to understand itself as implicated in the injustice caused by unregulated speech, and further, that it respond to this insight by taking an active role in righting the wrongs that it has set in motion. One significant objection to my project will come from those – including, notably, Foucault and Butler – who feel that the state, however implicated it is in injustice (and they of course would say 'very'), is not necessarily to be trusted to take part in its own self-correction. Thus, a major task of this chapter and the next is to demonstrate that the state is able to undertake the process of its own self-examination and reworking. I will argue that this is possible, first by recalling how claims about the nature of rights that I have canvassed so far are consistent with the idea that the state can and must correct its own illiberalities, and second by showing, in the next chapter, through the US, European, and Canadian jurisprudence, that Canada and Europe are already in the business of engaging in such a project. While the US jurisprudence can be seen to mark a strong departure from the Canadian and European jurisdictions, there is nevertheless a strand of academic liberal thought – found in recent works by Owen Fiss and Cass Sunstein – that reads the US decisions compatibly with the activist state that I have been advocating. I will briefly discuss their work in this chapter as well.

Another objection to the idea of an activist egalitarian liberal state comes not from a suspicion of the state but from a critique of the nature of the harms of pornography and hate speech. How is the violation of equal concern and respect evidenced? How do we know when it has occurred? In other words, how is even a well-intentioned state to identify and remedy such nebulous harms? To answer this question, I will discuss Andrew Kernohan's notions of cultural oppression and accumulative harms in order to characterize more firmly the nature of the harms involved in hate speech and pornography. Here we can also recall Mill's arguments in *The Subjection of Women*, which were considered in Chapter 2. In *Subjection*, Mill argues that the subordination of women to men is so thoroughgoingly normalized by various cultural forces as to ensure that women never become aware of their own preferences, desires, or conceptions of the good life in any authentic way. Rather, women living under such conditions are the victims of a profound cultural conditioning which teaches that autonomy is distasteful and undesirable for them.

Mill's view is of a piece with Kernohan's characterization of the nature of cultural oppression – that views about the unequal moral worth of women and minorities are in such wide and diffuse circulation as to impede women and minorities from being able to formulate a conception of the good life that does not incorporate those oppressive views in a fundamental way. Thus it seems that the Mill of *Subjection* would take the contemporary idea of cultural oppression quite seriously and sympathetically. I will now turn to an examination of Kernohan's work in order to develop a more robust vocabulary about the nature of the harms of racist, sexist, and homophobic speech, as well as how an activist state may appropriately tailor its response to these harms.

## 7.2   Cultural oppression, accumulative harms, and advocacy

Cultural oppression, according to Kernohan, arises when a society permits the unchecked cultural formation of attitudes and beliefs about inequality to such a degree that these beliefs infuse the lives of those who are deemed to be unequal, such that they are no longer able to formulate authentically their own conceptions of their moral worth and their own conception of the good. If this in fact characterizes contemporary American society, there is a crisis in liberalism, since liberalism draws its justification and appeal through facilitating citizens' abilities to formulate their own good. Given that the charge from cultural oppression is so fundamental, much more needs to be said about cultural oppression's workings in order to demonstrate that this is an apt characterization of our contemporary situation.

The first step in examining cultural oppression is to ask how it is produced. The silencing and subordination arguments hold that cultural oppression is produced by the speech acts of pornographers and hate speakers, but these arguments prove problematic in light of speech act theory: in order for a speech act to be efficacious, it must be backed by the appropriate social authority of the speaker. Pornographers and hate speakers are on the very margins of society, and thus would be among the last people to claim such authority. If this is the case, it is difficult to assign responsibility to them for the culturally oppressive effects of their speech.

However, Kernohan more plausibly contends that cultural oppression may act as cumulatively and nebulously as air pollution. It is what he calls an 'accumulative harm' – a harm '...done *by* a group, not *to* a group. It is a harm to another person brought about by the actions of a group of people where the action of no single member of that group can be seen, by itself, to cause the harm.' (Kernohan 1998: 72; emphasis as in the original). He gives an example of pornography as an accumulative harm, as follows:

> Pornography, as a cultural practice, reinforces men's false beliefs about sex and male dominance. It contributes to eroticizing the submission of women, and incidentally to women's beliefs about their own self-worth. Yet the solitary consumption of pornography by one individual man may be totally harmless. It is the accumulative power of the whole system of production, distribution, and consumption which does the harm, a system of which the solitary consumer is but a small part. But if a culture of pornography is to be understood as a harm to both men and women, it will be an accumulative harm, not an individual one. (Kernohan 1998: 84–5)

Therefore, although pornographers, or the average male consumer of pornography, may lack the social authority to enact an efficacious speech act, they certainly could still be viewed as having at least as much role in cultural oppression as the average automobile driver has in air pollution. In other words, saying that pornographers or consumers lack the social authority for efficacious speech acts is not to say that they are not causing harm. Indeed, collectively, the harm is grievous. This harm does not seem to stem, however, from an illocutionary speech act – given that its speakers lack the requisite social power to perform one – nor does it seem to be the kind of harm for which the state might seek to prosecute individual offenders.

This second point is clearer when we return to the air pollution analogy. Though every individual driver of a car is indeed contributing to the air pollution that in its totality is no doubt a great harm to others, and each driver is at least in some sense responsible for that harm, nevertheless, no single driver's contribution is efficacious enough to the overall total that we could be justified in assigning legal blame to each driver for the effects of the whole. Instead, the state ought to regulate the emissions of new cars produced and fine only those individual drivers whose emissions exceed some standard allowable levels. Accordingly, the silencing and subordination arguments' discussion of the harms of pornography and hate speech may be better cast as accumulative harms, so long as we are speaking of the harms caused by individual producers of pornography or hate speech. To prosecute individual speakers would be to miss seeing, crucially, where the responsibility for these actions really lies. The important sense of responsibility, I want to maintain, lies with the state, and a characterization in terms of speech acts remains an appropriate conceptual model for analysis on that level.

It would miss the mark to blame each individual speaker for the overall atmosphere of cultural oppression, for the reason that any individual act is not equal to the cumulative harm, which is harmful only in its cumulative state and not necessarily on an individual level. When we inquire as to how we reached this cumulative state of cultural oppression, however, we find that the answer refers not only to the cumulative actions of every individual utterance of racist, sexist, or homophobic speech from time zero, but also – and more importantly – to the state, whose ineffective regulation of such speech or altogether lack thereof caused the preconditions for what resulted in a culturally oppressive culture. And indeed, the efforts of the international community have been focused on having states sign and abide by anti-pollution treaties for just this reason. Examining cultural oppression as an accumulative harm, then, leads back yet again to investigating the state's role in the proliferation of hate speech and pornography.

Further, to deny that individual private actors ought to be prosecuted for accumulative harms in certain instances is in no way to suggest that accumulative harms ought to go unaddressed by the state. On the contrary, Kernohan suggests that accumulative harms ought to be considered as falling within the scope of Mill's harm principle, such that if they harm an interest worthy of being protected by a right, then the state should depart from its neutral stance to remedy them. However, remedies are not limited to individual prosecutions. They may also encompass what Kernohan calls the 'advocacy strategy' wherein state resources are expended in order to advocate for the equal moral worth of citizens. The advocacy strategy would

> ...act on the beliefs and attitudes of both speaker and audience. It would endeavour to dissuade the former from the attitudes that led to the expressive activity, and to persuade the latter that beliefs in inequality acquired from the cultural environment are false and should be abandoned. (Kernohan 1998: 97)

This would require the state to weigh the level of harm posed by the speech in the particular cultural circumstances of the time. Kernohan maintains that, for example, racist speech in a racist culture would meet the bar both in terms of the harm principle and as an accumulative harm worth taking state action to remedy.

Kernohan argues that the advocacy strategy ought to replace unqualified state neutrality as an underpinning of egalitarian liberalism. He ties the strategy to citizens' highest-order interest in knowing the good:

> The advocacy strategy recognizes that citizens have a highest-order interest in knowing the good, undertakes to protect that interest from deceptive cultural practices, and will use the economic and educational state apparatuses to oppose inegalitarian cultural oppression. Accepting the core liberal principle of the equal worth of persons, it will oppose practices falling into the following category: cultural practices that lead people to believe in the unequal moral worth of persons belonging to different groups, with people relying on these false beliefs about inequality in forming their beliefs about value. (Kernohan 1998: 100–1)

This seems of a piece with the argument of this book, as well as with Mill's arguments in *Subjection*. Importantly, it diverges from the views of MacKinnon and others who focus on the individual user or producer of pornography or hate speech and concentrate their critique of the state solely on its not prosecuting these individuals. The force of Kernohan's advocacy strategy, combined with the critique of state neutrality I have developed here, suggests that the state still needs to play an important role – a role that departs from neutrality – whether or not that role includes legislation that would punish individuals for culturally oppressive views.

The noted legal scholar Owen M. Fiss, in his book *The Irony of Free Speech*, makes points that are very compatible with Kernohan's advocacy strategy. Writing within the liberal tradition, Fiss feels that the dominant reading of the US jurisprudence as upholding state neutrality to guard against state incursions on free speech is wrongheaded. Rather, Fiss argues that the state is by no means necessarily the enemy of free speech, and state neutrality is by no means necessarily the means by which free speech is facilitated.

In a similar vein, Sunstein notes (1995: 251): 'We do not have enough substantive discussion of public issues, and we are not exposed to sufficient diversity of view. Democratic deliberation about remedies should not be foreclosed by the First Amendment. Some forms of apparent government intervention into free speech processes can actually improve those processes. They should not be understood as an objectionable intrusion into an otherwise law-free social sphere. Intervention should not always be seen as an impermissible "abridgment" of the free speech right.'

Instead of such a blanket approach, Fiss argues that we must ask on a case by case basis whether the state's action of limiting or facilitating speech in a particular instance is facilitating or hindering the workings of public debate. Facilitating public debate, going back to Mill, is of course one of the central aims of a liberal state.

Fiss comments here on state neutrality:

> The principle of content neutrality bars the state from trying to control the people's choice among competing viewpoints by favoring or disfavoring one side in a debate. So understood, the principle has powerful appeal and can be profitably applied in many contexts.... On the other hand, content neutrality is not an end in itself and should not be reified. The principle responds to some underlying concern that the state might use its power to skew debate in order to advance particular outcomes, and this purpose should always be kept in mind. Accordingly the principle should not be extended to situations like hate speech, pornography, and political expenditures, in which private parties are skewing debate and the state regulation promotes free and open debate. In those cases, the state may be disfavoring certain speakers – the cross-burner, the pornographer, or the big spender – and make judgments based on content, but arguably only to make certain that all sides are heard. The state is simply acting as a fair-minded parliamentarian, devoted to having all views presented. (Fiss 1996: 21)

While Fiss does not go as far as I have in maintaining that state neutrality is impossible, he argues that neutrality alone is by no means sufficient to guarantee that the state is acting in the service of promoting debate. Rather, in order to advocate for the state's acting in the service of promoting debate, Fiss invokes the ideal of the state as a 'fair-minded parliamentarian, devoted to having all views presented.' This ideal is very much of a piece with what Kernohan and I are calling the activist liberal state in the service of equality. Fiss is very much in favor of an activist court in his explicating this parliamentarian ideal as follows:

> Those in charge of designing institutions should place the power to regulate content – to act as a parliamentarian – in agencies that are

removed from the political fray.... [A] heavy burden of scrutinizing the state's action should fall to the judiciary, especially because it stands apart from the political fray.... The court must ask itself: Will the regulation actually enhance the quality of debate, or will it have the opposite effect? (Fiss 1996: 24)

This test question – will regulation of speech actually enhance the quality of debate? – is exactly the way that he feels judges ought to proceed in adjudicating free speech cases, and during the tenure of the Warren Court, they did. Fiss asserts that under the Warren Court, the key decisions of *New York Times v. Sullivan*[1] – which protected freedom of the press by limiting the ability of public figures to sue for defamation and libel – and *Red Lion Broadcasting Co. v. FCC*[2] – which allowed the FCC to regulate private broadcasting in order to ensure that these companies carry on a discussion of public issues, and that such discussion present each side of those issues – were correctly decided according to this principle, even though superficially the decisions appear to stand in opposition to one another.

While a surface, and dominant, reading of the two decisions would see *Sullivan* as the state being, correctly, hands-off – in disallowing causes of action which would inhibit free speech – and see *Red Lion* as the state being, incorrectly, hands-on and attempting to regulate the free speech decisions of television broadcasters, Fiss instead sees the decisions as both compatibly and correctly decided with reference to the test question of whether or not regulation would enhance debate. In the case of *Sullivan*, the decision was made that would best enhance debate – by disallowing most libel and defamation suits, the decision ensured that the press would be able to achieve fuller reporting without fear of legal action. In the case of *Red Lion*, while the active, hands-on regulation of broadcasters by the FCC would constitute a limitation of the free speech of the broadcasters, it would nonetheless facilitate a more robust public debate because the decision ensured that all sides of the debate be presented.

In conclusion, Fiss writes (1996: 26), quite radically for a writer in the liberal tradition: 'We should never forget the potential of the state for oppression, never, but at the same time, we must contemplate the possibility that the state will use its considerable powers to promote goals that lie at the core of a democratic society – equality and perhaps free speech itself.' It is exactly this possibility that this book hopes to render plausible. Fiss's reading of the Warren Court jurisprudence and of the ideals of a liberal state, while far from mainstream and far from having been adopted in more recent US court decisions, nevertheless offers hope for the possibility of a functioning activist liberal state in the service of equality.

Political thinkers outside of liberalism, however, including Foucault and Butler, tend to be even more deeply suspicious than most liberal thinkers about the state's ability to act as anything but an agent of unexamined power. I want to argue that while we cannot, and ought not, return to the traditional liberal view of the state as innocent in power relations and neutral about the content of speech, there is reason – as Fiss has shown and the Canadian and European jurisprudence on hate speech and pornography will show – not to go as far as Butler and Foucault have gone in denying the possibility of the state's protection of equality. On my view of the activist state, the state is able to take its own complicity into account in the operation of power, both productive and repressive, and to respond to its shortcomings through more egalitarian, and truly public debate-enhancing, jurisprudence going forward.

Further, Foucault and Butler not only doubt that the state is well-intentioned enough to correct its own wrongs, but they also doubt that the state is powerful enough to do so. For both thinkers, the modern state is by no means a sovereign power in the traditional sense. Even if I grant this point, however, we are dealing not with the question of whether the state has absolute power, but rather only with the question of whether it has enough power to produce efficacious speech acts when enacting laws. It seems uncontroversial that the state does. Thus, I can accept at face value Foucault and Butler's point that we are living in a post-sovereign age, with its limited application to the state in this context, and focus instead on Foucault's discussion of the relationship between power and discourse. It is the production of knowledge/discourse that establishes, produces, and reifies power. In this regard, the state is certainly a noteworthy discourse producer, especially in its enactments of laws and the jurisprudence of its courts, each considered as discourses.

To put the role of the state in Foucauldian terms, these two powerful sites of law and jurisprudence play a large role in the enactment of the moral norms of our culture. Certainly, as Foucault well knew, the enforcement of these norms is carried out at other sites to a greater or lesser degree removed from the state – such as schools or prisons. Additionally, the state in its judicial role can be seen as having a crucial part in discourse production, with all of the attendant implications for power that this entails.

The efficacy of state speech offers an even stronger reason to support Kernohan's advocacy strategy. Kernohan maintains:

> In an inegalitarian and oppressive culture, the egalitarian liberal state should take an active role opposing inegalitarian beliefs in public forums. Such opposition should involve vigorous educational efforts and active financial support for associations and groups striving to combat inegalitarian cultural practices.... Instead of coercing people, the advocacy state would persuade them. Final evaluation of ideas would be left to the public, in forums of deliberation outside the state. The state should not be impartial in these forums, but instead should be the major participant on the side of equality. (Kernohan 1998: 102–3)

The advocacy strategy, then, would necessarily involve the state first taking an active and conscious role in correcting the failures of the marketplace that arise in culturally oppressive cultures, and then putting resources behind its speech in advocating equality. Such speech, it is important to note, is not sovereign – it is not the binding, and necessarily efficacious, illocutionary speech that we see in the state's judicial decisions. Nevertheless, advocacy speech is an important adjunct to that illocutionary speech.

Kernohan's advocacy strategy initially sounds radical, but it increases in force and persuasiveness when we recall that the state is already a powerful speech actor, whose voice in a debate necessarily carries authoritative, and, depending on the context, illocutionary, weight. Advocacy speech, by virtue of its albeit post-sovereign state authority, would still stand a great chance of being persuasive to the private citizen whose collective acts, sanctioned by the state, result in accumulative harms.

It is here that the notion of accumulative harms, along with its remedy of the advocacy strategy, dovetails quite nicely with the analysis of speech act theory and Foucauldian power developed in Chapters 4 and 5. It is only with an understanding of the nature of state speech, even outside of its lawmaking function, that we can begin to see how the advocacy strategy may prove to be effective. The state's speech and resources directed towards egalitarian ends have much greater weight than does the speech of private speakers, or even of non-governmental groups. Using the advocacy strategy in particular, then, to chip away at the accumulative harm of a culturally oppressive environment may greatly expedite the task of becoming a more truly egalitarian society.

One reason that liberals have traditionally feared state activism is its potential, they feel, for arbitrary enforcement: the state would simply choose to regulate, or to impose its advocacy strategy on, just those ideas of which it disapproved. I would like to suggest that such a problem at the operational level should not be confused with the theoretical issues that exist prior to any operational considerations. If it turns out that, in practice, the state is acting in an unprincipled way, there is no reason to believe *a priori* that it cannot correct its own failures.

Kernohan argues that the advocacy strategy delineates fairly strict criteria for when the state's activism should be triggered – when expressive activities contribute to an inegalitarian cultural environment. Since there is a certain amount of ambiguity in this formulation, the state should first deploy its resources towards challenging its audience's attitudes and only secondly target the expressive acts themselves (Kernohan 1998: 107). Prioritizing in that way ought to minimize the concerns of those who fear the slippery slope effects made possible by placing this matter in the state's hands.

The advocacy strategy also has the crucial benefit of sidestepping many of the traditional liberal concerns with censorship, though it too, along with activist judicial speech, requires a move away from state neutrality in cases of cultural oppression. The only difference is that the move required is not directly towards regulation of speech, but rather primarily towards the expenditure of state resources on counter-speech. I want to maintain that this move away from neutrality is much more important than the more specific and operational question of what actions the state makes after it commits to its departure from neutrality. The departure from neutrality is the moment when the state truly commits to equality, and it is this commitment and this move away from neutrality that I have argued is requisite for a truly egalitarian liberal state. Again, the advocacy strategy may go hand-in-hand with explicit, legally binding regulation of speech if necessary; it is my view that such a two-pronged approach is desirable. What matters, ultimately, is that as long as there is a serious commitment to advocacy, the neutrality criterion has been compromised, which leads us to rethink the character of liberalism.

The advocacy strategy overcomes a number of problems raised by liberals who are wary of censorship as a remedy, and thus challenges these liberals to clarify whether their problem lies at the level of remedy (and thus opposed to censorship) or more deeply at the level of neutrality (and thus opposed to advocacy). For example, one issue that arises, especially in the US context, is the idea that hate speech (as opposed to pornography) is political speech and thus much more closely tied to the fundamental values of freedom of expression that we as a culture want to protect. Insofar as this Millian argument is compelling, it is compelling only as an argument against the remedy of censorship and not at the level of departure from neutrality. Indeed, the advocacy strategy operates on the very same Millian principles as the hate-speech-as-political-speech argument does, but from the counter-speech end. On the advocacy view, it is the state that will become active in the counter-speech, and such counter-speech is seen as a Millian remedy to inegalitarian speech.

Similarly, the advocacy view meets another objection that is really only an objection at the level of remedy, rather than an objection brought in favor of state neutrality. This objection notes that culturally oppressive speech occurs in far-ranging venues – from fashion magazines (especially with regards to subordinating views of women) to academic journals (especially with regards to racist and homophobic speech) – and to censor these venues would be absurd. This objection is sound, as far as it goes, but the question remains: would the same objector be averse to state-funded counter-speech aimed at readers of these publications? If state funding of counter-speech is unobjectionable, then all parties agree on a state departure from neutrality in order to promote speech affirming the equal moral worth of subjects, and this departure is far more crucial than a debate about censorship versus advocacy strategies to achieve those aims.

It has been the aim of this book to demonstrate that the liberal state's departure from neutrality is key to operationalizing the commitment to equality that the liberal state claims to have. I have introduced speech act analysis in order to show that the state, and not individual speakers, has the power to effect speech that will decisively advocate in favor of equality. The idea of cultural oppression has been introduced to demonstrate that notions of harm and evidence of harm need to be problematized. Taking these two frameworks of cultural oppression and speech act theory together, then, finally creates the space to investigate what the state can do – namely, utter efficacious illocutionary speech acts – in order to remedy cultural oppression. Kernohan's activism strategy appears to be a good first line of action in this regard, and ought to assuage many of the fears that plague traditional liberals about unprincipled state activism.

However, I depart from Kernohan insofar as I wish to consider state speech in the form of laws that may prosecute individuals for contributing to cultural oppression, as well as state speech invoked in the name of non-binding advocacy towards the elimination of cultural oppression. My focus lies not on prosecuting particular individuals for their parts in cultural oppression, but rather on aiming to change the individuals' opinions in a less direct and less coercive way. There seems on the surface to be a tension within my two-pronged approach, in that the judicial arm aims to prosecute individuals, while the advocacy arm is concerned with using speech to reach a wider group without the use of the legal system as such. More strongly, the tension may be highlighted by the fact that the advocacy strategy, at least implicitly, rejects the prosecution of individuals for a situation to which each individual contributed only slightly.

How can I advocate both strategies simultaneously? These two routes can indeed be compatible, in much the same way that many crimes are also, or even primarily, social problems, requiring a two-tiered structure of remedies – criminalization as well as advocacy. This can be seen clearly, for example, in the state's handling of illegal drugs, which may involve both public education campaigns and prosecutions in some cases. This is indeed the approach of the Canadian Court, which remarked in *Butler*:

> It should be emphasized that this [criminalization of pornography] is in no way intended to deny the value of other educational and counseling measures to deal with the roots and the effects of negative attitudes. Rather, it is only to stress the arbitrariness and unacceptability of the claim that such measures represent the sole legitimate means of addressing the phenomenon. Serious social problems such as violence against women require multi-pronged approaches by government. Education and legislation are not alternatives but complements in addressing such problems. [*Butler* (1992), 509]

It is possible, as with illegal drugs, that prosecutions are wrongheaded in that they have unacceptably high levels of recidivism, as well as yielding unmanageably high levels of incarcerations. It is nevertheless the case that, as a culture, we frequently employ both criminalization and advocacy simultaneously. If empirical data shows that either strategy is not working, then we can readjust the plan, but at the outset, a two-tiered approach seems best suited to capture the dual character of hate speech and pornography.

Further, the deterrent function of criminalization needs to be more fully considered in determining whether criminalization is justified. It is certainly true, as proponents of the advocacy strategy maintain, that an individual is not solely responsible for a culturally oppressive environment. However, punishment might be justifiable if the deterrent function to others of having laws restricting culturally oppressive speech is such that these laws provide more overall utility for fighting cultural oppression than would advocacy strategies alone. Further, the state in its judicial function is operating at the pinnacle of its sovereign power, as each speech act in this forum has the force of law. Thus, to employ merely the advocacy strategy – which only invokes non-binding, non-judicial speech – is to fail to use the most powerful weapon in our arsenal: state advocacy of egalitarianism, which has the force of law. That said, I will now consider whether and how judicial speech might function effectively as an instrument of state power used to further the core egalitarian liberal goal of treating citizens with equal concern and respect.

In the next chapter I will turn to a brief examination of the leading US, European, and Canadian hate speech and pornography cases to see how a legal system might succeed or fail to use its judicial speech in the service of equality. Prior to case discussion, Section 7.3 will provide a brief overview of the Canadian constitutional adjudication framework, as familiarity with this will be necessary in order to understand first, the reasoning in the Canadian cases, and secondly, how they depart from the framework established in the US. I will argue that the Canadian framework allows the liberal state to interrogate its own speech and ensure that it is in fact acting in the service of equality. Chapter 8 will provide a brief overview of the hate speech and pornography decisions in all three of these jurisdictions, and conclude that the European and Canadian courts provide real-life models of effective activist, post-sovereign liberal states.

## 7.3    The Canadian *Charter's* rights-balancing approach

Viewing rights as instrumental, reciprocal, and protective of the common good – which Chapters 1 and 2 suggested as a viable strand of egalitarian liberal thought[3] – comes into play in a very practical sense when we examine the Canadian *Charter* jurisprudential framework (see Appendix A for the text of relevant sections of the *Charter* ). All of the *Charter's* enumerated rights are subject to limitation under section 1 (hereinafter s.1), which provides: '*The Canadian Charter of Rights and Freedoms* guarantees the rights and freedoms set out in it subject only to such reasonable limits prescribed by law as can be demonstrably justified in a free and democratic society.'[4] In other words, if a limitation on a right has been validly enacted as a law and can be demonstrably justified in a free and democratic society, then the right will be so limited and the law limiting it will be upheld as constitutional. There is thus a two-tiered test for an impugned piece of legislation in any *Charter* case: first, has the enumerated right been violated, and, if so, is the violation permissible under s. 1? Impugned legislation can be upheld under either of two ways: the court may hold that the legislation does not in fact violate the enumerated right, or that it did violate the enumerated right but that such violation was justified under s.1.

The very fact that a rights limitations clause exists already distinguishes the Canadian *Charter* from many other rights-granting instruments, including, notably, that of the United States. A limitations clause entails that the state views rights not as absolute or inviolable. Rather, they exist in order to protect instrumentally the important interests of a democratic culture up to the point when protecting those interests is less in the interest of the common good – what the words of the *Charter* call a 'free and democratic society'– than limiting those interests is. In other words, it seems that the s. 1 clause is consistent with the idea that rights are to be seen as instrumental, reciprocal, and in the service of the common good. That this is indeed the case will become clearer as I examine what is known as the 'balancing framework' for adjudication of s. 1.

The balancing framework was developed by the Supreme Court in *R v. Oakes* to determine whether or not a limit on a right is 'demonstrably justified in a free and democratic society.'[5] Known now as 'the *Oakes* test,' this balancing framework sets out a two-part test for adjudication under s.1. The *Oakes* test is as follows:

1. *Legislative objective*: The purpose of the legislation must be sufficiently 'pressing and substantial' to justify limiting the right.
2. *Proportionality*: The means employed by the legislation must be proportional to the objective to be achieved. The proportionality test subdivides in turn into three parts:
   (a) Rational connection: There must be reasonable grounds for expecting the legislation to be effective in achieving its objective.
   (b) Minimal impairment: The legislation must limit the right no more than is necessary in order to achieve its objective.
   (c) Proportional effects: The costs of the limitation must not exceed the benefits to be gained from achieving the objective.[6]

A piece of legislation must first pass step 1 of the *Oakes* test, which is usually understood as a low threshold to pass. In other words, if a government has succeeded thus far in enacting a controversial and potentially unconstitutional law, it likely has what it, and probably the Court, feels is a good reason for doing so. Once the legislation has passed step 1, it moves on to the three proportionality tests, all of which aim to make sure that the law is narrowly tailored to effect its pressing and substantial objective with minimal infringement to the right in question. The law must be rationally connected to the objective, such that it is reasonable to expect that it will have some degree of success in meeting that objective; it must minimally impair the right; and the cost of the limitation of the right must not exceed the benefits to be gained from reaching the objective of the law. A law must pass all three subsections of step 2 of the *Oakes* test in order to be upheld as constitutional.

In *The Hateful and the Obscene*, Wayne Sumner suggests that step 2 of the test, with its three subsections, is best considered as a 'balancing act,' in which the expected benefits of the impugned legislation are weighed against its expected costs. He writes:

> Once the government's objective has been deemed sufficiently weighty, the first two proportionality requirements focus respectively on the benefit and the cost sides of the equation, in order to ensure that the intended benefits can be rationally expected and that the costs (to free expression) have been minimized. But only at the last step are the cost and benefit sides brought together and compared in a calculation meant to determine whether the government's objective is worth pursuing in this particular way, in the face of its predictable costs. The previous steps have the function of feeding necessary information into the final cost-benefit balancing, but they do not conduct that balancing. It is only at the final step that it can be determined whether a limit to free expression is 'demonstrably justified,' all things considered. (Sumner 2004: 66)

While the overall *Oakes* scheme facilitates rights-balancing, the scheme only crystallizes, and the rights only truly get balanced, at the last step. The fine-grained character of this framework insists that each case is considered on its very particular set of circumstances, rather than abstractly.

Sumner cites numerous examples of the Canadian Supreme Court justices themselves characterizing the *Oakes* test in this way. What is being balanced, of course, are rights – for our purposes, the right to freedom of expression versus the right to equality. The Supreme Court stops short of calling the *Oakes* test 'rights-balancing' and instead uses terms such as 'values' or 'interests' to describe what the process balances. At root, however, this seems tantamount to rights-balancing, with a marked emphasis on the particularity of the facts of the case and the nature of the rights at play in it. For instance, Justice McLachlin in *Keegstra*, a leading Canadian hate speech case, held: '[T]he judge must situate the analysis in the facts of the particular case, weighing the different values represented in that context.'[7] Indeed, Justice McLachlin recognizes that having a rights-balancing, or cost-benefit, approach at all necessarily entails context-specificity – costs and benefits of course depend on the specific facts of the matter at issue, and cannot be measured abstractly. This approach can be contrasted with an approach that looks at the issue simply based, for example, on the abstract principles of the right to freedom of expression versus the right to equality, as in US jurisprudence. Instead, the Canadian approach is nuanced enough to weigh the particular kind of expression at issue against the particular harms that the restriction on the expression was designed to protect. This approach is much more in keeping with a view that rights are not absolute since they are explicitly limitable by s. 1. Rather, rights are instrumental and capable of being overridden by the common good – the democratic society itself – that s. 1 is designed to protect.

If this is the case, it follows that the Canadian Supreme Court is subscribing to an instrumentalist view of rights: since the Canadian *Charter* has a limitations cause at all – which necessarily entails that rights are not inviolable – and the limitations clause is about rights-balancing, such a framework would preclude rights being viewed as constitutive. Further, the Court is arguably subscribing to a view of rights as in the common interest, since the idea behind s. 1 clearly indicates that the interests of a 'free and democratic society' may trump the interests of the individual, or in fact be shared by the individual and the larger society. If this is correct, and indeed it seems that the jurisprudence supports this instrumentalist reading, then the *Charter* is an ideal testing ground for the liberal state to act in the interests of equality in a principled way. The structure of s. 1 is consistent with the idea that Dworkin and I have been maintaining: that the interest in equality to a free and democratic society is paramount. The logic of s. 1 is such that it would preserve that key interest in equality over other, lesser, interests. Indeed, this is exactly how then Chief Justice Dickson framed the role of s. 1 in *Oakes*:

> The Court must be guided by the values and principles essential to a free and democratic society which I believe embody, to name a few, respect for the inherent dignity of the human person, commitment

to social justice and equality, accommodation of a wide variety of beliefs, respect for cultural and group identity, and faith in social and political institutions which enhance the participation of individuals and groups in society. The underlying values and principles of a free and democratic society are the genesis of the rights and freedoms guaranteed by the Charter and the ultimate standard against which a limit on a right or freedom must be shown, despite its effect, to be reasonable and demonstrably justified. [*Oakes* (1986), 136]

This formulation not only clearly identifies equality as a key value to a free and democratic society, but it also states unequivocally that the enumerated *Charter* rights are logically posterior to the values underlying those of the free and democratic society that gave them birth. Again, then, the Canadian *Charter* and its jurisprudence hold the potential to realize the notion that I have been trying to advance – state commitment to and advocacy of equality as a central value in its judicial speech.

Even more specifically, Sumner suggests that the *Oakes* test, and in particular the final proportionality requirement, bears resemblance to the kind of test invoked by Mill in articulating the test for the harm principle. The second step of the harm principle requires that curtailing a right due to a harm must produce an outcome with more utility – that is, benefits over costs – than not curtailing the right would have yielded. This is exactly what the proportionality component of the *Oakes* test requires. Again, while such a balancing framework does not commit us, or the Canadian Supreme Court, to an overall utilitarian framework, it certainly seems to commit us to the idea of rights treated instrumentally and in the service of the common good, rather than conceiving of rights as in the service of the individual right-holder. That the *Oakes* test has this Millian element, and that the *Oakes* test has been adopted by a progressive democracy like Canada, provides reason for optimism that egalitarian liberal principles can be enshrined and acted upon in an actual democracy. Whether or not such principles produce more egalitarian results than are found in a jurisdiction such as the United States, which has no such enshrined principles, is the topic of investigation in the next chapter.

The contrasting view – of rights treated abstractly, rather than being subjected to a balancing approach – can be seen more clearly in the jurisprudence of the United States, which takes the approach that rights in general are presumptively absolute. The language of the US Constitution offers no hints of a rights-balancing approach, let alone anything as explicit as that offered by Canada's s. 1. This lack of a rights-balancing preamble to guide judicial interpretation has led to an approach that sees rights as absolute, which thus means that any governmental infringement upon rights is taken to be presumptively unjustified. This is to be contrasted with the two-step approach of the Canadian Court, which holds that identification of an infringement is only the first step in the inquiry to determine whether legislation violates the *Charter*. Here, the second step is the s. 1 analysis of reasonable limitation, which is where the rights-balancing takes place.

Because the US doctrine of absolutist rights interpretation suggested in the preamble to the Bill of Rights is too rigid to be workable in practice, the First Amendment jurisprudence in the US has worked out a hierarchy of values that freedom of expression is supposed to protect; the likelihood of a particular piece of impugned speech's protection depends on where in the hierarchy it has been deemed by the court to fall. Political speech – taken to be at the pinnacle of democratic values – traditionally receives the highest level of protection. Obscenity and defamation, on the other hand, traditionally receive no protection, as they are seen to fall quite far from the values that freedom of expression is held to protect. This hierarchical approach, however, should not be mistaken for a rights-balancing approach. There is nothing about the practice of identifying where speech fits into a hierarchy of values that suggests that that speech is to be weighed against *other* rights.

In the next chapter, I will offer but a brief sketch of the kinds of questions that rights-balancing and speech acts frameworks, taken together and in the service of equality, raise, and perhaps resolve, when looking at the leading hate speech and obscenity decisions in the United States and Canada. Here I will argue that the jurisprudence in the US, Europe, and Canada reveal that a rights-balancing approach, combined with a state commitment to equal concern and respect that acknowledges the role of its own power in its judicial speech acts, produces more egalitarian results than approaches that seem to lack either or both of these components.

# 8

# The Courts and the Constitution: Hate Speech and Pornography in the United States, Canada, and Europe

## 8.1 The hate speech jurisprudence

### 8.1.1 The US decisions

In the landmark 1969 case of *Brandenburg v. Ohio*,[1] the United States Supreme Court upheld the right of the Ku Klux Klan to advocate at rallies for the return of all Jews to Israel and all African-Americans to Africa, a result appearing to privilege the liberty of the speakers at the expense of the equality of their targets. The Court held that since the advocacy was not intended to incite direct action towards those ends – and thus did not trigger a 'fighting words' exemption from First Amendment protection – it must be protected as political speech, the most protected class of speech in the US First Amendment framework.

If, however, that same content included a direct incitement to riot on behalf of its aims, then the speech, presumably, would not be protected. *Brandenburg* thus stands for the American Court's application of a strict 'time, manner, and circumstance' restriction on political speech, originally advocated by Mill, which holds that content *per se* is not to be restricted. Rather, only the time, manner, and circumstance of the utterance – provided that these latter considerations cause some compelling risk of harm to the public, such as if the words in question are deemed to be 'fighting' – can face curtailment by the state. Such an approach, whatever its merits, certainly does not balance the right to freedom of expression with the imperative to treat all citizens with equal concern and respect. Such a balancing could come either from a consideration of the targets' Fourteenth Amendment rights under the

Equal Protection Clause, or from a consideration of how the speakers' words undermine the speech of the targets, thus vitiating the First Amendment rights of the targets. Neither analysis was undertaken in *Brandenburg*, and thus this leading US decision is at odds with the approach I am advocating ought to be taken by an egalitarian liberal state.

Further, the decision in *Brandenburg* fails to take the historical context of the utterances into consideration: these statements were uttered during the height of the civil rights movement in the US and hence had greater force. Thus, *Brandenburg* must be read as an inegalitarian decision that privileges the liberty of the speakers at the complete expense of even a discussion of the equality owed by the state to all of its citizens.

However, even though hate speech is political speech according to the US Court, it may alternatively be construed as 'fighting words,' or words that can reasonably be taken to be incitements to violence, and in that case be deemed unworthy of constitutional protection. In 1992, in *R. A. V. v. City of St. Paul*,[2] the Court was confronted with such a potential scenario. In this case, a group of teenagers had burned a cross on a black family's lawn. The perpetrators of the act, who were juveniles at the time, were charged under a city hate crimes ordinance, which explicitly prohibited the display of any symbol 'which one knows or has reasonable grounds to know arouses anger, alarm or resentment in others on the basis of race, color, creed, religion or gender.'[3] The ordinance's wording aimed to frame hate speech as falling within the ambit of the unprotected 'fighting words' doctrine, rather than under the protected political speech jurisprudence, which only allowed time, manner, and circumstance restrictions on political speech. However, the Court decided that even though the ordinance indeed applied only to fighting words and was thus not over-broad in its reach, the wording was not viewpoint-neutral in that it prohibited speech targeting certain groups and not others. Because of the ordinance's particular prohibitions, the Court held, the legislation was imposing a content restriction on the speech and must be struck down.

Reading *Brandenburg* and *R. A. V.* together, then, reveals that the US jurisprudence with respect to hate speech is dominated by the view that hate speech, *qua* political speech, is to have no content restrictions whatsoever. Further, when political speech and fighting words exist side by side, the rules governing political speech – that is, not to employ any content restrictions – are read into the fighting words doctrine in order to ensure that the fighting words doctrine cannot be used to protect minorities in particular. Again, this approach does not entertain a rights-balancing framework, nor does it give any meaningful mention to the potentially conflicting compelling state interest in equal concern and respect. Finally, with respect to speech acts and the related topic of state power, neither case gives any indication that the state in its decision was itself acting as an instrument of power – either in the service of equality or in any other way.

Further, the tests employed by the US Court do not take rights to be instrumental for the preservation of a democratic culture, which is contrary to Mill's view, but rather to be constitutive of such a culture, as per Dworkin. For any case involving freedom of expression, the Court asks whether and to what extent the particular kind of speech at issue exemplifies the values central to a well-functioning democracy – political speech being understood as paramount. To the extent that the speech does exemplify prioritized values, it will enjoy constitutional protection. However, for the US Court, freedom of expression is not to be seen as instrumental for the cause of protecting and upholding democratic values; rather, the right to freedom of expression and democracy go hand in hand, rights forming a crucial part of a larger whole that is democracy. Sumner, in *The Hateful and the Obscene*, describes the relationship as follows:

> If we focus again on free speech rights, the larger whole of which they are an indispensable component is usually taken to be democracy itself. On this view, a well-ordered democracy is not a further end to which various rights, including freedom of expression, contribute as means. Rather, it is a political system which consists essentially in those rights: a system lacking them simply does not count as democratic. (Sumner 2004: 73)

However, as Sumner notes, such an approach is incomplete if it fails to account for the fact that rights other than freedom of expression – such as rights to equality – also constitute essential components of democracy. Once this is granted, and I have argued in the preceding chapters that it must be, we need some way of adjudicating between rights. If all rights bear such a close relationship to democracy, and if any two are in conflict in a particular case, how can we limit one in favor of the other without doing violence to the fabric of democracy itself? Here, an appeal to the underlying values that the rights serve, like the Canadian instrumentalist approach contemplates, may facilitate such an adjudication better than the American approach, which elides the problem by merely stipulating which rights are more central than others.

## 8.1.2   The Canadian decisions

We cannot conclude, however, that the American constitutive approach will always produce results that favor the upholding of rights to freedom of expression, while the Canadian instrumentalist approach will always favor the limitation of that right, at least in the context of hate speech. Notably, the two Canadian leading cases on hate speech, *Keegstra* and *Zundel*,[4] were decided in opposite ways and in very close votes. In *Keegstra*, a 4-3 Court decided to uphold *Criminal Code* of Canada hate speech legislation, which criminalized the 'willful promotion of hatred against an identifiable group.'[5] Yet two years later in *Zundel*, a 4-3 Court struck down a different section of the *Criminal Code*, which criminalized the 'spreading of false news.'[6] Sumner notes that these differing results suggest that there is nothing in an instrumentalist approach *per se* that would guarantee that freedom of expression rights in a hate speech context will be curtailed in the light of some other value, such as equality.

While there need not be any single, or even any principled, answer, to the differences between the US and Canadian jurisprudence, the spirit of s. 1 of the Canadian *Charter* makes clear that rights are not inviolable, which is exactly what a constitutive approach must deny. This in turn allows the Canadian Court the freedom to adjudicate between rights in a principled way and without the worry about violating rights that a court governed by a constitutive approach must have. Further, the Canadian Court is characterized by the fundamental idea, granted in s. 1, that what are to be upheld are whatever rights or *whatever lawful limitations of those rights* in a particular instance best facilitate the functioning of a democratic society. The American Court, which must protect political speech regardless of the social context in which it is uttered, seems to lack this flexibility.

*Keegstra* (1990) had facts similar to *R. A. V.* in that both cases dealt with the constitutionality of a statute intended to prohibit hate crimes against minority groups; the courts in the two jurisdictions, however, treated the issue very differently. Neither *Brandenburg* nor *R. A. V.* read the issue as one of rights-balancing between liberty and equality, but rather, both were wholly concerned with whether hate speech ought or ought not to fall within the categories of protected expression, *qua* political speech. *Keegstra*, on the other hand, treated the issue as a rights-balancing issue and arrived at quite a different result than did its American counterparts. In *Keegstra*, the facts involved a high-school teacher in Eckville, Alberta, who espoused anti-Semitic views in his classroom as part of the graded curriculum. When his classroom practices were brought to light, Keegstra was charged with the 'willful promotion of hatred' under the hate propaganda statute then in place. The Court, by a narrow 4-3 margin, ultimately upheld the hate propaganda law. The majority reasoned that though the statute, like any other imposing a content restriction on speech, infringed on the Canadian *Charter*'s section 2(b)'s guarantee of freedom of expression, such an infringement was justified under s. 1 (see Appendix A for the elaboration of the 'Fundamental Freedoms' under the *Charter*).

In applying the s. 1 analysis to the facts in *Keegstra*, both the majority and minority agreed that the first step of the *Oakes* test, the pressing and substantial objective of the legislation, was met by the legislature in its efforts to promote the values of equality and multiculturalism, which are themselves important enough to be enshrined in the *Charter*. However, the majority and minority differed with respect to the first two steps of the proportionality tests. Justice Beverley McLachlin, writing the minority opinion in *Keegstra*, held that the legislation failed both the rational connection and minimal impairment conditions.

In terms of rational connection between the intended outcome of promotion of equality for minorities and the actual effect of the legislation, McLachlin held that such a connection could not be found. Paradoxically, prosecutions under the impugned legislation would have the perverse effect of giving racist speech a more prominent voice than it otherwise would have had, especially given all of the publicity surrounding a high-profile *Charter* case. With respect to minimal impairment, she found that the law was over-broad because of the wide range of speech that could be considered hateful, and thus the law would likely have a chilling effect on legitimate forms of expression, whose speakers would fear prosecution under the impugned legislation. Furthermore, human rights legislation, which imposes remedies for hate speech that fall short of criminalization, may be as effective and less invasive on free speech than the legislation in question. Thus, the legislation in question was deemed not to be minimally intrusive by the Court.

The majority in *Keegstra* found that the rational connection test was met because the prosecution of hate speakers was more likely to have the beneficial effect of promoting the values of diversity and equality, and showing that the state is taking an active stand against racism, than it was to have the negative effect of promoting racist speech. This approach dovetails impeccably with my idea of the power involved in state speech. Then Chief Justice Brian Dickson, writing for the majority here, seems very aware of the state's exercise of power in making this decision. He sees himself as choosing to deploy this power in a way that will uphold the values that he feels to be central to a liberal society:

> It is undeniable that media attention has been extensive on those occasions when s. 319(2) has been used. Yet from my perspective, s. 319(2) serves to illustrate to the public the severe disapprobation with which society holds messages of hate directed towards racial and religious groups. The existence of a particular criminal law, and the process of holding a trial when that law is used, is thus itself a form of expression, and the message sent out is that hate propaganda is harmful to target group members and threatening to a harmonious society. [*Keegstra* (1990), 769]

This statement makes apparent the majority's recognition of the efficacy of the speech acts of the Court and of the media coverage of the Court's decision, and makes clear that this fact of state power exercised through state speech ought to be recognized by the Court and used in the self-conscious service of equality, rather than be shied away from. In this respect, Dickson's decision is a prime example of the kind of egalitarian jurisprudence I am advocating.

With respect to minimal impairment, Dickson held that the law's definition of hatred was narrow enough – given its insistence that the promotion of hatred be 'willful' – to be considered minimally intrusive. The availability of other, non-criminal remedies, such as human rights legislation, did not preclude the legislature from also employing a criminal remedy. The majority opinion in *Keegstra* stands for the kind of jurisprudence I am advocating – actively in favor of using the courts to promote equality, and having a self-conscious awareness of the power of state speech in making decisions that affect the way that democracy functions.

This approach is not, however, necessitated by the Canadian framework, as *Zundel*, decided on the same framework only two years later, amply demonstrates. In *Zundel*, the Court was considering a different provision used to regulate hate speech, the provision criminalizing the 'spreading of false news,' in the case of the false news of a Holocaust denier. In this case, the 4-3 majority found that the provision was outdated and failed to impair minimally the *Charter* right to freedom of expression. It was outdated because at the time the impugned provision was enacted, the stated legislative objective was to facilitate 'prevention of deliberate slanderous statements against the nobles of the realm to preserve political harmony in the state' [*Zundel* (1992), 733].

The Canadian Court had previously held that a new objective, such as the prevention of racism in the instant case, cannot be added in an ad hoc way.

Further, even if the Court were to allow that promoting racial tolerance was a pressing and substantial objective, the impugned provision would still fail to meet the proportionality test, due to its being overbroad: 'The phrase "statement, tale or news," while it may not extend to the realm of true opinion, obviously encompasses a broad range of historical and social speech, going well beyond what is patent or provable to the senses as a matter of "pure fact."' [*Zundel* (1992), 733]. In conclusion, the Court held that 'the value of liberty of speech, one of the most fundamental freedoms protected by the *Charter*, needs no elaboration. By contrast, the objective of s. 181, in so far as an objective can be ascribed, falls short of constituting a countervailing interest of the most compelling nature.' [*Zundel* (1992), 735].

Thus, the reasoning in *Zundel* demonstrates that the Canadian Court, at the very least, respects the s. 1 analysis enough so as not to use it disingenuously to justify its aims for the promotion of equality. Instead of being discouraged by the conflicting verdicts in *Keegstra* and *Zundel*, we can view these decisions with optimism that the Court will only use its voice for the promotion of equality if it can do so on facts that themselves support such a voice. This should serve to reassure those who are wary that an activist state will promote too zealous a state activism; the Canadian Court, at least, seems not to have gone this route.

As seen in these leading US and Canadian hate speech decisions, then, an instrumental, rights-balancing approach employed by a Court that is conscious of its power and is acting in the service of equality can produce results that uphold the liberal state's core commitment to treat its citizens with equal concern and respect. I will turn now to the European jurisprudence, which also evidences an activist state in the service of equality.

### 8.1.3   The European decisions

The atrocities of the Nazi Holocaust did much to shape European hate speech jurisprudence, which is the most obviously activist of the three jurisdictions considered here. That this historical event figures so prominently as motivation for the European jurisprudence is, importantly, in line with Foucault's prescient observation that understanding the historicity of a situation is crucial in accurately viewing the power relations embedded in it. European countries, at the international level of the European Union and of various treaty-making bodies, as well as at the state level, are epitomes of activist liberal states, explicitly prioritizing 'dignity' over freedom of expression. I will argue that this privileging of dignity is conceptually synonymous to the fundamental liberal idea of treating all citizens with equal concern and respect. Though every European nation recognizes a fundamental right to freedom of expression, each has been receptive to content-based regulation of that right in the case of hate speech.

The earliest and perhaps most influential international treaty to address the issue of hate speech explicitly is the International Convention on the Elimination of All Forms of Racial Discrimination (ICERD),[7] which entered into force by the United Nations in 1969 and was ratified by over 150 nations. Article 4 of the ICERD contains the hate speech provision and mandates that all signatories shall criminalize the 'dissemination of ideas based on racial superiority or hatred'. Although the US has ratified the ICERD, it has notably filed a reservation to the effect that it will not enact any laws violating its First Amendment. Thus, the US stands as an outlier amongst the other signatories in privileging freedom of expression over dignity.

Another important international treaty concerning hate speech is the 2002 Additional Protocol to the Convention on Cybercrime, Concerning the Criminalisation of Acts of a Racist and Xenophobic Nature Committed through Computer Systems. This treaty originated in the Council of Europe and was signed by twenty-three of its forty-seven member nations. The treaty enjoins its signatories to criminalize 'distributing or otherwise making available, racist and xenophobic materials to the public through a computer system.'[8]

At the state level, the signatories of the ICERD and the Additional Protocol to the Convention on Cybercrime have enacted criminal laws as mandated by these treaties, which have led to some quite strong speech regulations, particularly in Germany. Article 5 of the Basic Law of Germany provides that every individual has the right to freedom of expression, but then it states that 'these rights shall find their limits in...the right to personal honor.'[9] Article 1 declares that 'human dignity' is of the utmost value and article 18 allows for the forfeiture of other rights when the right to dignity is abused.[10] These ideas of honor and dignity resonate with the Dworkinian invocation of each citizen's entitlement to equal concern and respect, and, given that they are in practice invoked as trumps on hate speech, indicate that Germany operates within a rights-balancing framework very similar to that of Canada. Further, the German use of language like 'honor' and 'dignity' resonates with the comments from critical race theorists examined in

Chapter 2: hate speech is received by minorities as an assault on their dignity, and the German legislation attempts acknowledge and protect that dignity.

The most recent piece of relevant European legislation is the European Union's passage of the Framework Decision on Racism and Xenophobia in 2007. While the Framework Decision does not have direct effect on the EU member states, and the European Commission, the enacting body, does not act as an enforcement body, the Framework Decision asks EU member states to enact legislation against various forms of hate speech, most notably against speech that is 'publicly condoning, denying or grossly trivializing...crimes defined by the Tribunal of Nuremberg.'[11] Though the Framework Decision cannot be said to be illocutionary, in that it is non-binding, it is likely to inspire illocutionary, binding, legislation by the EU member states. Further, because of its direct reference to Nuremberg, this state speech is exemplary of my assertion that a self-conscious activist liberal state would be mindful of the historicity of its decisions and of the fact situations that come before its courts.

From this brief canvassing of the European hate speech legislation, at both the state and international levels, it is apparent that the EU and its member countries – Germany in particular – serve as prime exemplars of the activist liberal state in the service of equality. However, most European countries only regulate child pornography, rather than regulating other forms of pornography. The United Kingdom legislation on pornography is perhaps the most restrictive in Europe, and I will argue that although it has egalitarian aims, weaknesses in the drafting of the legislation have led to a lack of prosecutions. In the realm of pornography, it is clear that Canada is the most activist egalitarian state of the three jurisdictions.

## 8.2   The obscenity jurisprudence

On the surface, the leading obscenity decisions in the US, Canada, and the UK appear to take a similar approach: all three attempt to find a community standard of tolerance beyond which pornographic materials are considered obscene and thus not constitutionally protected. However, the rationale for this test is quite different in each country. In the US, obscene speech is seen as having limited relevance to the values that the First Amendment is intended to protect – values going to the heart of a democratic system, such as political speech. According to the US Court, obscene speech is as far as possible from political speech, and is thus worthy of little, if any, protection.

While the Canadian Court in its leading decision in *Butler* also observes the low value of obscene speech to a democratic culture, most of its justification for its decision rests on balancing the rights to freedom of expression of the pornographer with the harm that pornography causes women, where the harm is understood as stemming from the idea that degrading or dehumanizing representations of women cause reification of oppressive stereotypes.

In the UK, obscenity legislation is informed by the rights-balancing framework of the European Convention for the Protection of Human Rights and Fundamental Freedoms (also known as the 'European Convention on Human Rights' and 'ECHR.' Hereinafter, I will refer to this treaty as the ECHR).[12] In sum, then, the US Court takes a constitutive view of rights, and the Canadian and UK courts embrace a rights-balancing approach. This latter approach, as I have argued, facilitates a self-conscious liberal state acting in the service of equality.

### 8.2.1 The US decisions

In the leading US case of *Miller v. California*,[13] the Court formulated its three-part obscenity test that is still in use today. Under the *Miller* test, a work is deemed to be obscene if it: (1) would be found appealing to the prurient interest by an average person applying contemporary community standards, (2) depicts sexual conduct in a patently offensive way, and (3) has no serious literary, artistic, political, or scientific value. The equality rights of women were never even mentioned in this case's reasoning, and the three-step test is formulated solely in order to determine how far away a particular expressive instance strays from the core freedom of expression values. The *Miller* test's reasoning, then, is consistent with the American Court's constitutive view of rights and the Court's reluctance, given that approach, to engage in rights-balancing.

### 8.2.2 The Canadian decisions

In the leading Canadian decision of *R. v. Butler* (1992), decided almost twenty years after *Miller*, the Court adopted a similar test. The defendant, Donald Butler, had opened a store in Winnipeg that sold sex toys and videos. Butler was charged with, and convicted in the lower courts, on the following counts: possessing obscene material for the purpose of sale, selling obscene material, and exposing obscene material to the public view. At the time of hearing, the Supreme Court did not have a standard test for obscenity, and here it became the Court's task to develop one. Previous decisions had left three distinct tests competing with each other: the community standards test, wherein it would be up to the community to determine whether a work was obscene; the harm test, under which material would fail to enjoy constitutional protection if it was deemed to be harmful to others; and the internal necessities test, under which a work would not be deemed to be obscene if its creators could establish that the work needed its graphic content for the sake of another, artistic, purpose.

The Court in *Butler* adopted a version of the community standards test that subsumed the harm test. Justice Sopinka, writing for the 7-2 majority, held as follows:

> The courts must determine as best they can what the community would tolerate others being exposed to on the basis of the degree of harm that may flow from such exposure. Harm in this context means that it predisposes persons to act in an anti-social manner as, for example, the physical or mental mistreatment of women by men, or, what is perhaps debatable, the reverse. Anti-social conduct for this purpose is conduct which society formally recognizes as incompatible with its proper functioning. The stronger the inference of a risk of harm the lesser the likelihood of tolerance. The inference may be drawn from the material itself or from the material and other evidence. [*Butler* (1992), 485]

In other words, the way to determine whether material is harmful is to determine whether the community would tolerate that material being consumed by others. This approach appears to be beneficial by minimizing the risk that the decision would be made by judges acting in a vacuum and applying their own standards of morality to the public at large.

However, the community standards test has two serious and related drawbacks. First, there does not seem to be any kind of national consensus on what the community's level of tolerance in fact is, and thus we are left effectively with a standard of what the majority's level might be. This is obviously problematic because, as Dworkin mentions, one important function of rights is to trump majoritarian interests, not to reinforce them. Second, if we indeed live in a culturally oppressive society, the public, or at least the majority, may not necessarily be in a position to judge what is harmful to others – either the harm will have been so normalized and naturalized as not to appear harmful at all, or what is in fact innocent may appear harmful, due to culturally oppressive programming. One need only look to situations of domestic abuse for an example of the former, or to religious intolerance for an example of the latter.

The Court in *Butler*, without the aid of an actual empirical study of what most Canadians felt to be harmful, nevertheless concluded in the face of only inconclusive, equivocal, social science evidence on the related, though by no means equivalent, question of whether pornography does in fact lead to increased violence against women, that it would follow the decision in *Irwin Toy*.[14] This latter case found that in situations of inconclusive empirical data, the Court must maintain a high level of legislative deference and conclude that as long as the legislature acted with a 'reasonable basis' in assessing that evidence, the legislature's decision should stand [*Butler* (1992), 502–3] .

In *Butler*, the Court proceeded to find that regardless of the tenuous link between pornography and violence:

> [t]he clear and unquestionable danger of this type of material is that it reinforces some unhealthy tendencies in Canadian society. The effect of this type of material is to reinforce male–female stereotypes to the detriment of both sexes. It attempts to make degradation, humiliation, victimization, and violence in human relationships appear normal and acceptable. A society which holds that egalitarianism, non-violence, consensualism, and mutuality are basic to any human interaction, whether sexual or other, is clearly justified in controlling and prohibiting any medium of depiction, description, or advocacy which violates these principles. [*Butler* (1992), 493]

This statement is alarming in two ways. It seems to gloss over the fact that the Court is switching focus from the harm of violence to the harm of stereotyping, and it concludes that because there was no conclusive proof for the former, the truth of the latter was simply obvious. This shift enables the Court to get around its evidentiary burden of harm: in shifting from violence to stereotyping, the Court moves from a well-mined and equivocal body of social science evidence to a much murkier, much less developed, and possibly – in principle – unempirical realm.

Further, the Court makes the equally bold move of concluding that since there is a clear connection between pornography and stereotyping, it is obvious that an egalitarian court is justified in prohibiting such expression. Is there anything that can be considered sound in this reasoning, from my perspective of advocating self-reflective state speech in the service of equality? I will address this question shortly after first continuing to outline the basics of the Court's decision in *Butler*.

The Court then provided three-tiered criteria for what material would be too harmful, on the level of stereotypes or any other considerations, to be tolerated. Justice Sopinka maintained that explicit sex with violence would almost always be obscene and hence prohibited; explicit sex without violence but which subjects people to treatment that is degrading or dehumanizing may be obscene if the risk of harm is substantial; and explicit sex without violence which is neither degrading or dehumanizing will not be obscene unless children are employed in the production [*Butler* (1992), 484–5]. While the Court was ostensibly guided by the desire to curtail the putative harm to women that it believed pornography brings, it nevertheless seems to have been guided not by evidence of that harm, since no such evidence was actually adopted by the Court, but rather by its own opinions on what the community ought to tolerate.

What should we make of *Butler*, in terms of our discussion of cultural oppression and state speech? On its face, the decision seems glaringly paternalistic and undemocratic – with judges effectively legislating the community's morality for the community itself, while denying that they were doing so. However, the logic of cultural oppression, like Mill's logic in *Subjection*, raises the difficult problem of what to do in circumstances where first-hand reports of harm or well-being may be unreliable. Whether pornography is harmful to women, on the level of contributing to cultural oppression in general and to stereotypes in particular, might not be a question that the public can answer correctly or about which academic social science can devise a well-constructed experiment. Accordingly, the question of whether autonomy was desirable for women in Mill's time may not have been correctly answerable by the women themselves, nor could social scientists have necessarily gauged cultural oppression – at that time or any other. In other words, that there was no independent empirical evidence – any kind of academic study or public opinion survey – adopted by the *Butler* Court to support its conclusions need not be prohibitive if we are in a cultural environment that, because of its deeply oppressive views on the unequal moral worth of some of its members, could not produce such evidence for the reason that such views have been thoroughgoingly normalized.

Further, the vast majority of studies have investigated male responses to pornography – both in terms of violence, and less frequently, in terms of male attitudes towards women – and have produced inconclusive results on these questions. It is entirely possible, however, to conceive of a case where pornography has failed to produce any kind of negative effect on men but still produces negative effects on the women who view it themselves, encounter it in the marketplace, or know their male partners view it. The effects on women of pornography have been quite under-investigated – itself a sexist fact – and it would only further this sexism to conclude that because the male studies were inconclusive, pornography is safe enough to be decriminalized in the absence of better, non-sexist, egalitarian research.

In a similar vein, while an activist egalitarian approach such as the one I am advancing would shun a court acting, even in the name of equality, *against* established empirical evidence, the question of what a court should do in the absence of insufficient, or equivocal, evidence is by no means obvious. To hold that the right, say, to freedom of expression should be upheld until such time as decisive evidence is produced in the other direction is to beg the question – why is it any more obvious that we should lean in this direction in the interim than to lean in the direction that would favor, say, the right to equality, if only until such time as decisive evidence is produced? This returns to our primary question – how to respond when liberty and equality are in tension?

In other words, in my view, the fact that the Court made a unilateral, and non-empirically based, pronouncement in the name of equality was not in itself problematic under circumstances of cultural oppression, for all of the above reasons. What was problematic, however, was its disingenuousness in doing so. The Court should have honestly discussed that it was making this move in an activist way, in the name of egalitarian liberal values, rather than hide behind the thin veil of community standards that the Court itself enacted.

Many critics have attempted to discount the reasoning in *Butler* in its entirety by seizing on the point that the Court was telling the community what and what not to find obscene, and indeed doing so without any external evidence to support its ruling. In my view, the Court may be excused for ruling in the absence of external evidence, but only in either of two cases, as discussed above: First, if the absence of external evidence in principle or in practice results from a culturally oppressive scenario that precludes fair studies from taking place. An example of such a scenario is one in which a community is so programmed to believe in women's unequal moral worth that studies are biased to consider only men's views on the question, or biased in some other way that makes proper data difficult or impossible to obtain. A second case rendering excusable the Court's absence of external evidence is when research results are inconclusive and the Court determines that in such a situation, it would better serve the interests of equality to err on the side of the equality-preserving option – rather than on the side of the liberty-preserving option – while waiting for conclusive research to be produced. In either situation, the Court, in my view, would be performing its job in fighting cultural oppression by erring on the side of equality until the time that new data tilts the scale decisively toward freedom of expression.

To this extent, the Court could be excused from Sumner's requirement (Sumner 2004: 181) that '[g]iven the importance of the values, both personal and social, advanced by freedom of expression, the default presumption for any form of expression must be free circulation rather than suppression. Overcoming this presumption will require reliable evidence of harm.' Sumner's statement, however, pointedly fails to give consideration to the importance of the values – personal, societal, social – of equality itself. In the absence of reliable evidence of harm, from my point of view, the Court should ask: First, is there reliable evidence of cultural oppression whose harm may be difficult or impossible to ferret out? And second, given equal evidence on both sides, which value is most important to promote? In a committed egalitarian culture, we ought to answer 'yes' to the first question and 'equality' to the second, given the present social circumstances of pervasive racism, sexism, and homophobia.

The evidence for saying 'yes' to the first question comes from the multitude of media – advertising in print and on television, movies, and video games that portray women and minorities as subordinate, to name a few – that seem unlikely, given their vast proliferation, to be benign in their influence on cultural attitudes towards women and minorities. Interestingly, the media that liberals frequently offer as a *reductio* argument against the censorship of pornography can now be harnessed to advance an argument for the existence of cultural oppression and an activist liberal state to fight it on all fronts. Since an effective fight against inequality through censorship would mean engaging on this multitude of fronts – an absurd prospect, they claim – it would be arbitrary to fight it on just one front, pornography. While criminalization of video games is likely untenable, here the state can use its less authoritative speech, as per the advocacy strategy, to encourage other forms of entertainment.

Further, as I have argued in various instances throughout this study, the idea of cultural oppression has support from Mill's writings in *Subjection*, as liberal theory can accommodate the notion that first-hand accounts of preferences may not be the end of our inquiries into the good life.

However, while the *Butler* Court may appear to be activist in the name of equality when it effectively answered 'yes' and 'equality' in its result, it cannot be seen as an exemplar of the approach I am advocating, because it answered these questions on the so-called behalf of the community itself. Failing to speak in its own voice as the Court, and instead claiming to speak for the Canadian public, is deeply problematic given my argument that state speech is necessarily the voice of state power. Since the state did its bidding not through its own mouth, the state to some degree subverted the legitimate authority that that state speech should convey. Since the Court supposedly acted in the name of the community, the *Butler* decision had the effect of the public resenting being told backhandedly what it found to be offensive. This, I believe, was the fault of the decision's wording, which reads as anything but a transparent effort by the Court to prescribe standards for obscenity that would have upheld the values of egalitarian liberalism. To be sure, such an effort would also have had many detractors, but there would, most likely, have been some who would have welcomed the effort, and still others who would have been persuaded by the court's reasoning over time.

The point, though, from the viewpoint of speech act theory and Foucauldian power analysis, is that for state speech to have the desired effect – of promoting equality – it must be imparted transparently by the state as speaker. For all of the reasons that Austin provided about the relevance of social position and power to the kinds of speech acts that will prove to be effective, the state must speak *as* the state to avoid undercutting the power of its speech. The Court in *Butler* gave a hint of this direct and powerful state speech in the service of egalitarianism in the passage quoted above, when declaring that an egalitarian society is justified in taking action against inegalitarian speech; however, that sentiment was undercut by the Court's claim to express the feeling of the public, rather than by simply issuing the mandate from the Court itself.

Again, then, we can learn a great deal by paying attention to the notion of state power and state speech when investigating rights jurisprudence as a discourse. From this brief look at the leading obscenity decisions, we learn a cautionary lesson in both the US and Canadian cases. The US Court in *Miller* suffered for its failure to incorporate the notion of equality, as a rights-balancing approach would have, in creating its obscenity test, and the Canadian Court in *Butler*, while informed by a rights-balancing approach, nevertheless failed to produce a truly just result because it failed to take proper ownership of its own speech acts.

### 8.2.3   The UK decisions

While most of Europe has very permissive legislation with respect to pornography that is both produced and consumed by persons over the age of 18, the UK is an exception in that it has legislation for the regulation of obscenity based on a community standards of tolerance test. I will focus on this legislation because of its egalitarian content. The UK obscenity legislation must of course remain consistent with the ECHR and the Constitution of the European Union, both of which prioritize the dignity of the human person and provide for rights-balancing frameworks similar to that of Canada.

The UK's statute on the regulation of pornography is the Obscene Publications Act of 1959,[15] which establishes a community standards test for determining whether speech is obscene and therefore subject to regulation. Article 1 of the Act lays out this community standards test as follows:

> For the purposes of this Act an article shall be deemed to be obscene if its effect or...the effect of any one of its items is, if taken as a whole, such as to tend to deprave and corrupt persons who are likely, having regard to all relevant circumstances, to read, see or hear the matter contained or embodied in it.

This test, understandably, has proven difficult to utilize, since it is difficult to determine what would 'tend to deprave and corrupt' persons. As a result, the Act has not given rise to many prosecutions, and those that have arisen tended to be exonerated by the defense that the impugned work has literary merit.[16]

It is a stretch, though not an impossible one, to view the desire to prevent moral corruption of the consumers of pornography as egalitarian in its morality, rather than merely Victorian. However, the language of the Act leaves open the clear possibility that the Act could be used by an egalitarian state that interprets 'corruption' as meaning the fostering of culturally oppressive attitudes. However, this interpretation is hypothetical at this point.

A more compelling argument for the UK, and Europe as a whole, as an activist egalitarian state comes from the two central human rights statutes governing Europe, the ECHR, adopted by the Council of Europe in 1950, and the *Charter of Fundamental Rights of the European Union* (hereinafter, the CFREU),[17] which came into force as law concurrently with the entering into force of the *Treaty of Lisbon*,[18] on December 1, 2009. The CFREU explicitly provides that it does not supersede any of the provisions of the ECHR, though it may in some cases provide more human rights protection than the earlier statute.

What is notable in both statutes is that each contains rights-balancing language, and the CFREU contains prominent and central reference to the primacy of human dignity within the scheme of enumerated rights. The ECHR is one of the most stringently enforced international treaties, as it enacted the European Court of Human Rights as a tribunal to adjudicate claims under the ECHR.[19] That a court was formed to enforce this treaty ought to impact the way that the illocutionary and sovereign nature of state judicial speech is viewed – the ECHR makes more of a claim to illocutionary force the closer it comes to being law in the paradigmatic case of the indisputably binding nature of law enacted at a national level. The founding of the European Court of Human Rights ensures that the ECHR will not be toothless in the event that member states fail to enact compatible legislation, and thus, I would argue, the very founding of the Court gives the ECHR binding illocutionary force.

The freedom of expression provisions of the ECHR, contained in Article 10, contain explicit limitation provisions, and are in this respect distinct from the rest of the treaty's enumerated rights, which contain no such provisions. Article 10 reads as follows:

1. Everyone has the right to freedom of expression. This right shall include freedom to hold opinions and to receive and impart information and ideas without interference by public authority and regardless of frontiers....
2. The exercise of these freedoms, since it carries with it duties and responsibilities, may be subject to such formalities, conditions, restrictions or penalties as are prescribed by law and are necessary in a democratic society, in the interests of national security, territorial integrity or public safety, for the prevention of disorder or crime, for the protection of health or morals, for the protection of the reputation or the rights of others....

The language of subsection 2 is clearly egalitarian: the right to freedom of expression is subject to the necessary limits of a democratic society, which entails that this right must be understood as, in most cases, instrumentally valuable to a democratic society, but where it is not valuable, it is to be limited. That it is to be limited when it interferes with the rights or reputation of others shows that there is a balancing between the right to freedom of expression and other rights. That the ECHR exists alongside the hate speech legislation I canvassed earlier strongly demonstrates that hate speech is considered a case where the 'rights or reputation of others' can justify a limitation on freedom of expression.

The CFREU has similar rights-balancing language, although in this case it spans over the entire document and not just over the freedom of expression provisions. The rights-balancing provisions are set out in Title VII, Article 52, Subsection1, and provide as follows:

1. Any limitation on the exercise of the rights and freedoms recognised by this Charter must be provided for by law and respect the essence of those rights and freedoms. Subject to the principle of proportionality, limitations may be made only if they are necessary and genuinely meet objectives of general interest recognised by the Union or the need to protect the rights and freedoms of others.

Here it is evident that the EU sees rights as in the general interest, as per Raz and Mill, and that rights may need to be limited to 'protect the rights and freedoms of others.' Of course, since the CFREU has yet to come into force, as of the time of this writing, it remains to be seen under what circumstances the EU courts will see it fit to limit rights. However, I venture to predict that they will do so in the case of hate speech, given the hate speech statutes canvassed earlier, and given the priority of human dignity in the drafting of the CFREU. The right to human dignity appears in Title 1, Article 1 of the CFREU and reads as follows: 'Human dignity is inviolable. It must be respected and protected.' If the right to human dignity is inviolable, it follows that any other right curtailing it must be limited in order to preserve human dignity. Again, following the remarks of the critical race theorists canvassed in Chapters 2 and 3, the very problem with hate speech is that it is received by its targets as affronts to their dignity.

Thus, the preceding discussion of human rights and hate speech legislation has shown that the EU and its member states have taken a rights-balancing approach in their rights enacting and limiting legislation, which places the EU on a solid footing to make egalitarian activist decisions under these laws.

## 8.3   Conclusion

We have seen that egalitarian liberalism and continental theories of power and speech, taken together, provide a strong argument in favor of state activism in the name of equality. It is important, once again, to clarify that in my view, neither path – of legislation or of advocacy – should be taken alone. Rather, together, they provide a persuasive justification for activism.

Even within the brand of egalitarian liberalism that I have sketched – which would allow for state activism in the name of equality and thus necessitate dropping the neutrality requirement in such cases – key reservations about the desirability and feasibility of state activism remain. Such reservations are centered on the pervasive grip of liberalism's neutrality requirement: how to ensure that the state is not entrusted with too much power in its activism decisions, and how to ensure that the state is in fact acting in the name of equality rather than some other, less vital, interest. The neutrality requirement was intended to guard against these issues ever arising, but the force of arguments from theorists such as Foucault and Butler demonstrate that the neutrality requirement does not necessarily provide the assumed protection. Foucault's and Butler's theories, in effect, state that given that the neutrality requirement does not keep us safe from state excesses and biases, and given the overwhelming inequalities that persist alongside liberalism, we should not be afraid to drop the neutrality requirement as part of an activist program for equality.

The theories of speech and power canvassed in this study, then, serve to demonstrate that neutrality is not a salve for inequality, but rather in many instances an enactor of it; they function to highlight the role of state power in the hope that making the liberal state more aware of its own power will serve to curb its potential excesses when given the responsibility to engage in activism on behalf of equality. Further, these theories offer a space for the voicing of minority discourse, which the contemporary liberal state may otherwise not hear. If the liberal state cannot hear minority discourse, it will not fully understand the extent of cultural oppression. Finally, these theories of speech and power offer a view of censorship that ought to alleviate traditional liberal fears of censorship, since they locate the latter at a level necessarily implicating the state. If the state is, of necessity, implicated in censorship, then it follows that there is no need to attempt to avoid such implication. These views, combined with the activist-friendly egalitarian liberalism I outlined in the early chapters, and the advocacy strategy outlined in Chapter 7, are sufficient to justify an egalitarian activist state.

All of the work on the theoretical side of justifying an activist, egalitarian liberal state is vastly enhanced if evidence can be produced that such a state can work not only in theory but also in practice. To this end, the brief canvassing of hate speech and pornography legislation and jurisprudence in this chapter have shown that Europe and Canada engage in a self-reflective, rights-balancing approach that facilitates egalitarian decisions in cases of hate speech and pornography.

# Conclusion

An activist egalitarian liberal state is not nearly as radical a possibility as mainstream liberal discourse supposes. Rather, as I have shown in these pages, there is support for the idea within liberalism itself – both implicitly, in thinkers such as Mill and Dworkin, and explicitly, in thinkers such as Fiss and Raz. Further, there is support for an activist state from traditions outside of liberalism, such as speech act theory, feminism, and continental political philosophy. It has been the task of this book to weave these strands of thought together in order to show that criticisms of the inequitable consequences of liberal neutrality can in fact be adopted by the liberal state, and that such adoption will ultimately strengthen the liberal state and its ideals.

This project's novelty has in no small part arisen due to disciplinary boundaries between contemporary Anglo-American political philosophy and contemporary continental political philosophy that, in my mind, are far too infrequently bridged. Beyond my central argument that continental theories of speech and power can and ought to inform the Anglo-American debate about freedom of expression, I hope that this book is also taken as an example of the many potential problems in political philosophy – and perhaps in other sub-fields as well – that may be illuminated by the engagement of Anglo-American and continental traditions.

From the premise, taken as basic, notably by Ronald Dworkin, but also adopted by many prominent liberal thinkers, that the liberal state's fundamental commitment is not to liberty, but rather to the treatment of its citizens with equal concern and respect, I have argued that the hard cases in freedom of expression – pornography and hate speech – do well to point out the contours and fissures of the liberal state's putative commitment to equality over liberty.

Taking pornography and hate speech jurisprudence as test cases in examining the nature and extent of liberalism's commitment to equal concern and respect for all its citizens reveals that, in the United States and in the bulk of the contemporary academic literature, the commitment to equal concern and respect is understood as having been met so long as the state is neutral with regard to the content of speech in enacting limits on the right to freedom of expression. It has been my aim to show, both from within liberalism and outside of it, how and why this dominant line of thinking is misguided and how liberalism fails in its commitment to equal concern and respect by adhering to it. Further, I have attempted to show that in this very failure a space is created for liberalism finally to live up to its egalitarian core commitment by abandoning its policy of content neutrality and instead using its significant state power to advocate for equality, both within and outside of legally binding channels.

While Dworkin espouses equal concern and respect as the core commitment of liberalism, he maintains at the same time that the state can meet this commitment by acting neutrally with respect to the content of speech, even in the cases of pornography and hate speech. In this regard, he echoes the dominant strand of liberal thinking on the topic of freedom of expression from Mill onwards. However, I have shown that there is room, within even this line of thinking, for the activist egalitarian state, since Mill's *Subjection of Women* reveals his sensitivity to the idea that social forces, left unchecked, can so constrain an oppressed population even at the basic level of preference formation that that population may not be able to formulate their own true sense of the good life.

If Mill in *Subjection* is correct in his diagnosis of the problem of what I am calling cultural oppression, then the dominant idea governing the policy of neutrality – the liberal state as merely passively facilitating, through a 'marketplace of ideas,' the privately formed conceptions of the good life of its citizens – becomes deeply problematic, since a culturally oppressive society means that a significant percentage of the population – namely, women and minorities – are denied the authentic opportunity to form their own good, due to dominant oppressive views of their inferior moral worth that have flooded the marketplace of ideas. The controversy, from most quarters in the classical and contemporary egalitarian liberal debate, is not about whether this is the case, but rather what the proper remedy for it ought to be.

This skewed marketplace full of culturally oppressive ideas is the first failure of a liberalism wedded to content neutrality. The marketplace of ideas facilitated by a neutral state works to fulfill the Millian goal of free and wide-ranging discourse about diverse conceptions of the good life only if people holding those diverse conceptions – women and minorities surely among them – are allowed to participate. However, what the silencing and subordination arguments have suggested is that in actuality, such participation by women and minorities is precluded in the marketplace due to the chilling effect that extremely racist and sexist comments have upon their speech. In Mill's vision of the marketplace, of course, subordination and silencing would not exist, no one's ideas would be precluded in advance of their being voiced, and open-mindedness and a spirit of genuine inquiry would be effectively facilitated by state neutrality about content. The problem, as I see it, is that our culturally oppressive society falls far short of the Millian paradigm, and the reification of neutrality in mainstream liberal discourse as a core value of the marketplace, rather than a merely instrumental means toward achieving a diversity of voices, ties the hands of the liberal state to do anything to remedy this failure.

A liberalism committed to content neutrality fails on two levels, then. First, it fails when allowing for silencing and subordination to skew the marketplace of ideas so strongly as to preclude diverse voices from speaking or from being heard. Neutrality liberalism then fails in a second way, and even more tragically, when it cannot correct for that marketplace failure by inserting its own culturally liberatory speech, or using its power to discourage culturally oppressive speech. The liberal state wedded to content neutrality as a value, rather than as an instrument, ties its own hands first in allowing the production of a culturally oppressive culture to flourish in its neutrally facilitated marketplace of ideas, and then, having its hands tied, is impotent to act to remedy this culturally oppressive, skewed marketplace – because to do so would of course require a departure from content neutrality, which this liberal state takes to be anathema.

I have argued that without some compelling reason to do so, the liberal state ought not to tie its hands in this way, in so grave a circumstance: a culturally oppressive society, which is the very antithesis of the authentically Millian marketplace of ideas. The reasons advanced by mainstream liberalism as compelling – the need to preserve neutrality as a check on abuse of state power, the need to preserve equality between citizens by not favoring one person's viewpoint over another, and the need to avoid state censorship – have both been shown, in the preceding pages, to be flawed.

Neutrality as justified and necessitated by its efficacy in checking state power has been undermined in three ways in this account. First, it has been undermined through speech act theory which, I argued, reveals the judicial discourse of the state as an illocutionary speech act, and as such is necessarily powerful and efficacious regardless of whether the state takes a hands-off, neutral approach (which it still must speak its intentions to do in its judicial decisions), or a more directly interventionist approach. In either case, the state is using its power, through its speech, in order to enact particular circumstances which cannot help but favor some speakers over others. Such an outcome, of course, is anything but neutral.

Second, examining Foucault's thought revealed that power runs through discourse, and though the state in modernity does not have the sovereignty that it had in monarchical times, the idea that the modern state's discourse – *whatever its content* – is always the chief way in which it wields its power exposes the freedom of expression judicial discourse as *itself* the pinnacle of a power-producing discourse, because its content in fact delimits the scope of all future state-sanctioned discourse. Again, if Foucault's account is persuasive, state speech cannot ever achieve neutrality, and the state is always speaking, even if only to proclaim (falsely) its own neutrality. Even if the liberal state is unaware of its own speech as power-producing discourse, or as efficacious illocutionary speech acts, it nevertheless operates as such.

Third, the 'new censorship' theories put forward by Butler and Schauer reveal as misguided liberalism's frequently voiced fear that non-neutrality would be tantamount to censorship. Censorship as liberals envision it – as occurring after speech has been spoken – misses the mark on how censorship operates at a deeper level: to 'foreclose' speech that has yet to be spoken, to delimit the range of acceptable speech in advance of its being uttered, or even, perhaps, to restrict thought. On a new censorship perspective, then, the liberal state is, once again, acting non-neutrally in spite of its best attempts to remain neutral. A new censorship understanding of the freedom of expression judicial discourse would hold that discourse operates to set the boundaries of acceptable speech – permitting some speech to be uttered in the future and foreclosing other speech to be uttered in the future. If this is the case, and it is hard to see how these decisions can be seen to do otherwise, then the liberal state cannot help but censor in this sense, by necessarily delimiting – and hence foreclosing – some speech in advance of its utterance.

The thrust of all three lines of argument – speech act theory, Foucauldian analysis of power, and the new censorship – all lead to the idea that state neutrality is impossible in principle, rather than merely undesirable. Thus, my account is meant as a twofold critique on neutrality – if the reader is unpersuaded by the three theories offered to the effect that state neutrality is impossible in principle, she may still be persuaded that a marketplace so skewed by cultural oppression as to preclude Mill's diversity of viewpoints from being heard is undesirable enough that the liberal state ought to depart from its otherwise tenable neutral stance in order to remedy cultural oppression.

In either case, though, the treatment of pornography and hate speech as constitutionally protected in the US jurisprudence and in the bulk of the influential academic Anglo-American literature ought to be seen as deeply problematic, as it both instantiates and promotes a society profoundly at odds with liberal goals and commitments.

I have intended in the preceding pages to clarify the heart of liberal commitment – the imperative to treat all citizens with equal concern and respect and to encourage a society where diversity flourishes. Further, I have meant to show not merely that this commitment cannot be met through a state that is neutral about the content of freedom of expression, but more importantly that liberalism would benefit from insight into its own non-neutrality and the consequences of that non-neutrality.

If I am correct in assessing that liberalism's core commitment is to treatment of its citizens with equal concern and respect, and that a well-functioning liberal state would be characterized by a fruitful and robust debate about diverse conceptions of the good life, then the liberal state has no inherent conflict with taking to heart the arguments in this book. Neutrality has never been at the core of liberalism, and the liberal state's core commitments have a much better chance of being met without it.

# Appendix A: Relevant sections of the *Canadian Charter of Rights and Freedoms*

Being Part I of the *Constitution Act, 1982*
Enacted by the Canada Act 1982 [U.K.] c.11; proclaimed in force April 17, 1982. Amended by the Constitution Amendment Proclamation, 1983, SI/84-102, effective June 21, 1984. Amended by the Constitution Amendment, 1993 [New Brunswick], SI/93-54, *Can. Gaz. Part II*, April 7, 1993, effective March 12, 1993.]

Whereas Canada is founded upon principles that recognize the supremacy of God and the rule of law:

## Guarantee of Rights and Freedoms

RIGHTS AND FREEDOMS IN CANADA.
**1.** The *Canadian Charter of Rights and Freedoms* guarantees the rights and freedoms set out in it subject only to such reasonable limits prescribed by law as can be demonstrably justified in a free and democratic society.

## Fundamental Freedoms

FUNDAMENTAL FREEDOMS.

**2.** Everyone has the following fundamental freedoms:
- **(a)** freedom of conscience and religion;
- **(b)** freedom of thought, belief, opinion and expression, including freedom of the press and other media of communication;
- **(c)** freedom of peaceful assembly; and
- **(d)** freedom of association.

## Equality Rights

EQUALITY BEFORE AND UNDER LAW AND EQUAL PROTECTION AND BENEFIT OF LAW/Affirmative action programs.

**15. (1)** Every individual is equal before and under the law and has the right to the equal protection and equal benefit of the law without discrimination and, in particular, without discrimination based on race, national or ethnic origin, colour, religion, sex, age or mental or physical disability.

**(2)** Subsection (1) does not preclude any law, programme or activity that has as its object the amelioration of conditions of disadvantaged individuals or groups including those that are disadvantaged because of race, national or ethnic origin, colour, religion, sex, age or mental or physical disability.

# Appendix B: Relevant sections of the *Bill of Rights of the United States*

## Amendment I

Congress shall make no law respecting an establishment of religion, or prohibiting the free exercise thereof; or abridging the freedom of speech, or of the press; or the right of the people peaceably to assemble, and to petition the government for a redress of grievances.

U.S. CONST. amend. I.

Amendment XIV
**Section 1.**

All persons born or naturalized in the United States, and subject to the jurisdiction thereof, are citizens of the United States and of the state wherein they reside. No state shall make or enforce any law which shall abridge the privileges or immunities of citizens of the United States; nor shall any state deprive any person of life, liberty, or property, without due process of law; nor deny to any person within its jurisdiction the equal protection of the laws.

U.S. CONST. amend. XIV, § 2.

# Notes

## Introduction

1 The idea behind this phrase can certainly be found in Mill's *On Liberty*, though the phrase itself is not uttered by him. The phrase dates to Oliver Wendell Holmes's dissent in *Abrams v. U.S.*, 250 U.S. 616 (1919), 624.

2 I owe the term and the above definition of 'cultural oppression' to Andrew Kernohan in *Liberalism, Equality, and Cultural Oppression*.

3 The idea of 'equal concern and respect' as liberalism's core value is Ronald Dworkin's. Since I agree with this very influential view, I am adopting it throughout this study. Dworkin's view will be discussed much more fully in Chapters 1 and 3. Throughout this work, unless Andrea Dworkin is specified, 'Dworkin' refers to Ronald Dworkin.

## Chapter 1

1 I am using the term 'egalitarian liberalism' synonymously with the idea of social welfare liberalism – that is, in the tradition of Rawls – as opposed to libertarian liberalism in the tradition of Nozick.

2 The theme of neutrality is central in the work of Rawls, Raz, Nozick, Dworkin, and Kymlicka.

3 This famous phrase is attributed to Plato but was popularized by Mill in Chapter 1 of *On Liberty*.

4 Rights, and their corollary duties, are famously viewed as constraints on freedom in Nozick's (1974) influential libertarian account, *Anarchy, State, and Utopia*.

5 Since the argument of this study can proceed with or without a utilitarian underpinning, I will not entertain the discussion of whether or not such an underpinning is desirable.

6 This was implicitly the approach of the majority in *R. v. Keegstra*, one of the leading Canadian hate speech decisions, which I will consider in Chapter 8.

7 Hart, Raz, and Mill are all advocates of a fundamental right to liberty.

8 It is of course a possibility, though one oddly not discussed in the literature, that rights are simply in some cases primarily about protecting choices, in other cases primarily about protecting interests, and in still other cases about both interests and choices equally. A proposition like this, wherein the primacy of protecting interests versus choice in the upholding of rights can vary, seems more plausible than there being a single overarching theory. In either case, though, for my purposes I need only argue that rights in the case of constitutional rights are about the protection of interests, rather than choices, whatever else they may concern in other cases.

# Chapter 2

1 Here I will rely on Dyzenhaus's arguments in (1992), 'John Stuart Mill and the Harms of Pornography.'

2 The notion of cultural oppression does not give rise to the need for empirical data to the same degree as does the idea of systemic discrimination, because cultural oppression centers on statements regarding the unequal moral worth of subjects, rather than on how those subjects fare in the marketplace with their moral worth thus diminished. It is uncontroversial that such culturally oppressive statements abound in our culture, and that their existence bears to some degree on the beliefs of at least some of its citizens. The existence of such statements and their resulting effects on some people's beliefs are all that we need to demonstrate in order to raise the issue of the utility or disutility of such views. To calculate the degree of harm caused by cultural oppression is admittedly a more difficult task, but not more difficult than many other calculations required by utilitarianism.

3 While it is of course outside of the scope of this project to canvass the history of censorship, a helpful text in this regard is Boyer (2000), *Purity in Print*.

4 Rae Langton provides this example.

5 Dworkin draws heavily on Isaiah Berlin's 'Two Concepts of Liberty,' in *Four Essays on Liberty*. Berlin claims that positive liberty is untenable because it is more likely than negative liberty to give rise to paternalism in determining what one's 'real' desires in fact are.

6 Notable proponents of the silencing argument include Frank Michelman in (1989), 'Conceptions of Democracy in American Constitutional Argument,' and later, Rae Langton and Jennifer Hornsby (1998), in the context of speech act theory. I will discuss Langton's and Hornsby's arguments in Chapter 4.

# Chapter 3

1 A question arises at this point. Even if we grant that some speech causes silencing and subordination, why believe that pornography and hate speech are the particular culprits? Dworkin addresses this question in his (1993) article, 'Women and Pornography.' Though a thorough discussion of this question is beyond the scope of this book, Dworkin's short answer is that there is enough empirical evidence to suggest that pornography in particular is efficacious in producing harmful views about women's sexuality. See especially the report of the 1986 US Attorney General's Commission on Pornography. However, there are other studies determining otherwise. In any event, an honest response to the data must grant that the empirical evidence is not sufficient to settle the matter on one side or the other – but that in the absence of sufficient evidence, both acting to regulate a potential harm and *not* acting have political consequences. That is precisely what the silencing and subordination arguments attempt to demonstrate: that maintaining the status quo legal framework *means to privilege the pornographers' and hate speakers' interests*.

2   It should be noted that while MacKinnon and her allies do believe that there is a close relationship between freedom of expression, moral agency, and democracy, these theorists still depart from Dworkin in that they hold that such a relationship is not constitutive, but rather strongly instrumental.

3   MacKinnon has repeatedly insisted that her arguments are for regulation of speech, and not outright censorship. She has maintained that her 1983 anti-pornography ordinance – drafted with Andrea Dworkin, and adopted by the city of Indianapolis before it was ruled unconstitutional by the Supreme Court – did not advocate state censorship because it did not place a prior restraint on pornographic materials. See MINNEAPOLIS, MINN., Rev. Ordinances, Title 7, Chapter 139 of the Minneapolis Code of Ordinances Relating to Civil Rights (1983).

## Chapter 4

1   This was the definition employed by Schauer in 'Causation Theory and the Causes of Sexual Violence' (1987: 752). Schauer credited Cartwright, in 'Causal Laws and Effective Strategies' (1979), for this formulation.

2   See Sumner, *The Hateful and the Obscene* (2004: 131–41), for a concise review of the social scientific literature.

## Chapter 5

1   See Foucault (1980d), *The History of Sexuality, Volume 1*, for a further elaboration of this term.

2   *R.A.V. v. City of St. Paul*, 505 U.S. 377 (1992).

## Chapter 6

1   Here, Butler's arguments recall her earlier work on the reproduction of gender norms in her groundbreaking (1999), *Gender Trouble*.

## Chapter 7

1   *New York Times Co. v. Sullivan*, 376 US 264 (1964).

2   *Red Lion Broadcasting Co. v. Federal Communications Commission*, 395 U.S. 367 (1969).

3   Mill, Raz and Dworkin all endorse at least some part of this view of rights.

4   *The Canadian Charter of Rights and Freedoms*, Part I of *the Constitution Act, 1982*, being Schedule B to the *Canada Act 1982* (U.K.), 1982, c. 11.

5   *R. v. Oakes* [1986] 1 S.C.R. 103.

6   The wording of this summary comes from Sumner's *The Hateful and the Obscene* (2004: 56).

7   *R. v. Keegstra* [1990] 3 S.C.R. 697, at 845.

# Chapter 8

1  *Brandenburg v. Ohio*, 395 U.S. 444 (1969).
2  *R.A.V. v. City of St. Paul*, 505 U.S. 377 (1992).
3  St. Paul, Minn., Legis. Code, Section 292.02 (1990).
4  *R. v. Zundel* [1992] 2 S.C.R. 731.
5  Canada, *Criminal Code*, [R.S.,c.C-34, s.1].
6  Canada, *Criminal Code*, [R.S.,c.C-34, s.1]. Interestingly, from the point of view of US jurisprudence, the results in *Keegstra* and *Zundel* were at odds with the principles in *Brandenburg* and *R.A.V.* The seemingly 'content neutral' provision of *Zundel* was struck down, while the *Keegstra* provision, which imposed a content distinction, was upheld.
7  International Convention on the Elimination of All Forms of Racial Discrimination, Jan. 4, 1969, 660 U.N.T.S. 195.
8  Convention on Cybercrime, Concerning the Criminalisation of Acts of a Racist and Xenophobic Nature Committed through Computer Systems, Council of Europe, Additional Protocol, November 7, 2002, chapter 2, article 3.
9  Grundgesetz [GG] [Constitution] art. 5, sec. 2 (F.R.G.).
10  Grundgesetz [GG] [Constitution] art. 1 (F.R.G.).
11  Council of the European Union, Framework Decision on Racism and Xenophobia, sec.2, Apr. 19, 2007.
12  Council of Europe, *Convention for the Protection of Human Rights and Fundamental Freedoms*, ETS 5.
13  *Miller v. California*, 413 U.S. 15 (1973).
14  *Irwin Toy Ltd.v. Quebec (Attorney General)* [1989] 1 S.C.R. 927.
15  Obscene Publications Act 1959 (c.66 7 and 8 Eliz 2).
16  The most famous of these was the case against Penguin Books for the publication of D.H. Lawrence's *Lady Chatterley's Lover*. Penguin was victorious, successfully claiming that the book's literary merit was a defense against its being cast as obscenity. See *R. v. Penguin Books Ltd.* [1961] Crim LR 176.
17  European Union, *Charter of Fundamental Rights of the European Union*, 7 December 2000, Official Journal of the European Communities, 18 December 2000 (2000/C 364/01).
18  European Union, *Treaty of Lisbon Amending the Treaty on European Union and the Treaty Establishing the European Community*, 13 December 2007, 2007/C 306/01.
19  Council of Europe, ECHR, sec. II, art. 19.

# Bibliography

References to most legal sources I employed in forming this work – case law, statutes, treaties, and other international instruments – are not included in this bibliography. Instead, at the first mention of a legal document, a full citation is given as a note in the text. All other sources consulted in the writing of this work are listed in full in this bibliography.

Althusser, Louis (1971) Ideology and Ideological State Apparatuses. In *Lenin and Philosophy and Other Essays*, translated by Ben Brewster. New York: Monthly Review Press.

Austin, J. L. (1975) *How to Do Things with Words*. 2nd edn. Cambridge, MA: Harvard University Press. [First published 1961].

Baker, Judith (ed.) (1994) *Group Rights*. Toronto: University of Toronto Press.

Berlin, Isaiah (1968a) Two Concepts of Liberty. In Berlin (1968b).

Berlin, Isaiah (1968b) *Four Essays on Liberty*. Oxford: Oxford University Press.

Bourdieu, Pierre (1991) *Language and Symbolic Power*. Cambridge, MA: Harvard University Press.

Boyer, Paul S. (2002) *Purity in Print: Book Censorship in America from the Gilded Age to the Computer Age*. Madison: University of Wisconsin Press.

Butler, Judith (1997) *Excitable Speech*. New York: Routledge.

Butler, Judith (1998) Ruled Out: Vocabularies of the Censor. In Post (ed.).

Butler, Judith (1999) *Gender Trouble: Feminism and the Subversion of Identity*. New York: Routledge.

*Canadian Charter of Rights and Freedoms*, Part I of *the Constitution Act, 1982*, being Schedule B to the *Canada Act 1982* (U.K.), 1982, c. 11.

Cartwright, Nancy (1979) Causal Laws and Effective Strategies. *Nous* 13: 419–37.

Derrida, Jacques (1988) *Limited Inc*. Edited by Gerald Graff, translated by Jeffrey Mehlman and Samuel Weber. Evanston, IL: Northwestern University Press.

Donner, Wendy (1992) *The Liberal Self*. Ithaca, NY: Cornell University Press.

Dworkin , Ronald (1984) Rights as Trumps. In Jeremy Waldron (ed.) (1984).

Dworkin, Ronald (1986) *A Matter of Principle*. Cambridge, MA: Harvard University Press.

Dworkin, Ronald (1993) Women and Pornography. *The New York Review of Books* 40, 17: 36–42.

Dworkin, Ronald (1997) *Freedom's Law*. Cambridge, MA: Harvard University Press.

Dworkin, Ronald (2005) *Taking Rights Seriously*. Cambridge, MA: Harvard University Press.

Dyzenhaus, David (1992) John Stuart Mill and the Harms of Pornography. *Ethics* 102 (April): 534–51.

Dyzenhaus, David (1994) Pornography and Public Reason. *Canadian Journal of Law and Jurisprudence* 7 : 261–81.

Fiss, Owen (1996) *The Irony of Free Speech*. Cambridge, MA: Harvard University Press.

Foucault, Michel (1977) *Discipline and Punish: The Birth of the Prison*. Translated by Alan Sheridan. New York: Pantheon.

Foucault, Michel (1980a) Two Lectures. In Foucault (1980c).

Foucault, Michel (1980b) The Confession of the Flesh. In Foucault (1980c).

Foucault, Michel (1980c) *Power/Knowledge: Selected Interviews and Other Writings 1972–1977*. Edited by Colin Gordon. New York: Pantheon.

Foucault, Michel (1980d) *The History of Sexuality, Volume 1: An Introduction*. Translated by Robert Hurley. New York: Vintage.

Foucault, Michel (1981a) Is it Useless to Revolt? *Philosophy and Social Criticism* 8 (Spring): 8.

Foucault, Michel (1981b) The Order of Discourse. In R. Young (ed.) *Untyping the Text: A Post-Structuralist Reader*. London: Routledge.

Foucault, Michel (1984a) Truth and Power. In Foucault (1984c).

Foucault, Michel (1984b) Space, Knowledge and Power. In Foucault (1984c).

Foucault, Michel (1984c) *The Foucault Reader*. Edited by Paul Rabinow. New York: Pantheon.

Foucault, Michel (1988a) On Power. In Foucault (1988b).

Foucault, Michel (1988b) *Politics, Philosophy, Culture*. Translated by Alan Sheridan. New York: Routledge.

Gray, John (1996) *Mill on Liberty: A Defence*. New York: Routledge.

Hart, H. L. A. (1979) Between Utility and Rights. In Alan Ryan (ed.) *The Idea of Freedom: Essays in Honor of Isaiah Berlin*. Oxford: Oxford University Press, pp. 77–98.

Kernohan, Andrew (1998) *Liberalism, Equality, and Cultural Oppression*. Cambridge: Cambridge University Press.

Kymlicka, Will (1995) *The Rights of Minority Cultures*. New York: Oxford University Press.

Langton, Rae (1993) Speech Acts and Unspeakable Acts. *Philosophy and Public Affairs* 22, 4: 293–330.

Langton, Rae (1998) Subordination, Silencing, and Pornography's Authority. In Robert Post (ed.) (1998).

Langton, Rae (1999) Pornography: A Liberal's Unfinished Business. Special issue, *Canadian Journal of Law and Jurisprudence*, pp. 109–33.

Langton, Rae, and Jennifer Hornsby (1998) Free Speech and Illocution. *Legal Theory* 4: 21–37.

Lawrence, Charles R. III (1993) If He Hollers, Let Him Go. In Matsuda *et al.* (eds.).

MacKinnon, Catharine (1987) Francis Biddle's Sister: Pornography, Civil Rights and Speech. In *Feminism Unmodified*. Cambridge, MA: Harvard University Press.

MacKinnon, Catharine (1996) *Only Words*. Cambridge, MA: Harvard University Press.

Matsuda, Mari J. (1993) Public Response to Racist Speech. In Matsuda *et al.* (eds.).

Matsuda, Mari J., Charles R. Lawrence III, Richard Delgado, and Kimberlè Williams Crenshaw (eds.) (1993) *Words That Wound: Critical Race Theory, Assaultive Speech, and the First Amendment*. Boulder, CO: Westview Press.

Michelman, Frank (1989) Conceptions of Democracy in American Constitutional Argument: The Case of Pornography Regulation. *Tennessee Law Review* 56, 3: 291–319.

Mill, John Stuart (1977) *Utilitarianism*. In Steven M. Cahn (ed.) *Classics of Western Philosophy*. Indianapolis: Hackett. [First published 1861.]

Mill, John Stuart (1978) *On Liberty*. Edited by Elizabeth Rapaport. Indianapolis: Hackett. [First published 1859.]

Mill, John Stuart (1997) *The Subjection of Women*. New York: Dover Publications. [First published 1869.]

Nozick, Robert (1974) *Anarchy, State, and Utopia*. New York: Basic Books.

Post, Robert (ed.) (1998) *Censorship and Silencing: Practices of Cultural Regulation*. Philadelphia: Getty Research Institute.

Rawls, John (1971) *A Theory of Justice*. Cambridge, MA: Belknap Press of Harvard University Press.

Raz, Joseph (1984) On the Nature of Rights. *Mind* 93: 194–214.

Raz, Joseph (1992) Rights and Individual Well-Being. *Ratio Juris* 5, 2 (July): 127–42.

Ryan, Alan (ed.) (1979) *The Idea of Freedom*. Oxford: Oxford University Press.

Schauer, Frederick (1987) Causation Theory and the Causes of Sexual Violence. *American Bar Foundation Research Journal* 4: 737–70.

Schauer, Frederick (1998) The Ontology of Censorship. In Post (ed.).

Sumner, L.W. (2004) *The Hateful and the Obscene*. Toronto: University of Toronto Press.

Sunstein, Cass (1995) *Democracy and the Problem of Free Speech*. New York: The Free Press.

U.S. Attorney General's Commission on Pornography (1986) *Final Report of the Attorney General's Commission on Pornography*. Edited by Michael J. McManus. Nashville, TN: Rutledge Hill Press.

Waldron, Jeremy (ed.) (1984) *Theories of Rights*. Oxford: Oxford University Press.

# Index